№ 16919
PRICE $15.00
SUBJECT HISTORY

GERMANY AND EUROPE
1919–1939

Germany and Europe 1919–1939

Second Edition

John Hiden

Longman
London and New York

Longman Group UK Limited,
Longman House, Burnt Mill,
Harlow, Essex CM20 2JE, England
and Associated Companies throughout the world.

Published in the United States of America
by Longman Publishing, New York

©John Hiden 1977, 1993

All rights reserved; no part of this publication may be reproduced, stored in a retrieval system, or transmitted in any form or by any means, electronic, mechanical, photocopying, recording, or otherwise without either the prior written permission of the Publishers or a licence permitting restricted copying in the United Kingdom issued by the Copyright Licensing Agency Ltd., 90 Tottenham Court Road, London W1P 9HE.

First published 1977
Second Edition 1993

ISBN 0 582 08722 8

British Library Cataloguing-in-Publication Data

A catalogue record for this book is
available from the British Library

Library of Congress Cataloging in Publication Data

Hiden, John
Germany and Europe, 1919-1939/John Hiden. – 2nd ed.
p. cm.
Includes bibliographical references and index.
ISBN 0-582-08722-8 (PPR)
1. Europe—Relations—Germany. 2. Germany—Foreign relations–Europe. 3. Germany—Foreign relations—1919–1933. 4. Germany––Foreign relations—1933–1945. I. Title.
D727.H44 1933
327.4304 – dc20 92-21845
CIP

Set by 9 in 10/12pt Bembo
Printed in Malaysia by PA

Contents

List of Tables

Acknowledgements

We are grateful to the following for permission to reproduce copyright material:

George Philip Printers Ltd for reproduction of a map from *New Cambridge Modern History Atlas* based on copyright map © George Philip & Son Ltd; Phoebus Publishing Company for reproduction of a table from *History Of The Twentieth Century* by Purnell.

Introduction

The literature on German foreign policy between the two World Wars is, naturally, even more extensive than it was when the first edition of this book appeared in 1977. Yet the reasons then given for publishing an analysis covering the interwar period as a whole remain valid. The variations in the scholarly treatment of the different areas and eras of German foreign policy after 1919 are still noticeable; some of the gaps in coverage, particularly concerning the Baltic states and other parts of Eastern Europe, have been closed since 1977, but others remain; the then patchy treatment of key aspects of German–British and German–French relations has been improved, but more needs to be done.

I have been persuaded to offer a revised edition of the book, integrating new work since 1977, largely because there is still no comparable short account in English which analyses the interwar period as a whole from the German side. Much of the foreign-language literature where debates on German foreign policy have taken place cannot even be used by many English students. The absence of a concise overview of the 1920s, which I remarked upon in 1977, has admittedly been partly remedied for English readers, notably by Marshall Lee and Wolfgang Michalka.[1] Yet by far the most impressive recent study of the Weimar Republic's foreign policy is in German.[2]

The balance of literature is still, as it was in 1977, heavily tilted towards coverage of German policy during the 1930s, where the

[1] M. Lee, W. Michalka, *German Foreign Policy 1917–1933. Continuity or Break?* (Leamington Spa, 1987).

[2] P. Krüger, *Die Aussenpolitik der Republik von Weimar* (Darmstadt, 1985).

introductions by William Carr and Klaus Hildebrand continue to be invaluable, and where in addition Ian Kershaw's useful survey of *The Nazi Dictatorship* provides background material for the consideration of foreign policy in the Third Reich.[3]

I made the point in the first edition of the book that I was anxious to give roughly equal weight to the 1920s and 1930s. In the first place the decision saved me from having to give my own blow-by-blow account of the last years of peace and spared me from competing with the many excellent studies of the immediate origins of war, of which the most impressive now is that by D.C. Watt.[4] Secondly, and more importantly, it enabled me to treat the study of the Weimar Republic and its foreign policy as valuable in its own right, rather than as a prelude to the Third Reich. Mild issue was taken with the marked tendency at the time, above all of German historians, to emphasise – at the expense of more benign but no less important traits in German foreign policy – the continuity of aggression from Bismarck to Hitler.

My original concern to bring out the positive and not just the all too obvious negative aspects in twentieth-century German foreign policy has been deepened by the momentous event of German reunification. Initial media and public reactions to this were often characterised, in Britain particularly, by sensationalist speculation about likely new German threats to Europe. The dispassionate study of the policies of the former Federal Republic provided no evidence to substantiate such fears, which arose from viewing Germany through the prism of the Third Reich, rather than from any balanced historical assessment.

Because the process of German reunification overlapped with the decline and ultimate collapse of the Soviet Union and the beginnings of reconstruction in East Europe, the familiar siren songs also sounded, about the inherent menace of German economic domination in Eastern Europe. In reality, German economic penetration of Eastern Europe is not in itself threatening, a point obscured by memories of the Third Reich's rule there. Nothing could be more unlike that than the current German quest to find, with the European Community (EC), a suitable role in the massive task of rebuilding in the states of East Europe and the members of the Commonwealth of Independent States, as well as their reintegration into a wider Euro-

[3] W. Carr, *Arms Autarky and Aggression. A Study in German Foreign Policy 1933–1939* (London, 1972); K. Hildebrand, *The Foreign Policy of the Third Reich* (London, 1973); I. Kershaw, *The Nazi Dictatorship. Problems and Perspectives of Interpretation* (London, 1985).

[4] D. C. Watt, *How War Came. The Immediate Origins of the Second World War, 1938-1939 (London, 1989).*

pean order. And it is this venture which conjures up, however faintly, echoes of the foreign policy developments slowly emerging during the short lifetime of the Weimar Republic.

My gratitude to former colleagues at Aberdeen University, where I first wrote this book, remains. Since then I have also enjoyed the many benefits of working in the Department of European Studies at Bradford University. Not least of these has been the opportunity to travel and research widely in West and East Europe, as well as contact with students, all of whom speak at least one foreign language. The gains for a teacher of European history are self-evident. Countless discussions of German history with my students have played their part in shaping my own work, including the changes to this new edition.

My biggest debt remains to Juliet, Hugo and Jessica. I am still some way from discharging this.

PART ONE
Germany

CHAPTER ONE

From War to Peace, 1918–21

What happens when a nation's external and internal situation is subject to sudden change, as was the case with Imperial Germany when it suffered military defeat and revolution in the space of a few weeks at the close of the First World War? It is a truism to argue that such a collapse provided the opportunity to think afresh the tenets of foreign policy,[1] but this barely does justice to the speed of events in Germany. In early October 1918, the German Army High Command (OHL) unexpectedly but insistently urged the stunned civilian leaders to ask the Allied Powers for an armistice and a peace treaty based on the American President Wilson's famous 'Fourteen Points' of January 1918. Prince Max of Baden was appointed to head a new, if short-lived government. His task was to prevent a new and crushing military attack by the *Entente*, but it signalled the end of the 'military dictatorship' which Generals Ludendorff and Hindenburg had exercised since 1916 in their capacity of war heroes extraordinaire. In late October, Germany transformed itself into a constitutional monarchy and on the 24th of that month Ludendorff was dismissed. By 9 November, the Kaiser had been compelled to abdicate as the revolution got under way. Wilhelm Solf, the last Foreign Minister of the Empire, woke up, as it were, the first Foreign Minister of the Republic, servant to the all-socialist Provisional Government which was composed on 10 November 1918, the Council of People's Commissars.

[1] O.E. Schüddekopf, 'German foreign policy between Compiègne and Versailles', *Journal of Contemporary History*, **4** (1969): 81. Cf. P. Grupp, *Deutsche Aussenpolitik im Schatten von Versailles 1918–1920. Zur Politik des Auswärtigen Amtes von Ende des Ersten Weltkrieg und der November Revolution bis sum Inkrafttreten des Versailler Vertrags*, (Paderborn, 1988).

It was a time almost for reflexes rather than long-sighted planning in the field of foreign policy as elsewhere. Certainly, a study of German foreign policy in these months offers no neat solution to the political scientist's problem about the relative importance of internal and external factors.[2] The near-simultaneous transition from war to cease-fire, from Empire to Republic demonstrated, rather, the interaction between domestic and foreign events. President Wilson's insistent calls for proof positive of a genuine change in Germany's power structure played an important part in the general slide towards revolution. The demands were made in the exchange of notes which Prince Max of Baden's government conducted with Wilson prior to the Armistice. Consequently, the Kaiser's failure to confirm the extent of the October reforms by a more ready abdication appeared to the German masses as *the* obstacle to the conclusion of a speedy and reasonable peace; the more intolerable in that the shattering news of imminent defeat made the whole war effort seem tragically wasted. Conversely, when the Kaiser had gone it was apparent that there was a connection between the way in which internal order was restored and the sort of policy pursued towards the outside world.

A mere ten weeks separated the formation of the revolutionary Provisional Government of 10 November 1918 from the appearance in January 1919 of the first Republican parliamentary government which was responsible to the newly elected National Assembly. In that brief period the vision of radical reforms which had helped to fuel the revolution in the first place faded. This process was charted by the growing split between the two main wings of the German socialist movement, the Independent Social Democrats (USPD) and the Majority Social Democrats (SPD) and by the final resignation of the USPD from the Council of People's Commissars on 27 December 1918. Along with the burial of the ideal of socialist unity which had inspired the provisional goverment in the first place went the demise of the still more revolutionary plans of the radical shop stewards and the Spartacists, later to become the German Communist Party (KPD). Their leaders, Rosa Luxemurg and Karl Liebknecht were buried too, literally, in January 1919, after their bloody execution at the hands of the *Freikorps* (volunteer forces).

The failure of revolution was only in part the result of policies pursued by the SPD leaders; only in part the reflection of their own preference for a return to normalcy and the restoration of their links with the moderate bourgeois parties of Germany. These contacts had

[2] Cf. W. Wallace, *Foreign Policy and the Political Process* (London, 1971), p. 17.

been nurtured in the Empire and had culminated in the reforms of October 1918 only to be rudely interrupted by the revolution.[3] Under Friedrich Ebert's guidance, the top SPD leadership sought to resume the dialogue with other parties and groups as soon as possible. Many have regretted that the SPD did not instead concentrate on forcing through sweeping reforms of the social and economic system. The reality was, however, that hardly anybody in Germany wanted a Bolshevik-style revolution. Moreover, the established forces of imperial Germany remained influential. The maintenance of the Imperial bureaucracy, symbolised by Solf's continuing presence in the German Forign Office, the survival of the German officer corps, founded on Ebert's use of the Army to maintain internal order after 10 November, the successful evasion of socialist reforms by German business – all of these come as no real surprise when the magnitude of the problems thrown up by the transition from war to peace is taken into account.[4] Germany was not Russia after all. The German Workers' and Soldiers' councils were modelled along Russian lines, but on 16 December they voted themselves out of power by agreeing to the elections for the National Assembly. The extent to which the conceptions of Ebert and the SPD found general support was reflected in the voting at these elections. The SPD, together with the moderate bourgeois parties willing to support the new Republic, the Centre Party and the Democrats, received the overwhelming share of votes.

Such internal realities helped to define the range of choices immediately open to German foreign policy. Most obviously, its commitment to prevent more radical revolution in Germany made it impossible for the provisional government to pursue an active policy of *rapprochement* with Lenin's Russia. A network of contacts had sprung up between the German Workers' and Soldiers' Councils and representatives from the Russian Soviets in the earliest days of the German revolution and this was hardly welcome to the SPD or USPD members of the government.[5] Joffe, the Soviet Ambassador to Berlin, had been expelled on 5 November for revolutionary

[3] R. N. Hunt, 'Friedrich Ebert and the German revolution of 1918' in L. Krieger and F. Stern (eds), *The Responsibility of Power: Historical Essays in Honour of H. Holborn* (London, 1968), p. 320. The strains and stresses of SPD–bourgeois co-operation can be followed in E. Matthias and R. Morsey (eds), *Die Regierung des Prinzen Max von Baden* (Düsseldorf, 1962).

[4] G.D. Feldman, 'Economic and social problems of the German demobilisation', *Journal of Modern History*, **47** (March, 1975): 1–2, 20–1. His critics comment, ibid., pp. 24–44. Cf. R. Rürup, 'Problems of the German Revolution 1918–1919', *Journal of Contemporary History*, **3** (1968): 109–35.

[5] H.G. Linke, *Deutsch–sowjetische Beziehungen bis Rapallo* (Cologne, 1970), pp. 21ff.

propagandising. To the domestic pressures preventing the premature development of closer relations between the new Germany and the new Russia was added the weight of external factors.[6]

THE IMPACT OF THE ARMISTICE

The Armistice which Germany signed with the Allied Powers on 11 November 1918 created additional obstacles to any normalisation of German–Russian relations. It demanded that Germany abrogate not only the Treaty of Bucharest with Romania but the Treaty of Brest-Litovsk, which had governed German–Russian relations since March 1918. Technically, this put Germany in a state of war with Russia. In fact Lenin had also declared Brest-Litovsk null and void in November and Germany's Embassy in Moscow had not been filled after the murder of their Ambassador Count Mirbach, in July 1918. The Armistice reflected the determination of the Western Allies to stop Bolshevism from spreading to Central Europe. In effect the Germans were associated with the Allied intervention against the Bolshevik regime. Whereas the territories occupied by German troops in Western Europe at the end of the war were to be evacuated more or less immediately, Germany was only to evacuate those occupied areas in the east formerly belonging to Russia when the Allies deemed the moment suitable (Article XII).

Other provisions in the Armistice included the predictable arrangements for the immediate repatriation of prisoners of war and the forbidding of Germany damaging property as it evacuated occupied territories. The financial clauses called for the return of gold seized from Belgium, Romania and Russia and, ominously, for 'reparations for damage done'. The overwhelming preoccupation of the Allies with their own security was reflected in the demand for the surrender of heavy arms and vehicles and for the immobilisation of the German fleet. Moreover the left bank of the Rhine was to be occupied by Allied troops, together with the bridgeheads of Mainz, Cologne and Coblenz and a surrounding stretch of thirty kilometres. The crippling blockade of Germany was to be continued for the time being and in effect this was made harsher by the ban on Germany's merchant naval

[6] Wolfgang Elben, *Das Problem der Kontinuität in der deutschen Revolution. Die Politik der Staatssekretäre und der militärischen Führung vom November 1918 bis Febuar 1919* (Düsseldorf, 1965), pp. 105–7.

activity. As a means of securing German's continued good behaviour until the conclusion of a peace treaty, the Armistice was made renewable after an initial period of thirty-six days.

The Armistice brutally underlined the extent of Germany's military defeat. The scale of adjustment required of German foreign policy may be seen from a brief look back at the conditions existing when Germany signed its victorious peace with the Bolshevik forces in March 1918 at Brest-Litovsk. In this present study it is impossible to discuss at any length the controversies about German war aims, 1914–18. No attempt can be made to answer the question to what extent the annexationist policies pursued by the Germans in Europe after 1914 were conceived before war broke out. All that can safely be assumed here is that the Imperial war aims at least fulfilled many of the requirements of Germany's rulers, of its military, landowning and industrial élites, and that these aims received at least the approval of large sectors of German society during the war. Fritz Fischer's summary of Germany's war aims as they stood in 1918 can therefore serve as a useful yardstick against which to measure the dramatic limitations imposed by the Armistice.

> A survey of Germany's war aims at the beginning and in the middle of 1918, when German self-confidence was at its peak in the expectation of early victory, discloses a picture of an *imperium* of grandiose dimensions. In the West: Belgium, Luxemburg, Longwy–Briey, linked with Germany on such terms as to make possible the adherence of France and Holland and to isolate Britain and force her to recognise Germany's position; in the East: Courland, Livonia, Estonia and Lithuania, from Reval to Riga and Vilno, the Polish Frontier Strip and Rump Poland all closely fettered to Germany; in the South-east: Austria–Hungary clamped into Germany as a cornerstone, then Rumania and Bulgaria, and beyond them the Ottoman Empire as an object of Germany's Asiatic policy. Command of the Eastern Mediterranean was to compel the adherence of Greece and secure the route through Suez, while the domination of the Black Sea guaranteed the economic mastery of the Ukraine, the Crimea and Georgia, and the command of the Baltic compelled Sweden and Finland, with their riches, to take the German side. On top of all this was the position of at least economic hegemony in Rump Russia.[7]

Such an extended European power base was to be the precondition of Germany's bid for world power. The Armistice obviously removed for the foreseeable future any prospect of reviving the imperial war aims in Western Europe. What remained was an aversion to the Western Powers and a determination to recover Germany's status at their expense which was nutured by the survivors of Imperial

[7] F. Fischer, *Germany's Aims in the First World War* (London, 1967), p. 607.

Germany's establishment, by its military leaders and by its unrepentant nationalists. They could capitalise on the resentment of the wider German public but they could do little directly in 1918/19, beyond trying to frustrate the slow and painful emergence in the German Foreign Office and in some of the political parties of a more realistic policy towards the Western Powers (p. 65). But what of East Europe where the situation was more confused owing to the continuing fighting of the Bolshevik forces and the highly uncertain outcome of the revolution in Russia? Could the unrepentant elements in Germany salvage something of Imperial war aims before it was too late?

On 18 November 1918, the Council of People's Commissars discussed the issue of German–Russian relations in order to clarify the policy to be pursued towards Lenin and the Bolsheviks, who were pressing precisely for this while still counting on revolution in Germany. There was unanimous agreement in the Cabinet that any suggestion of more friendly relations with Russia would prejudice Germany's prospect for a better peace. The USPD spokemen, who shared the general feeling that the Bolsheviks might well fall from power, endorsed the view that:

> The Entente is willing to meet the present bourgeois-socialist republic halfway in the matter of peace terms and food supplies, but only as long as the government adheres to its present composition under Ebert's leadership. The Entente would, however, intervene with all its might to forestall the rise of Bolshevism. If Joffe, for one, were to return, that alone would suffice to alter the prospect of peace.[8]

What was to be done? Ironically, Haase, leader of the USPD, provided the suggestion which kept even the Army leaders happy for the time being; namely to give a dilatory answer to the Russian overtures. A positive commitment to intervention against the Soviets was of course impossible for the USPD to support.[9] At the same time, delaying tactics towards the Bolshevik overtures offered the only chance of preserving even a limited freedom to manœuvre for the Berlin government. A dilatory answer to Lenin's overtures left open the future possibility of some *rapprochement* with the new Russia, if it survived, but did not exclude close co-operation with the Allied Powers against the Bolsheviks if this seemed likely to lead to a better peace for Germany. Exactly how the Army hoped to exploit this situation will be examined shortly.

[8] C.B. Burdick ad R.H. Lutz (eds), *The Political Institutions of the German Revolution 1918–19* (New York, 1966), p. 70.

[9] Elben, op. cit., p. 108.

THE GERMAN FOREIGN OFFICE UNDER BROCKDORFF-RANTZAU

When the government of Philip Scheidemann (SPD) took office in January 1919 the danger of revolution had receded to the point where both the Foreign Office and the Army leaders could exercise a more overt influence on the immediate peace strategy than had been possible when they worked in harness with the provisional government, which had been technically responsible to the Workers' and Soldiers' Councils. Nonetheless, the Foreign Office had not been unaffected by the revolution. The origins of the German Foreign Office (*Auswärtiges Amt* – AA) go back to the eighteenth century but its name, and importance, was not acquired until 1871, when the Prussian Ministry of Foreign Affairs was elevated to the central authority for the new German Empire. Under Bismarck the AA played a crucial role in the Imperial administration. It might be going too far to describe the AA as in 'eclipse' during the First World War and the military 'dictatorship' of Hindenburg and Lundendorff, although it was overshadowed.[10] Like the rest of the Imperial bureaucracy it continued to function after the Republic was proclaimed and its officials were influential, although flanked by the political watchdogs of the socialist parties.[11] In short, it was far more involved in the domestic political crossfire than it had ever been in Bismarck's day, a point to which this book will return later. It was the intention of the Foreign Minister appointed in December 1918, Count Ulrich Brockdorff-Rantzau, to gather together more firmly the various strands of German foreign policy as the Peace Conference loomed nearer. As a member of the aristocracy who nonetheless accepted the need to adjust to changed circumstances he was the classic 'wanderer between two worlds', a description which could be applied to many during the November revolution.[12]

[10] Cf. W. Baumgart, *Deutsche Ostpolitik 1918: Vom Brest-Litovsk bis zum Ende des Ersten Weltkrieges* (Vienna–Munich, 1966), pp. 85–6, 90–2. More generally see A.R. Carlson, *German Foreign Policy 1890–1914 and Colonial Policy to 1914: A Handbook and Annotated Bibliography* (Metuchen, New Jersey, 1970), pp. 32–9; M. Kitchen, *A Military History of Germany: from the Eighteenth Century to the Present Day* (London, 1975).

[11] Matthias and Morsey, op cit., pp. 545–6; Eberhard von Vietsch, *Wilhelm Solf. Botschafter zwischen den Zeiten* (Tübingen, 1961), pp. 212–22.

[12] Short surveys of Rantzau's policies and attitudes can be found in Elben, op. cit., pp. 107–14, 120ff; Schüddekopf, op. cit., p. 189; Leo Haupts, 'Zur deutschen und britischen Friedenspolitik in der Krise der Pariser Friedenskonferenz. Britisch–Deutsche Separatverhandlungen im April/Mai 1919?' *Historische Zeitschrift*, **217** (1973): 54–98; Udo Wengst, *Graf Brockdorff-Rantzau und die aussenpolitischen Anfänge der Weimarer Republik* (Frankfurt am Main, 1973).

Rantzau had to hand a special organisation attached to the AA under the leadership of Graf Bernstorff, numbering some forty officials and a staff of 120 experts. Its function was to consider in detail the problems expected to arise during the peace negotiations and to act as a sort of information office and co-ordinating agency once the talks had actually got under way. Also waiting was a six-man peace delegation for the forthcoming negotiations. At this stage the German goverment's preparations for the coming peace talks were based on the assumption that ultimately Germany would be allowed to *negotiate* and that peace would be based on the Fourteen Points. This, too, was Rantzau's starting point. In an important speech to the National Assembly in Weimar on 14 February 1919, he developed most clearly his appeal to the moral basis of the forthcoming peace. That peace was to be based on the Fourteen Points, without additions or alterations. It would have to include the League of Nations and the obligation to accept international arbitration. Not surprisingly, given Germany's defeat, the peace would have to include a general renunciation of armaments. The pressing social questions of postwar Europe, so tied up with the cause of international peace, were to be subject to international solutions. The principle of self-determination was to be accepted and applied to frontier settlements and of course to the problem of German–Austrian relations.[13]

Brockdorff-Rantzau looked therefore towards the United States, relying on President Wilson's influence in the first instance. He did not only depend on moral arguments but also on the assumption that in the last resort America and Britain would perceive the disastrous implications for themselves of a harsh peace with Germany, particularly in the economic field. It was a corollary of his approach to emphasise, too, the pre-Armistice exchange of notes, when the Fourteen Points had been agreed as providing the basis for the peace. The strict application by Brockdorff-Rantzau of such tactics undoubtedly aggravated his opponents at home and abroad, but it has been argued that the Foreign Minister's strategy was an unavoidable consequence of Germany's exclusion from the preliminary inter-Allied exchanges at the Paris Peace Conference. Before the final negotiations took place, public opinion – at home and abroad – had to be made to see the folly of an unfair peace, and above all to grasp

[13] Gerhard Schulz, *Revolutions and Peace Treaties* (London, 1972), pp. 177–8. See M. Knoll, 'Anmerkungen zu Brockdorff-Rantzau's Rede in Versailles', *Geschichte in Wissenschaft und Unterricht*, No. 2 (1987): 108–111.

the fact that Germany was not alone guilty of the war.[14] On the other hand, Rantzau's policy did not permit any piecemeal bargaining with the Allies over details of the peace prior to the settlement. There were various semi-official exchanges between Compiègne and Versailles, but Brockdorff-Rantzau remained sceptical of the value of these, believing rightly that Britain, France and America would barely conceive of a different power stucture than that provided by the outcome of the war.[15]

This makes all the more remarkable the failure of Rantzau to take proper account of the impact on the Allied governments of their own electorates, which were determined to regard Germany, as guilty and to exact retribution for damages suffered as a result of German aggression.[16] The first setback to the German plans came when the Allied invitation for the Germans to attend the conference in Paris spoke not of negotiations but of Germany receiving the draft peace terms of the Allies. In part this procedure arose from the difficulties within the Allied camp of coming to agreement among themselves over the peace terms; the delay in presenting these might have been intolerably long in a war-torn Europe if Germany had been involved in their formulation. This is not the place to rehearse the well-worn arguments about the wisdom or justice of the Allied approach to peace-making. Although the Allies amended their invitation to the extent that 'negotiation' was mentioned the German Cabinet had a slightly clearer idea of what treatment it might receive in Paris. This was reflected in Brockdorff-Rantzau's *Richtlinien* (guidelines) for the German Peace Delegation of 21 April 1919. These envisaged a process of picking holes in the Allied terms, leading eventually to the Allies accepting the need to negotiate with the Germans.[17] In fact, negotiations as such did not take place between the Allies and the German delegation. When the draft peace terms were eventually handed over

[14] Haupts, op. cit., pp. 70ff. More critical is W. Baumgart, 'Brest-Litovsk und Versailles. Ein vergleich zweier Friedensschulüsse', *Historische Zeitschrift*, **210** (1970); 605–6. Also see I. Geiss, 'The outbreak of the First World War and German war aims', *Journal of Contemporary History*, **1** (1966): 75–8.

[15] Haupts, op. cit., pp. 70ff. An example of such contacts is given by F.T. Epstein, 'Zwischen Compiègne und Versailles. Geheime amerikanische Militärdiplomatie in der Period des Waffenstillstandes 1918/19. Die Rolle des Obersten A.L. Conger', *Vierteljahrshefte für Zeitgeschichte* (Oct. 1955), pp. 412–45.

[16] A.J. Mayer, *Politics and Diplomacy of Peacemaking. Containment and Counterrevolution at Versailles 1918–19* (London, 1968), pp. 623–4, 649ff., 789–90; Klaus Schwabe, *Deutsche Revolution und Wilson Frieden. Die amerikanische und deutsche Friedensstrategie zwischen Ideologie und Machtpolitik 1918–19* (Düsseldorf, 1971).

[17] Hagen Schulze (ed.), *Akten der Reichskanzlei. Das Kabinett Scheidemann* (Boppard am Rhein, 1971), pp. 193–204.

to the Germans on 7 May 1919, Rantzau's fury expressed itself in his celebrated insistence on remaining seated; an obvious proof for many ever since of Rantzau's pig-headed patriotism. In truth it was an action which reflected his bitter disappointment. His policy was not one of resistance for its own sake, but it was a gamble aimed at persuading the Allies to be more pliable.

THE BALTIC CAMPAIGN AND THE 'RUSSIAN FACTOR'

Before the German government's reaction to the draft peace terms is examined more closely, it will be as well to retrace events in East Europe during the spring of 1919. Here the German Army leaders had been trying to exploit the freedom of movement provided by Article XII of the Armistice in a way which threatened to endanger Rantzau's peace strategy. Their alliance with the provisional government in November 1918 to protect Germany from internal disorder enabled the Army officers to survive and to remain at the centre of things, bringing with them the germ of the new Army. The *Freikorps*, gathered together late in 1918 and early 1919 to restore internal order, remained under the command of the old officers. The Army laws of February 1919, which provided the basis for the Republican Army, sanctioned this process and were unable to prevent the continuity of values and ideals of an élite corps which was hardly pro-Republic.[18] Nonetheless, their world was vastly different now, with the prospect of a peace settlement which would curtail Germany's armed forces to a minimum. Such considerations amply reinforced the OHL's inclination to play the 'Russian card' for all it was worth. It was the policy of General Groener, who temporarily guided the OHL after Ludendorff's departure, to exploit to the maximum the notion of Germany as a bulwark against Bolshevism and to take part with the Allies in a military crusade against Russia. In so doing it was hoped that Germany would retain a strong Army and achieve a more favourable peace treaty.[19] Early in 1919, German *Freikorps* units began to leave the Baltic front in fulfilment of Article XII of the Armistice and to help hold the front against the advancing Red Army.

[18] F.L. Carsten, *Reichswehr und Politik* (Cologne/Berlin, 1964), pp. 57ff.

[19] See Groener's remarks on 'The situation in the east' at the Cabinet meeting of 24 April 1919. Schulze, op. cit., pp. 210–18.

The problems posed for German foreign policy thereafter arose from a number of anomolous factors. The Army headquarters were transferred to Kolberg, the better to supervise the conflicts in the east. Remote from Berlin, the Army leaders on the spot were able to influence the course of events in East Europe and this in itself created headaches for the civilian government. It gave rather more scope for the commanders in the field, notably General Rüdiger von der Goltz, who took over the Eighth Army Corps in the Baltic at the beginning of February 1919.[20] Confusion was compounded by the underhand activities of Reichskommissar August Winnig. His job was to hand over to the new Baltic governments the reins of administration after the end of Germany's wartime occupation of the Baltic provinces, but he sympathised with the efforts of von der Goltz to create *faits accomplis* in East Europe which would be more advantageous to Germany when peace was made.[21] Alongside such efforts were those of the White Russian generals in the interventionist forces set up to oppose the Soviet troops. The network of official, semi-official and personal ties which sprang up between German and White Russian military adventurers hardly made for far-sighted policies or planning. To make matters worse, the military campaigns in the Baltic, ostensibly against the Bolsheviks, soon involved conflict between the native Baltic peoples and the *Freikorps* element. On 16 April the Latvian provisional government was overthrown and replaced by a Baltic–German dominated administration under A. Needra.

It would be going too far to say that the Berlin government fully supported such adventurism although some, like the SPD Defence Minister Gustav Noske, were more sympathetic than others. The activities of the *Freikorps* threatened to do long-term damage to Germany's relations with the Baltic nations. This the SPD, above all, could not accept. Nonetheless, the twilight relationships between civilian and military command were not conducive to a decisive stand by Berlin. In addition it was impossible to separate the Baltic campaign from the question of German–Polish relations. Since the end of the war, frontier conflicts between German and Polish forces had raised the spectre in Berlin of an East Prussia cut off from the Reich as well as the loss of the territories of Posen and Upper Silesia to the new Polish state, whose independence was promised by Wilson's thirteenth point. As Wipert von Blücher, of the Eastern

[20] Rüdiger von der Goltz, *Meine Sendung in Finland und im Baltikum* (Leipzig, 1920), pp. 146–8.

[21] August Winnig, *Heimkehr* (Hamburg, 1935), pp. 28–30.

Department of the AA wrote, it was impossible to see at that point if anything useful would come from the undertaking in the Baltic.[22]

These events confirm the obvious. Brockdorff-Rantzau could not alone decide the course of Germany's foreign policy. In spite of his growing disappointment at the outcome of his peace tactics he remained firmly wedded to the idea of getting American support. It was consistent with this that he should want Germany to appear loyal to the Allies in the joint defence against Bolshevism. Nevertheless, he did not yet think the time right for a joint crusade with the Allied Powers against the Bolsheviks, as some of the Army leaders wanted. Two additional points urged for caution. In the first place, the policy of the Allies towards Russia continued to show the most alarming contradictions. It was by no means clear by the spring of 1919 that there *was* an 'Allied' policy towards the Bolshevik regime. Secondly, if the Bolsheviks managed to survive – and as 1919 progressed the signs indicating this possibility multiplied – the rigid application of Groener's plans would prove embarrassing and positively damaging to German–Russian relations in the future. Such considerations were mirrored in the Cabinet meeting of 24 April 1919.[23] Indeed, the meeting was occasioned by the events in Latvia and the Baltic. The differences between Rantzau and Groener were patched up under the compromise formula: 'The Cabinet was, however, agreed, that the present front be held where it was. Offensive plans were not to be followed.'[24] In effect this was a continuation of the 'wait and see' policy of the Council of People's Commissars. It was not, regrettably, an effective deterrent to the German military leaders in East Europe.

This naturally worried another key figure in German foreign policy, Matthias Erzberger, the head of the German Armistice Delegation. As such, he had played a vital role in helping to create the context in which Brockdorff-Rantzau had to operate. The Armistice in effect prejudiced aspects of the peace settlement. Examples were Germany's financial commitments and the qualifications to the general concept of freedom of the sea which Germany had accepted during the Armistice exchanges. In the negotiations between Erzberger and the Allies over the extension of the Armistice – prolonged for

[22] Wipert von Blücher, *Deutschlands Weg nach Rapallo* (Wiesbaden, 1951), p. 74; Otto Meissner, *Staatssekretär unter Ebert, Hindenburg, Hitler* (3rd edn, Munich, 1950), pp. 39–40. Linke, op. cit., pp. 65ff. gives a balanced account of the Baltic campaign from the German viewpoint. So too does H.-E. Volkmann, *Die russische Emigration in Deutschland 1919–1922* (Würzburg, 1966), pp. 61–74.

[23] Schulze, op cit., p. 221.

[24] Ibid., p.225.

the third and last time on 16 February 1919 – the German minister had invitably moved even nearer to the centre of the policy-making process. This produced a striking clash between Erzberger and Rantzau whose severity cannot be explained in terms of foreign policy differences alone.[25]

The most obvious point to make is that Erzberger's activity as head of the Armistice Commission was circumscribed by the demands of the Allies. Even the Army leaders had accepted that better Armistice terms would not have been obtained if Erzberger had been replaced by somebody else. It can hardly be doubted, either, that Erzberger gave nothing to Brockdorff-Rantzau in terms of patriotism. It was rather that Erzberger appeared to favour a more flexible approach, being more ready to enter the shady world of pre-peace making and semi-official bargaining; apparently more ready in the last resort to come to terms with the inevitable and opposed to the seemingly inflexible stand of his Foreign Minister. Undoubtedly, Erzberger was correct in worrying about the Army policies and in being apprehensive about the effects of these in hardening Allied attitudes. This was indeed an important consequence of the Baltic campaign. Events in Latvia certainly played a part in directing the fears of the Allies more towards the dangers of a German–Russian alliance. This helped to shift Allied preferences towards creating a strong political cordon sanitaire of the smaller Eastern European states in line with French desires as the prospects of a military defeat of the Bolsheviks dwindled.[26] As yet, however, Erzberger was not able to persuade the Cabinet to accept the view he put forward in the meeting of 24 April: that Germany ought to conclude an armistice with the Soviets as soon as possible.

It is important to set the differences between the key makers of German foreign policy during the transition from war to peace in the context of the uncertainty about what the Allies actually wanted from the forthcoming peace. This in itself does much to explain the differing conceptions of peacemaking in official circles in Germany. Knowledge of Allied plans was partial, derived from newspaper sources, personal impressions from observers and the sort of semi-official contacts which often promised much but which had no obvious backing from the governments concerned. There is that much truth at least in the familiar argument about the German delegation at

[25] Ibid., pp. 254–5; K. Epstein, *Matthias Erzberger and the Dilemma of German Democracy* (Princeton, 1959), pp. 290–1.

[26] For references see note 2, Chapter 5 (p. 138).

Versailles being isolated from the victor powers, if that isolation was also a consequence of the difficulties the Allies had in coming to agreed terms between themselves. A discussion of the differing conceptions of some of the main characters in Germany's policy-making élite, cannot therefore be sufficient to explain German foreign policy in 1919.

Moreover, differences in emphasis and principle plagued the coalition of political forces on which the Scheidemann government was founded – the Social Democrats, the Centre Party and the Democrats. Then there were the arguments developed by the nationalist parties in the National Assembly. These aspects of Weimar foreign policy have been treated more fully in Chapter 2, for in 1919, prior to the signature of the Peace Treaty, the emphasis was on getting peace at all costs and to some extent the looming internal conflicts were suppressed in this interest. Without peace, in any event, long-term political planning was impossible. But the conflicts were hardly unimportant, even if kept roughly in their place. They reinforced Brockdorff–Rantzau's insistence on a close and faithful interpretation of the Fourteen Points to unite the most important internal forces, above all those of the socialists on the one hand and those of the business communities on the other. The latter's dominant role, in a government headed by the SPD, can be gauged from the fact that the early phase of Germany's reparations policy was chiefly determined by the entrepreneurs and the big banks. They insisted on the closest possible interpretation of the Fourteen Points in the interest of limiting Germany's liabilities and in order to maintain at least the economic power base of the German state.[27]

THE TERMS OF PEACE

The differences in Cabinet and country became immediately evident when on 7 May 1919 the draft treaty terms were presentd to the German delegation at Versailles under Brockdorff-Rantzau. There could be no further illusions about the spirit in which the Fourteen Points would be interpreted. The German Peace Delegation had already discovered on their arrival at the conference that their general

[27] Haupts, op cit., p. 67; P. Krüger, *Deutschland und die Reparationen 1918/19. Die Genesis des Reparationsproblem in Deutschland zwischen Waffenstillstand und Versailler Friedensschluss* (Stuttgart, 1973), pp. 210–13.

remit to examine the peace in terms of the Fourteen Points was of little help when it came to considering the countless practical details arising from day to day.[28] On 7 May, they came face to face with the full results of the inter-Allied bargaining over an acceptable peace. The severity of the shock of the terms on the German public as a whole can hardly be disputed. No doubt this was one of the consequences of the government's policy of propagating the idea of a peace based strictly on the Fourteen Points, instead of preparing public opinion for the icy cold shower which the leaders of Germany suspected very well might be in store for them. This is the usual criticism of the Scheidemann government's peace strategy. Exactly how such a task could be accomplished by even a stable government, when faced with the overwhelming belief of the German people that they were not solely guilty of the war, is difficult to imagine; the problems multiply in mathematical progression if the composition of the Scheidemann government is properly taken into account.

The emphasis in the draft terms on Germany's responsibility for the war and its effects ensured that: 'The fear of the odium associated with the responsibility for signing the Peace Treaty formed the strongest obstacle on the road to a decision.'[29] The most spirited resistance to accepting the peace terms inside the government parties came from the Democrats, but even the SPD and Centre parties could express no united opinion. What made matters worse was the background of continuous discussion in the National Assembly at Weimar where it soon emerged during the debates that, irrespective of the decisions in Berlin, there was virtually unanimous agreement (the USPD excepted) over the need to reject the thesis of German aggression. Above all, the voice of the so-called 'national opposition' was already making itself heard. It is in such a context that Erzberger's attempts to prevent a headstrong reaction to the peace terms are so remarkable. Erzberger sought to emphasise the consequences to Germany of a refusal to accept the terms, the possibility of the unity of the Reich being destroyed and the end of the chance to effect its economic and political reconstruction in more settled conditions. To some extent he was successful in that the Centre Party accepted the compromise of agreeing to sign under protest as long as items in the peace terms which affected Germany's honour were removed, par-

[28] For colourful descriptions of the arrival of the Germans at the Conference see A.M. Luckau, *The German Delegation at the Paris Peace Conference* (New York, 1941), pp. 115ff.

[29] Schultz, op. cit., pp. 183–4.

ticularly the insistence on holding Germany responsible for the war and the proposal to try war criminals.[30]

Unfortunately, during the critical days after the presentation of the draft peace terms, discussion inside Germany drifted into the hysterical reaction against the so called 'war guilt' thesis and away from a more reasoned critique of the detail of the terms themselves. This was regrettable, but reflected the efforts of Brockdorff-Rantzau and the Peace Delegation in Paris. Without co-ordinating his actions with those of the Cabinet in Berlin, Rantzau proceeded to bombard the Allies with notes emphasising the intolerable nature of central aspects of the Peace Treaty. Although this procedure was in keeping with his *Richtlinien* of April, in attempting to show the disparity between the voiced ideals of the victors and their behaviour in practice, it undoubtedly helped to set the tone for the reaction in Germany. It made considerably more difficult what efforts were made by the government to devise a realistic response to the challenge of the draft terms. The German Cabinet grew increasingly affronted by Brockdorff-Rantzau's paper war because it only served to worsen the atmosphere in Paris and threatened to prejudice the reception of the more measured formal German counter-proposals. These were handed over by the government on 29 May, somewhat later than the fifteen-day deadline originally imposed by the Allies for a reply. It remains difficult, however, to see what differences would have been made to the peace terms in the absence of the concentrated argument against the 'war guilt' clause, although the painful process of re-educating German public opinion *might* have been made easier later.

Such a suspicion is confirmed by the fate of the German counter-proposals which were marked by an attempt to approach the Allied position on some of the more important conditions. The notion of a Regular Army reduced to 100,000 men was accepted, notwithstanding the predictable objections of the military leaders; effectively, the loss of Alsace-Lorraine was accepted since the outcome of the proposed plebiscite for the area was hardly to be doubted. The Foreign Office line prevailed over that of the military in the German government's readiness to transfer some territory to Poland and to provide the new Polish state with free ports at Danzig, Königsberg and Memel, together with rail connections guaranteed by treaty.[31] As to reparations, the Germans mentioned the sum of 100 milliard gold

[30] R. Morsey, *Die deutsche Zentrumspartei 1917–33* (Düsseldorf, 1966), pp. 180ff.

[31] C.M. Kimmich, *The Free City, Danzig and German Foreign Policy 1919–1934* (New Haven/London, 1968), pp. 19–21.

marks as interest-free compensation payment. As yet the proposed peace terms put no final figure forward. This was to be considered by the Allied Reparations Commission not later than 1 May 1921, until which time Germany was to make an incredible twenty milliard gold mark advance. The German counter-proposals also offered to supply coal to France until the mines destroyed in the war were restored, and they also offered direct aid for rebuilding the war-ravaged regions of Belgium and Northern France. In return, the Germans reinforced their appeal to the moral basis of peace by asking for guarantees that the Germans in Austria and Bohemia be allowed to decide their own fate. As to the matter of Germany's responsibility for causing the war, this was to be examined by neutral commissions. These counter-proposals were rejected, although some of the objections later found expression in partial modifications of the final Peace Treaty, as will be seen.

The extent to which rejection kindled the mood of defiant uproar among the German parties is well enough known and described. The divisions within a government which unanimously resented the terms were confirmed by the seven against seven vote during the Cabinet meeting of 18–19 June over the question of signing the treaty. The Scheidemann government resigned on 20 June 1919. However, once the question of what to do next had been posed, its answer was a foregone conclusion. The Allied ultimatum implied the threat of invasion if it were rejected, with the prospect of a renewal of the blockade's damaging effects on Germany's food supplies and the disintegration of the Reich's unity. It is possible from today's vantage point to wonder if in fact the Allies *could* have renewed military operations. The view of Hindenburg that military resistance against the *Entente* troops was useless was indeed accompanied by the suggestion of risking an honourable defeat. Many of the Army leaders toyed with the idea of exploiting the situation in the East against Poland and went far beyond this in their dreams.

In the last resort the impossibility of generating a fighting spirit in troops or population convinced Groener of the need to accept the terms, providing the dishonourable mentions were erased from them.[32] This was a view sanctioned by the 237 votes for the signature of the treaty against 138 in the National Assembly debate of 22 June. Included in the 138 were the nationalists and all but six of the

[32] Carsten, op. cit., pp. 44–56. cf. H. Mühleisen, 'Annehmen oder Ablehnen? Das Kabinett Scheidemann, die OHL und der Vertrag von Versailles', *Viertelfahrshefte für Zeitgeschichte*, 35, 3 (1987): 419–81.

Democrats. The Allies, however, preserved a united front, and the new SPD–Centrist coalition government, under the Social Democrat Gustav Bauer, was finally forced to sign: 'Surrendering to superior force but without retracting its opinion regarding the unheard-of injustice of the peace conditions the government of the German Republic therefore declares its readiness to accept and sign the peace conditions imposed by the Allied and Associated Governments.'

Few would dispute that, given the remarkable range of conditions and factors bearing on the task of peacemaking in war-torn Europe, the Treaty of Versailles was a remarkable achievement. But this is a judgement from the historian's study. In 1919, neither on the Allied nor on the German side was there the time or desire to balance niceties. The terms had to be reconciled with the conflicting views of the Allied powers. The detailed investigation of forces at work in Britain, France and America, the quest to determine how the compromise was hammered out in London, Paris and Washington, can hardly detain us here.[33] The failure of the Germans to grasp the *forces profondes* at work in the Allied camp was tragic, but hardly surprising in a Europe where no one power yielded much to the other in terms of following national interests.

If the British response, taking its cue from Wilson's much-vaunted idealism, has invariably been regarded as milder towards Germany than France's attitude, this was because Britain's global position was for the moment rather more favourable than that of France. Moreover, when it came to the crunch, both British and French leaders treated the Anglo-French *entente* as vital to their respective futures in the face of mounting evidence that the United States' involvement in Europe would be somewhat less than emphatic as peace progressed.[34] It has been said, for example, of Lloyd George that he

> followed the middle road. In the event of American withdrawal from Europe he kept open the door in 1919 to an alternative strategy for the upholding of European peace: Anglo-French collaboration based upon a policy of combined moderation and firmness in the treatment of Germany. A major tragedy of interwar history was the inability of England and France to travel this road together.[35]

In fact, it might be argued that the two *did* travel this road in the 1920s and together, if uneasily and with some pain on both sides (p. 69).

[33] For a useful aid see M. Gunzenhäuser, *Die Pariser Friedenskonferenz 1919 und die Friedensverträge 1919/1920. Literaturbericht und Bibliographie* (Franfurt am Main, 1970).

[34] Schwabe, op. cit.

[35] H.I. Nelson, *Land and Power. British and Allied Policy on Germany's Frontiers, 1916–1919* (London/Toronto, 1963), p. 382.

This was not entirely appreciated by many Germans, partly because they preferred to exaggerate the significance of Anglo-French differences towards Germany. As it was, some modification of the French concept of peacemaking was achieved by Anglo-American pressures, but it made little difference to the impact of the treaty on German opinion. The military provisions of the Versailles Treaty graphically underlined the Allied determination to safeguard their own future security against German aggression. Germany was rendered virtually defenceless. Its Army was reduced to 100,000 men, its Navy to 15,000. Conscription was forbidden to prevent the training of more men and the period of service for the new Regular Army was to be twelve years for men, twenty-five for officers. Not more than 5 per cent of the effective forces were to be replaced each year. Offensive weapons were not permitted, nor were aeroplanes, tanks and submarines. What weapons were allowed were detailed carefully. The famous Great General Staff was to be abolished, together with the military academies and cadet schools. Measures of mobilisation or preparation for mobilisation were forbidden. The manufacture or import of poison gas and war materials was prohibited, and in general the German armaments industry was placed under the severest restaint and Allied control and inspection. The demilitarisation and occupation of the Rhineland completed Germany's military impotence in the face of France's military power. The fact that Germany's treatment under these clauses was 'in order to render possible the initiation of a general limitation of the armaments of all nations' was of little comfort to the German leaders, left with an Army which was in effect a glorified police force, suited only to the internal preservation of law and order. Few Germans gave any thought to the great fear of France of Germany's enormous potential which informed these provisions.[36]

Similarly, the Germans did not think much of the changes effected in the territorial settlement as a result of international pressures on France and of Germany's own efforts. The return of Alsace-Lorraine to France was a foregone conclusion, settled by the Fourteen Points and the Armistice, but the original plans for the Saar were modified. True, the valuable mines passed into French hands. The decision to hold a plebiscite after fifteen years of the Saar being governed by an International Commission of the League was a plus for Germany, if hardly seen as such in 1919. Small areas were lost to Belgium – Moresnet, Eupen and Malmedy. As to the Rhineland, the terms were

[36] Cf. M. Salewski, *Entwaffnung und Militärkontrolle in Deutschland 1919–27* (Munich, 1966), pp. 30ff.

an improvement on the original French demand for its detachment from Germany. The French agreed to German sovereignty continuing over the territories of both banks of the Rhine on two conditions. Firstly, the German territories to the west of the Rhine, together with the bridgeheads of Mainz, Coblenz and Cologne were to be occupied by Allied troops. Evacuation was to be effected at five-year intervals if Germany fulfilled the conditions of the Versailles Treaty. After a concession made in June 1919, the period of occupation could be shortened if Germany gave proof of its goodwill and satisfactory guarantees of fulfilling its obligations. The demilitarisation of the west bank of the Rhine was enforced, together with a fifty-kilometre-wide strip on the east bank of the river. Finally, the French received a guarantee of military support from America and Britain in the event of an attack by Germany, concluded on the same day as the Versailles Treaty. The fact that the later rejection of the whole treaty by America nullified the British treaty of guarantee helps to explain the French determination to uphold the Rhineland terms thereafter, as well as France's efforts to encourage separatist movements in the Rhineland in the early years of peace.[37] From Berlin the whole situation was simply regarded as impossible. In comparison with this, the settlement of the German–Belgian and German–Danish borders paled into insignificance. As a result of a plebiscite in 1920, Southern Schleswig stayed with Germany. Northern Schleswig joined Denmark.

It was in East Europe that Germans felt themselves most ill-treated. To give the new Polish state the access to the sea which Wilson's points had demanded, the 'Polish corridor' was created – the provinces of Posen and West Prussia being lost to Poland. According to the terms of the draft treaty, Upper Silesia was also to go to Poland. Anglo-American pressures and German protests produced a relative improvement of the final situation. In July 1920 East Prussian territory was enlarged by the addition of the Allenstein and Marienwerder zones after the plebiscites held there. In March 1921 some two-thirds of Upper Silesia voted for Germany, with the result that Poland eventually obtained only a third of this area, although this part contained the greater mineral wealth. Danzig was not given to Poland outright. It was made a free city under the supervision of the League, although Poland had special rights, a customs union and control of

[37] Nelson, op. cit., pp. 130ff.; more generally see J.C. King, *Foch versus Clemenceau: France and German Disarmament, 1918–19* (Cambridge, Mass., 1960); D.R. Watson, 'The making of the treaty of Versailles', in N. Waites (ed.), *Troubled Neighbours: Franco-British Relations in the Twentieth Century* (London, 1971), pp. 67–99.

the city's foreign affairs. However, the overwhelming reaction in Germany was dictated by the knowledge that the Polish frontiers were now only 100 miles from the German capital and East Prussia was isolated.[38] The extent to which Germany's resentment was concentrated against Poland was seen by the relative lack of fuss made about the cession of the Hultschin district to Czechoslovakia and by the fact that Germany's policy towards Lithuania, which in 1923 seized the former German-owned Memelland from Allied supervision, was dictated by a desire to secure the aid of the small Baltic country against Poland (p. 141). Apart from the damage to Germany's national pride of Poland's victory, there was the fact that Poland, along with the other small states in Europe, became the centre of France's policies in East Europe.

This aspect of the East European settlement at Versailles became more important to the Allies, and France in particular, as the intervention against Soviet Russia continued to fade throughout 1919. By December 1919, Clemenceau had formulated more explicitly the concept of a cordon sanitaire of the East European states. These new states, instead of Russia, were to help France keep Germany in check and the new status quo intact. The cordon sanitaire also operated against Bolshevik Russia. By an irony that has often been remarked on, Germany's policy in 1918 of pushing Russia back and erecting a ring of satellite states in East Europe, which climaxed with the German–Soviet Treaty of Brest–Litovsk in March 1918, was turned against the new German Republic.[39]

In fact, many question-marks were left hanging over the eastern peace settlement until 1921 because of the continuing fighting between the Red Army and the so-called border states. Indeed, this was not lost on the German military leaders in the Baltic. When the peace terms were made known, they made a last desperate attempt to salvage what was left of the campaign by trying to arrange for their men to join the remnants of the White Russian troops, thus avoiding the German government's orders to evacuate the Baltic. The venture was doomed from the start, not least because the Red Army was too strong for its White Russian opposition. More importantly, once the Allies had seriously decided to get the German troops back, it was only a question of time. The fact that the last of the *Freikorps* did not

[38] For an illustration of the way in which anti-Polish sentiments were shared by all the political parties see Peter Nitsche, 'Der Reichstag und die Festlegung der deutsch–polnischen Grenze nach dem ersten Weltkrieg,' *Historische Zeitschrift*, **216** (1973): 335–61.

[39] Baumgart, 'Brest-Litovsk und Versailles', p. 608.

leave the Baltic until December 1919 was a result less of defiance by the Berlin government than of the confused nature of civil–military relationships in Germany. There was also a genuine difficulty in convincing the military leaders on the spot that the orders from Berlin to evacuate were serious.[40]

Given the disappointment to the hopes of securing a better peace by co-operation against the Bolsheviks, even some of the key Army leaders were beginning to favour instead accommodation with the Soviet forces and the Baltic campaign of 1919 was a serious obstacle to this. In contrast to its more hesitant forerunners, the Müller government was at least markedly more ready to consider normalising relations with the Soviets. Although the official 'wait and see' line on Russia continued, by the opening of 1920 some progress was being made in restoring economic relations with the Russians, albeit for some time at the level of private contacts.[41] Political relations developed more hesitantly because of the need to avoid antagonising the Allied Powers. Thus, the German–Russian agreement of 1 April 1920 to regulate the exchange of prisoners of war allowed the German and Russian plenipotentiaries quasi-diplomatic functions. Although the defeat of the Red Army by the Poles in August 1920 ended any prospect of an early revision of the eastern frontiers by the Bolshevik forces, the episode left a network of contacts between Russian and German military leaders on which to build later (p. 110).

At the same time, key political and business figures, such as Walther Rathenau and the industrialist Felix Deutsch, were arguing that Germany should and could take initiatives in improving their standing with Bolshevik Russia and with the territories on former Russian soil. Such arrangements would have to be 'provisional' in the sense that Germany was forced by the Treaty of Versailles to recognise the arrangements for Russia which the Allies eventually hoped to make, but they could help to influence later developments in Germany's favour.[42] This helps to explain the importance attached by the German Foreign Office to developing relations with the Baltic states once the German troops had evacuated them. During 1920 more serious efforts were made to get friendly relations with these, in part because they were regarded as economic 'stepping-stones' to Russia's markets, in part to frustrate Poland's attempts to gain control

[40] Cf. H.-E. Volkmann, 'Der Bericht des Generalleutnants Walter von Eberhardt – Meine Tätigkeit im Baltikum', *Zeitschrift für Ostforschung*, **13** (1964: 728–33.

[41] Linke, op. cit., pp. 82–3.

[42] G. Rosenfeld, *Sowjetrussland und Deutschland 1917–1922* (East Berlin, 1960), pp. 260–1

of the nascent regional Baltic alliance schemes. The outlines of a possible Baltic 'bloc' were thrown into relief at a conference at Balduri near Riga, at the height of the Polish–Russian war. The Baltic states, Finland and Poland, considered projects for regional economic, political and military collaboration. Germany's early initiatives in normalising relations with the Baltic countries were vindicated when the Allies proceeded to recognise their independence in 1921. Lithuania remained particularly important to Germany as we have already suggested because it, too, was in conflict with Poland after the latter's seizure of the Lithuanian capital of Vilna in 1920 (p. 142).

With little sympathy for the Polish predicament, the Germans viewed with proportionately greater anger the failure of the Allies to sanction self-determination when it worked to the Republic's advantage. Thus the *Anschluss* desired by Austria and Germany was, not surprisingly, forbidden by the Versailles Treaty.[43] This issue was left to cast its shadow on the already knotty problems of the new East European settlement and will be raised again in due course (p. 144). As to territories abroad, the German obligation to surrender its colonies was the more irritating in that the system of mandating these under the general supervision of the League of Nations became in effect a share-out for the victorious powers, rooted in their own wartime alliances and secret agreements.

To what extent Germany's early economic difficulties were caused by the imposition of reparations was not a difficult question to answer in that country. Reasoned responses were not the order of the day. The final ruling of the Allies on the amounts due was eventually given in May 1921 and the whole issue soon began to plague Germany's relations with the Western Powers (p. 66). Economic arguments for and against could barely conceal the fact that the issue was also a political one. Few now accept that the reparations themselves caused Germany's early economic and financial crises. Nevertheless, they can hardly have been an unimportant part of the 'economic consequences of the peace', to refer to the celebrated book by the famous Maynard Keynes, which provided the Germans with some useful ammunition in due course. At the very least reparations must be seen in the context of the harsh economic provisions of Versailles. The lost resources of German territories handed over at Versailles have been reckoned to include some 14.6 per cent of its

[43] Cf. L. Kerekes, 'Zur Aussenpolitik Otto Bauers 1918–19', *Vierteljahrshefte für Zeitgeschichte*, **22** (1974): 18–45; A.D. Low, *The Anschluss Movement 1918–1919 and the Paris Peace Conference* (Philadelphia, 1974).

arable land, 74.5 per cent of its iron ore, 68.1 per cent of its zinc ore, 26 per cent of its coal production as well as the potash mines and textile industries of Alsace. To this must be added the confiscation of Germany's overseas investment and property in enemy countries and the restrictions imposed on Germany's foreign trading by the compulsion to give the Allies most-favoured-nation treatment and the five-year ban on protective tariffs. Then there were the losses of merchant ships over 1,600 tons, half the merchant ships between 1,000 and 1,600 gross tons, a quarter of the fishing fleet and large quantities of rail locomotives and rolling stock.[44] But lists do not convey the essence of the problem, compounded by the need to pay a colossal debt incurred from financing the war. There was ample material here for fuelling the strife between the domestic pressure groups inside Germany as peace got under way and this will be examined in the next chapter.

The peace settlement imposed on Germany can hardly be judged without remembering that it had to be executed, and that much still depended on the active co-operation between the Germans and the Allies, working through a range of mixed commissions and committees. Many able studies exist which try to take a more rational look at a settlement which the Germans criticised so bitterly. The questions posed by Gerhard Schulz offer a useful insight.

> The fundamental problem which is also at the heart of the more penetrating subsequent criticism of the 'System of Versailles' continued to exist after the conclusion of peace. This was the problem of establishing a sound political equilibrium in Europe not based merely on the distribution of power as it was at the end of the war. Yet how could a new balance of power be achieved while the Western Powers were fighting Russia or trying to isolate it and while Russia was threatening to expand westwards? How could there be an equilibrium when a number of new states were emerging at the European periphery of old Russia and others resulting from the break-up of the Danube monarchy, and when their internal situation, their reactions in the international sphere and their economic potential were totally unknown quantities? How could there be an equilibrium if it was impossible for statesmen accurately to take into account the invisible forces of both great and small states that had been irresistibly mobilised by the war? How could there be a lasting settlement that took account of all the elements that would be of importance in a radically changed world? There is a serious lack of logic in all verdicts passed on the peace treaty which ignore the fact that the pre-war policies

[44] See the chapter on the effects of peace in G. Stolper, K. Häuser and K. Borchardt, *The German Economy 1870 to the Present* (London, 1967); W. Fischer, *Deutsche Wirtschaftspolitik 1918–45* (Opladen, 1968), pp. 16–17.

> could not prevent war and which fail to appreciate the essential continuity of the pre-war period, the war, peace-time and the era of revision.[45]

There is little remarkable about the German public's virtually unanimous endorsement of the quest to revise the Treaty of Versailles. *How* to go about this was another matter. There were, as we shall see, debates about 'Eastern' or 'Western' orientations to German foreign policy in the Wilhelmstrasse and elsewhere after 1918, which have since been earnestly taken up by historians. Today, however, it is easier than ever to recognise the folly of assuming that Germany could develop a viable foreign policy by playing off East and West. Germany could no more afford to lose touch with both West and East than, for example, France and Britain could do without each other in any major European conflict.

Equally, where France, Britain, America and others behaved with exemplary regard for their past histories, and where the foreign policy of each power continued to show unsurprisingly familiar traits, it does not seem so remarkable that 'continuity' was also present in German policy before and after 1918. Is there not, as it were, 'continuity for all'? Within such a framework the study of German foreign policy after the First World War makes much more sense.

[45] Schulz, op. cit., p. 223. Cf. A.J. Mayer, 'Post-war nationalisms 1918–1919', *Past and Present*, **34** (1966): 114–26.

CHAPTER TWO

The Domestic Context of Policy-making, 1919–39

One result of the abortive revolution of 1918/19 was that the Weimar Republic had to endure the marriage of a novel political system with archaic social structures inherited from Germany's imperial past. Just as before 1918, so afterwards, opposed socio-economic groups were represented in the elected assembly, the Reichstag, by the political parties which had either survived or were formed during the revolution. Unlike imperial administrations, however, republican governments were directly responsible to the Reichstag. The conflicts in this could now be taken to Cabinet level, there to influence policy-making directly through the parties composing the administration of the day. The outcome of the revolution left no single party with an absolute majority of the vote and coalition governments were the norm. This could hardly be without its effect on German foreign policy after 1918. As the Republic's most celebrated Foreign Minister regretted: 'The German always sees foreign policy only from the stand-point of domestic party conflicts and thereby loses any sense of what is necessary.'[1]

That there would be conflict over foreign policy and that this would in turn affect the domestic life of the Republic was ensured by the shock impact of the Treaty of Versailles. How to conduct policies based on such a treaty was a crucial question for Germany's future. The various responses to it of the conflicting social, political and economic interest groups provided a most important key to achieving domestic harmony. Hajo Holborn's maxim about German foreign policy after 1918 was that 'The great decisions, as far as they were at

[1] Cited by G.A. Craig, *From Bismarck to Adenauer. Aspects of German Statecraft* (New York, 1965), p. 60.

all in German hands, were inherent in the outcome of the internal social struggle.'[2] While this was no argument for the 'primacy of domestic policies',[3] the qualification about being in 'German hands' was an important one. Just as domestic factors could affect foreign policy so the latter could influence the shape of domestic relations. This was not unique to Germany. Less common was the viciousness of the interaction between external and internal realities and this overshadowed the entire history of the Weimar Republic.[4]

Before this is examined more closely, it is well to remark also that the 'institutions' of foreign policy-making were not as untouched by the domestic setting as might be supposed from a reading of some diplomatic studies.

Adequate recognition has only recently been given to reformist impulses developing within the Reich during 1918/19. Pressure came from a number of sources for a newer policy of international understanding: from within the political parties who had proposed the 'peace resolution' in 1917; from sectors of the business community anxious to see foreign policy more responsive to Germany's interest in international trade, and even from a small group of officials within the German foreign service, for whom reform of the AA gradually became a priority. The so-called Schüler reforms of the AA in 1920 expressed many of the newer concerns. The consular and diplomatic services were merged and the AA was reorganised into departments dealing broadly with various regions. Above all, the fusion of political and economic affairs ensured that thereafter 'economic issues in particular received far more emphasis and became an integral part of foreign policy'.

The Schüler reforms provided the framework of the AA until 1936, although in many respects the development of a broader social and political basis to the German Foreign Office during this period was arrested by the mid-1920s, when the AA had become once more the preserve of a long line of professional diplomats from more exclusive social backgrounds. Moreover the German Foreign Office developed its own aura and, under a powerful Foreign Minister like Gustav Stresemann (1923–29), a momentum which helped to give

[2] H. Holborn, 'Diplomacy in the early Weimar Republic', in G. Craig and F. Gilbert (eds), *The Diplomats 1919–39* (Princeton, 1953), pp. 157–8.

[3] Cf. V.R. Berghahn, *Germany and the Approach of War in 1914* (London, 1973), pp. 2–3.

[4] Cf. A. Nicholls and E. Matthias (eds), *German Democracy and the Triumph of Hitler* (London, 1971), p. 17.

continuity to German diplomacy in the 1920s.[5] To suggest, however, that even under Stresemann the AA 'had reasserted its independence from control by parties and interest groups' and that 'although susceptible to movements of public opinion, Weimar foreign policy after 1923 was usually framed and executed by the Foreign Minister and his department of professionals',[6] is to minimise the domestic context in which foreign policy categories are 'framed'.[7] Although the Weimar constitution made the AA the sole agency for foreign affairs, it was placed under a minister responsible to the Reichstag, as was the case with the other departments of state. Stresemann's power as Foreign Minister was directly related to his commanding position in domestic affairs, as will become apparent later.

Under normal circumstances therefore, the 'policy' of the AA had to command at least sufficient support from the parties making up the government. This was underlined by the meetings between the Minister of Foreign Affairs and the foreign affairs experts of the government parties. Considerations of coalition politics could restrict the Chancellor's right, as head of the government, to lay down guiding principles of foreign policy and he could override his own foreign minister in the broader interest of his government. Over and above such considerations there was the interest of the government in securing general support for its policies in the Reichstag. This was reflected by the soundings taken in the 'Foreign Affairs Committee of the Reichstag', a body which remained in being between sessions.[8] Such restraints were effectively more important than the powers given to the President of the Republic to make treaties and to appoint diplomatic officers since both presidents, first Ebert and later Hindenburg, tended to try to avoid conflict with the AA as far as possible.[9]

All of the above factors mirrored the more general process taking place in Europe after the war and the move towards greater public debate of foreign policy in reaction against the menacing prewar 'secret' diplomacy.[10]

[5] Holborn, op. cit., p. 153; W. Zechlin, *Diplomatie und Diplomaten* (Stuttgart, 1935), p. 74. Quote from P. Krüger, *Die Aussenpolitik der Republik von Weimar* (Darmstadt, 1958), p. 27; see also K. Doss, *Das deutsche Auswärtige Amt im Übergang vom Kaiserreich zur Weimarer Republik. Die Schülersche Reform* (Düsseldorf, 1977).

[6] Gaines Post Jr, *The Civil–Military Fabric of Weimar Foreign Policy* (Princeton, 1973), p. 20.

[7] Cf. L. Hill, 'The Wilhelmstrasse in the Nazi era', *Political Science Quarterly*, **82** (1967): 552–3.

[8] W. Apelt, *Geschichte der Weimarer Verfassung* (Munich–Berlin, 1964), p. 189.

[9] Holborn, op. cit., p. 49; G. Arns, 'Friedrich Ebert als Reichspräsident', *Historische Zeitschrift*, Beiheft **1** (1971): 1–30.

[10] Mayer, *Politics and Diplomacy of Peacemaking. Containment and counter-revolution at Versailles 1918–19* (London, 1968), p. 13.

As we have suggested, Germany was emphatically not excluded from this process. At the same time, it would be misleading not to recognise that, as in other countries, a 'foreign office' view on key issues existed. Although older diplomats in particular may have been unhappy with the Republic, their loyalty to the 'state' was not in question. Other officials went on to play a positive and key role in the formulation of the policy of understanding (*Verständigungspolitik*) in the 1920s. Broadly speaking, it is true, the AA was concerned to 'revise' the Versailles settlement. A convenient summary of the AA view on this is provided by Hans-Adolf Jacobsen's description of Neurath, Hitler's foreign minister until 1938.

> The foreign policy conception of Neurath and his closest colleagues in the AA was, in general terms, firmly fixed. It culminated in an evolutionary programme aiming at the systematic revision of the Versailles Treaty. The peaceful recovery of Germany, the struggle for international equality of rights and participation in the world's economy were not means to an end but ends in themselves.[11]

This might equally be a description of Stresemann and his foreign office. The judgement is also a convenient reminder that German 'revisionism' was not in itself inherently *destructive* of the European order. The Treaty of Versailles was so pervasive in its effects on Germany's political, social and economic life, that virtually any step taken by German governments after 1919 could be termed 'revisionist'. It is therefore important to stress that the concept of peaceful revision and *Verständigung* had enough support from major political parties, interest groups and individuals to be workable, at least as long as the extremist forces in Germany were kept in check.

Finally, not too much time will be given to the point that in modern states many parts of the specialised administrative apparatus influence foreign policy. Obvious examples in Germany were the Reich Economic Ministry and the Ministry of Finance. Because of the enormous importance to the Weimar Republic of economic recovery and the complexity of international economic agreements, the Economic Ministry was certain to play a major role, for example, particularly in policy-making towards Russia and East Europe after 1919, since here there were important new markets to be captured and developed.

Indeed, in the politically restricted circumstances in which Germany found itself as a result of the Versailles settlement, Germany's

[11] H.-A. Jacobsen, *Nationalsozialistische Aussenpolitik 1933–8* (Frankfurt am Main, 1968), p. 32. This massive study is indispensable.

economic policy virtually *was* its 'foreign policy', in the sense that economic weight could help achieve political goals.[12] The role of the Ministry of Finance in helping to define the limits of foreign policy is also self-evident in an era when reparations were a dominant theme. Reference has often been made also to the increased influence of legal experts, such as Friedrich Gauss, because of the problems of interpreting and drafting clauses in the postwar treaties. Significantly, after 1933 many of the ministries assumed growing importance in relation to the AA when its changing status reflected the changed priorities of the Third Reich.

COALITIONS AND POLICY-MAKING

If attention is once more concentrated on the broader domestic context, the obvious feature of the years 1919–23 was that executive power was chiefly in the hands of the parties making up the 'Weimar coalition', the Social Democratic Party (SPD), the Democrats (DDP) and the Centre Party. The name given to such a coalition expressed the conviction that these parties had most interest in the Republic's future. In the elections to the National Assembly in 1919 they polled some three-quarters of the votes. Yet even within this grouping there were important differences. The SPD was originally formed in 1865 and although its commitment to the Republic was self-evident it continued to suffer from its past struggles and its experiences in 1918/19. Its behaviour during the revolution and after showed that, even though no longer strictly speaking a 'workers' party, it remained a 'party of opposition' and found it hard to develop a clear and coherent response to the challenge of governmental responsibility. The pragmatism of the party, in itself promising, was in turn limited by the need to retain the support of its followers and not to lose face before the leftist parties that had sprung from the SPD ranks before and during the revolution: the Independent Socialists (USPD) and the Communists (KPD).[13]

The DDP, broadly speaking representing the more moderate and progressive strand of Wilhelmine liberalism, committed itself to

[12] Hill, op. cit., p. 547; Holborn, op. cit., p. 150. See H.-J. Schröder, 'Zur politischen Bedeutung der deutschen Handelspolitik nach dem Ersten Weltkrieg', in G. Feldman *et al.* (eds), *Die deutsche Inflation, Eine Zwrischenbilanz* (Berlin/New York, 1982).

[13] S. Neumann, *Die Parteien der Weimarer Republik* (Stuttgart, 1965), pp. 28–41; *The Road to Dictatorship. Germany 1918–1933. A Symposium by German Historians* (London, 1970), pp. 57–73.

supporting the new Republic in spite of many individual reservations and disillusionment with the revolution. Its mixed social composition, which gave it a chance to exercise power at the middle of the political spectrum, was at the same time a source of potential weakness in its organisation. This, too, echoed the past and the fateful split in German liberalism in the Empire during the 1880s.[14] The Centre Party was formed in 1870 and after the early struggles against Bismarck its leading lights had come to accept the Empire before 1914. It had, however, a history of defending parliamentary rights and its progressive democratisation under the impact of the First World War under Matthias Erzberger's leadership made it a natural enough ally for the other two 'republican parties'.[15] It has been argued however, that few of the leading Centrists went far beyond loyalty to the 'state' towards a positive commitment to the Republic.[16]

From the outset, foreign policy played an important role in the development of the Weimar coalition. In June 1919, most of the Centrist and SPD delegates to the National Assembly had taken the courageous step, together with six of the Democrats, of signing the Treaty of Versailles. Thereafter the Centre and SPD in particular found a common bond in their realistic acceptance of the danger to Germany's future unity and very existence which would follow rejection of the peace terms. The Weimar coalition committed itself logically to the only alternative to resistance, to the cause of international understanding and to the peaceful revision of Versailles through working with the victorious Allied Powers. This accorded both with the strong elements of pacifism in the German socialist movement and with the anti-doctrinaire stand of the Centre against the 'desperado' tactics of the German nationalists.[17]

This was not immediately clear at first. The SPD, which led two of the three governments between June 1919 and May 1921 (Bauer, Müller) has been charged with failing to formulate any clear foreign policy. The difficulties were considerable. Externally, the publicised differences between the Allies over the execution of the Peace Treaty encouraged German governments to exploit any available loopholes

[14] T. Wolff, *Through Two Decades* (London, 1936), pp. 38–9, 141–4; L. Albertin, 'Die Verantwortung der liberalen Parteien für das Scheitern der grossen Koalition im Herbst 1921', *Historische Zeitschrift*, **205** (1967): 573ff.

[15] Neumann, op. cit., pp. 41–3; R. Morsey, *Die deutsche Zentrumspartei 1917–33* (Düsseldorf, 1966), pp. 128–42; K. Epstein, *Matthias Erzberger and the Dilemma of German Democracy*, (Princeton, 1959), p. 286.

[16] Morsey, op. cit., p. 614.

[17] Neumann, op. cit., pp. 31, 47. W. Ribhegge, *Frieden für Europa. Die Politik der deutschen Reichstagsmehrheit 1917–18* (Essen, 1988), pp. 377–90.

and to try to keep open all possible policy options.[18] Such an approach also helped to reduce the very real internal threat from the rightist – nationalist forces, who were against the very suggestion of co-operation with the Allies. In that context it is easier to account for the obstructive attitude of German officialdom over the matter of war criminals, the over-zealous refutation of the charges of German 'war guilt' and the temporising over the execution of the military clauses of the Versailles Treaty (p. 22) as well as the German government's dilatory and uncertain handling of the German troops in the Baltic states during 1919, the policy of 'neutrality' during the Polish–Soviet war of 1920 and the exploratory moves towards Russia (p. 108). Only when the Allied Powers had taken a decisive stand against treaty evasion by occupying three Ruhr ports in March 1921 and by presenting the London Ultimatum on 5 May 1921, did the acceptance by the Weimar coalition parties of the need to work with the Allies find more formal expression in the policy of 'fulfilment'. The policy was articulated by the two governments of Chancellor Josef Wirth of the Centre Party, beginning on 10 May 1921.

As to the 'opposition' during this early period, its two main components were the German People's Party (DVP) and the German National People's Party (DNVP). It was not an opposition in the normal sense, being neither formalised nor consistent, and it was not in any position to launch a 'firm' policy against the Allied Powers. The DVP, founded on 15 December 1918, was made up largely but not exclusively from the right wing of the once great National Liberal Party of the German Empire under the leadership of the celebrated Gustav Stresemann. Its attitudes and values ranged from those shared by many of that other branch of the liberal forces, the DDP, to those common to the less extreme members of the DNVP.[19] The DNVP, set up in November 1918, was the umbrella for a mixture of not only the monarchist–traditionalist elements in Wilhelmine conservatism – so prominent in the Imperial and Weimar administration and bureaucracy – but also pan-German and anti-Semitic groups. Of the greatest importance, these two parties represented most of the economic interests of the powerful German bourgeoisie. While the DNVP also spoke on behalf of the great agrarian interests of Prussia, with their influential *Landbund*, (Agrarian League) to which half the parliamen-

[18] Wipert von Blücher, *Deutschlands Weg nach Rapallo* (Wiesbaden, 1951), p. 34; O. E. Schüddekopf, 'German foreign policy between Compiègne and Versailles', *Journal of Contemporary History*, **4** (1969): 181–97.

[19] H.A. Turner, *Stresemann and the Politics of the Weimar Republic* (Princeton, 1963), pp. 3–26; Albertin, op. cit., p. 573.

tary delegates of the party belonged,[20] the DVP was in effect 'the parliamentary mouthpiece of industry'.[21]

Inherent in both parties was the pull between a basic anti-Republicanism and the awareness of the advantages of participating in governments in order to mould policies. The hostility towards the Republic shared by both parties might be represented as growing in intensity from left to right, reaching its highest point at the extreme right of the DNVP. Here it would be difficult at times to distinguish some of the attitudes from those of the still more extreme extra-parliamentary rightist forces and paramilitary formations. Their activities were charted by the *putsch* against the government led by Wolfgang Kapp in March 1920 and elsewhere by the spate of political murders, many of the victims of which were associated with fulfilment, like Erzberger and later, Wirth's Foreign Minister, Walther Rathenau. More alarming still was the fact that the wider German public shared to a greater or lesser degree the opposition disillusionment with the new order of things. Thus, in the 1920 elections to the Republic's first Reichstag, the Weimer coalition, in startling contrast to its success in the National Assembly elections of 1919, could get the support of only a minority of voters. In foreign policy terms, the resentment towards the Republic was expressed by a widespread popular rejection of the will of the Allied Powers and a determination to resist the execution of the Peace Treaty.

Under such conditions the policy of fulfilment was bound to have disruptive effects on German domestic politics, although it was at the same time a revisionist strategy. The rigorous attempt to fulfil the Versailles terms was intended to prove that they were inherently impossible to fulfil. Once the Allied Powers had come to realise this, revision of the Peace Treaty was expected to follow fairly soon. It must be said that even the Weimar coalition parties on which Wirth based the policy of fulfilment were decidedly pessimistic about the tactics, as was evident during the prolonged and tortuous inter-party negotiations to get Wirth's first Cabinet formed.[22] All recognised that it was a policy of necessity, but at the same time feared the worst for Germany in the very attempt to meet the schedule of reparations payments set out in the London Ultimatum (p. 65). Such fears were grounded in the continued failure of German governments to tackle

[20] M. Stürmer, 'Parliamentary government in Weimar Germany 1924–8', in Nicholls and Matthias, op. cit., p. 67.

[21] Ibid., p. 66.

[22] E. Laubach, *Die Politik der Kabinette Wirth* (Lübeck/Hamburg, 1968), pp. 17ff.

effectively the financial and monetary crisis which had been building up prior to Wirth taking office.

The crisis had its origins in the financing of Germany's massive war effort. The decision to rely on loans, and in this way to avoid unpopular measures of taxation, contributed to the phenomenal government debt which had accumulated by the end of the war. The supply of goods in wartime could hardly keep pace with the available money and excess purchasing power, not absorbed by taxation, pushed prices up. The internal debt for the war effort was reckoned at 156 milliard marks by 31 March 1919 – over three times the prewar national income.[23] The strains on the German economy were all the greater when it was exposed once more to world contacts in 1919. Another factor was that government expenditure was demanded on an unprecedented scale after 1918. Inflation was therefore established by the time peace came and was not caused by the reparations demands of the Treaty of Versailles, as German governments tended to argue, along with German bankers, industrialists and journalists and even some economists.[24]

The stabilisation of the mark remained the government's declared aim but no effective steps were taken. War loans were not written off, state bankruptcy was not declared.[25] There was no exploitation of the new centralised system of taxation which Matthias Erzberger introduced as Finance Minister in 1919, before matters became markedly worse after March 1921. Instead, governmental resort to the printing presses to meet commitments became more marked. Certain groups and speculators actually profited from Germany's mounting inflation, but the recourse to printing money was not a deliberate attempt by Germany to wreck its own currency in order to escape obligations, as foreign opponents of the Weimar Republic were prone to argue. To an important extent, Wirth, like other German leaders before 1923, was a victim of the worldwide failure to understand the novel problems posed by payments between states on such a vast scale. The prevalence of the theory that the mark's continued fall was due to the inverse balance of payments caused by Germany's massive payments abroad, itself prevented more serious attempts to balance the budget.[26] Perhaps more important, however, was the psychology of fatalism engendered in Germany. It was

[23] W. Fischer, *Deutsche Wirtschaftspolitik 1918–45* (Opladen, 1968), pp. 12ff.

[24] R.A.C. Parker, *Europe 1919–1945* (London, 1969), p. 64.

[25] Cf. P. Krüger, *Deutschland und die Reparationen 1918/19* (Stuttgart, 1973), pp. 76ff.

[26] Parker, op. cit., p. 66.

ruinous for business confidence in general and militated against the sort of farsighted reforms which are more easily seen with the benefits of hindsight. In addition, reparations were as much a political as an economic problem because of their relationship to the broader hostility between Germany and the victor powers. Nor did the domestic balance of power in Germany make Wirth's task easier.

The sort of reform needed to stabilise Germany's currency required the co-operation of both the 'socialist' and 'bourgeois' political groupings and this in effect meant broadening the 'Weimar coalition' to the right. In practice, this resolved itself above all into the task of modifying the class conflict between the SPD and DVP (very roughly equated with employee and employer) which had been inherited from the Wilhelmine Empire.[27] Notwithstanding the promising impulses in both the SPD and the DVP, particularly from Stresemann, towards finding a *modus vivendi* during 1921 and early 1922, the pressures of the economic crisis were such that the respective party leaders could never properly control their followers. The intransigence and selfishness of the big industrialists and their ultimate failure to help Wirth raise the necessary money to pay off reparations, was matched on the other hand by the ideological war cry of the SPD for *Substanzerfassung* (seizure of capital).[28]

Although Wirth also shared a common belief that Germany's dilemma over reparations could be escaped by exploiting Anglo-French differences towards economic problems in Europe (p. 68), the crucial fact was that a timely solution to Germany's tax and currency problems eluded the Chancellor. Precisely the failure to mobilise Germany's resources to pay off the reparations promptly according to the London schedule intensified France's hostility. In turn this always threatened to deprive Wirth of the tangible gains from the Allies which he so desperately needed to convince the 'national opposition' of the viability of the policy of fulfilment. The pattern continued throughout Wirth's second administration from October 1921 to November 1922. At the same time these developments confirmed that the opposition to fulfilment had no practical alternative policy. The agreement with Russia which Wirth made at Rapallo in April 1922 was certainly never an alternative, although key *Reichswehr* leaders, nationalists and many business interests acted as though it were (p. 113). Wirth's final resignation in November 1922 was greeted

[27] M. Stürmer, *Koalition und Opposition in der Weimarer Republik 1924–8* (Düsseldorf, 1967), pp. 248–53, 254ff.

[28] Laubach, op. cit., p. 85; Albertin, op. cit., p. 569.

by rightist forces as proof of the bankruptcy of fulfilment and it opened the way, via Cuno's 'business' Cabinet, to the all-or-nothing policy of passive resistance after France invaded the Ruhr in 1923, to enforce fulfilment of the peace terms.

The failure had, however, as much to do with defects in the parliamentary system as a whole as it had to do with Wirth's own shortcomings. The important parties continued to have difficulties in throwing off the dead weight of past values and postures and in striking the essential balance between the vested interests they represented and the 'needs of state'. Emergency powers had been used plentifully to cope with the crisis and economic pressures made it even more difficult for the parties to adopt flexible tactics. For such reasons, Michael Stürmer's excellent study of coalition politics in the Weimar Republic suggests that the term 'parliamentary government' cannot be properly used at all of the years 1919–23.[29] This probably does insufficient justice to those many individuals who were striving for co-operation. However, only under the pressure of the extreme economic crisis of 1923 could the Weimar coalition be broadened at last under Stresemann's chancellorship in August of that year, when the DVP entered the government. This so-called 'Great Coalition' was itself an achievement for Weimar democracy, but the important question was, could Stresemann go beyond Wirth and weld together diverse interests in support of a coherent foreign policy?

STRESEMANN AND THE POLITICS OF REASON

Stresemann remained Chancellor until the end of November 1923. He was still unable to convince the extreme Right – against all the evidence of Germany's economic misery – that passive resistance could not continue, that it had to be abandoned before getting concessions from the Allies. The experience of catastrophe was also enough in itself to prepare opinion at large for Stresemann's decision to end passive resistance, to halt the printing presses, to stabilise Germany's chaotic financial situation and, after interim measures, to issue a new currency, the *Rentenmark*, on 15 November 1923. At last government, banks and industry worked together. In addition, the

[29] Stürmer, 'Parliamentary government', p. 60; *Koalition und Opposition*, p. 31; K.D. Bracher, *Die Auflösung der Weimarer Republik. Eine Studie zum Problem des Machtverfalls in der Demokratie* (4th edn, Schwarzwald, 1964), p. 64.

shocked reaction of the outside world to Germany's traumatic crisis in 1923 gave Stresemann a bonus that had escaped Wirth; namely the acceptance of the Allies of the need to take a much broader view of reparations and the recognition of the hopelessness of trying to enforce the payments in their original extent. The result was the Dawes Plan which, by relating Germany's future payments to its capacity to pay and by contributing towards its economic recovery by loans (p. 71), provided Stresemann with the vital context for his subsequent foreign policy. The ensuing German economic boom, overtaking prewar production figures by the end of the 1920s, is a matter of record. Economic growth did not by any means benefit all sectors of society. The continuing class conflict was underlined by the defection of the SPD from government on 2 November 1923, although the immediate occasion for this was the use of the *Reichswehr* against the socialist–Communist coalitions which had gained power in Saxony and Thuringia in 1923 and not against the rightist resistance in Bavaria under Gustav von Kahr, where Hitler, too, had made his first appearance on the wider public stage. Yet the absence of severe economic crisis 1924–28, made it easier to follow placatory social and economic policies.

With the socialists reverting to their 'habit of opposition' between 1923 and 1928, the middle years of the Republic were more openly dominated by the powerful bourgeois interest groups, formerly so influential in Wilhelmine Germany. During these years the only types of government which could be formed were those based on the DDP, Centre Party and the DVP (Marx's first and second cabinets, December 1923 to 15 January 1925, his third Cabinet, May 1926 to 29 January 1927, Luther's second Cabinet, 20 January 1926 to 17 May 1926) or those which included the DNVP (Luther's first Cabinet, January 1925 to 20 January 1926, Marx's fourth Cabinet January 1927 to 29 June 1928). The former were minority cabinets, compelled to secure the support of right or left or both by concessions. The latter type of government could command a parliamentary majority but it suffered from the divergences within the rightist/nationalist camp, which will be examined shortly. On the surface, then, *consistent* government or opposition was no more possible after 1923 than it had been before. On the positive side, however, experience *was* slowly accumulating, at least to the extent that a clear foreign policy line could be drawn for the next six years.[30]

Of course, the balance of political forces must be kept in mind

[30] Stürmer, 'Parliamentary government', pp. 64–5.

when examining the policy which Stresemann pursued as Foreign Minister in all of the governments between 1923 and 1929. The new element in diplomacy was the support given to Stresemann and therefore the government by his own party, the DVP, although this cost him constant and tiring effort. The socialists, if still opposed to the DVP on many internal issues, could be relied on to support Stresemann's version of revisionism. Related to 'fulfilment' was Stresemann's espousal of co-operation with the Allied Powers and, above all, the more conscious effort he made to placate French fears of insecurity. This explains the diplomatic manœuvres leading from the Dawes Plan to the Locarno Treaties of 1925', Germany's entry into the League of Nations in 1926 and the continuous exchanges with the Allied Powers until his death in 1929 (p. 72). Going beyond Wirth, however, Stresemann more systematically pursued the cause of peaceful revisionism and the restoration of full German sovereignty rather than waiting for it to happen. Thus, the concerted effort to get the Rhineland evacuated, the exploitation of the Locarno provisions for the East European settlement, the blocking of any suggestion for an *Ostlocarno*, the continuing links with Russia and the furthering of the revisionist cause against Poland (p.146). The key to Stresemann's policy, some have argued, is that in many respects it was not so very different from Wirth's, if more vigorously applied under changed circumstances and more explicitly directed at getting the support of both moderate and nationalist forces in the Republic.[31]

Understandably, Stresemann has exercised a major attraction to historians of the Weimar Republic. His role was subjected to particularly critical scrutiny during the often heated arguments from the 1960s onwards about foreign policy trends between Bismarck and Hitler. Stresemann's foreign policy, it was often pointed out, with his emphasis on active German economic expansion and his well-known concern for the fate of Germans outside the Reich, implied the existence of a greater Germany dominating Central and Eastern Europe which had affinities both with the aims of prewar Germany

[31] The literature on Gustav Stresemann is immense. A convenient recent survey is R. Grathwol's, 'Gustav Stresemann: reflections on his foreign policy', *Journal of Modern History*, **45** (1973): 52–70. This supplements H.W. Gatske's earlier, 'Gustave Stresemann: a bibliographical article', *Journal of Modern History*, **36** (1964): 1–13. For more detail see M. Walsdorff, *Bibliographie Gustav Stresemann* (Düsseldorf, 1972). Laubach, op. cit., pp. 313–14 brings out the similarities between Stresemann's and Wirth's policies. See also M. Lee, W, Michalka, *German Foreign Policy 1917–1933. Continuity or Break?* (Leamington Spa, 1987), pp. 73ff.; and W. Stresemann, *Mein Vater Gustav Stresemann* (Frankfurt, 1987).

and those of Hitler.[32] Communist writers went further and insisted that 'In the long run, Stresemann's policy helped to pave the way for warlike expansion.'[33] Arguably, Stresemann's success in furthering the revision of the Versailles peace terms made Hitler's task easier in the early years of the Third Reich, when the Führer was anxious to stress that he was like other German statesmen. Yet 'revisionism', as we have suggested, is an all-encompassing term, and distinctions must be made in its application. It is more important than ever today, with Germany reunited, not to lose sight of the signal differences between Stresemann's and Hitler's diplomacy, nor to underestimate the constructive aspects of the Republican minister's foreign policy. It is, of course, well known that Stresemann had been a convinced supporter of German annexations during the First World War and he was as bitterly against the Versailles terms as the next man. His 'nationalist' pedigree was impeccable. Given, however, the greater knowledge we now have both of the difficult German domestic context in which Stresemann worked and of the comparative European setting, it is easier to see that Stresemann's advocacy of 'national' interests was paralleled by the actions of politicians in other countries. Like theirs, his ideas evolved quite naturally into a conception of policy-making which increasingly found room for the give and take of international diplomacy in the changed postwar conditions.

At least historians have long tried to pinpoint the moment when Stresemann turned from the annexationist into the *Vernunftrepublikaner* (republican by conviction), and have increasingly stressed the impact made on him by the events of 1923. The experience of that difficult year confirmed his growing belief in the value of a united approach to policy-making and the overriding need to minimise internal disputes in the interests of foreign policy.[34] Wirth's policies had implied this too, but Stresemann's insistence on the 'primacy of foreign policy' became in turn a highly developed political strategem to integrate political forces in the Republic. More than any other Republican leader, Stresemann understood and exploited the interaction between external and internal realities which was mentiond earlier. Foreign policy successes were to help lessen domestic conflicts

[32] H. Graml, *Europa zwischen den Kriegen* (Munich, 1969), pp. 195–6; K. Hildebrand, *The Foreign Policy of the Third Reich* (London, 1973), pp. 9ff.

[33] W. Ruge, *Stresemann. Ein Lebensbild* (East Berlin, 1965), p. 226.

[34] Turner, op. cit., pp. 263–4; Grathwol, op. cit., pp. 63–4; L.E. Jones, 'Gustav Stresemann and the crisis of German liberalism', *European Studies Review,* **4**, No. 2 (1974): 151–2; A.E. Cornebise, 'Gustav Stresemann and the Ruhr occupation: the making of a statesman', *European Studies Review*, **2**, No. 1 (1972): 43–67.

as the solution to these was to strengthen the basis for further successes in the international arena. Stresemann's concern to integrate domestic forces through foreign policy differs in essentials from the diversionary purposes fulfilled by Wilhelmine policies and the revolutionary ones of the Third Reich (Chapter 7).

However, Klaus Hildebrand has argued that peaceful 'revisionism' was in the last resort too feeble a tool to integrate the diverse forces of the Weimar Republic.[35] Rightist opposition to Stresemann's policies remained formidable, notwithstanding the fact that the bourgeois governments after 1923 were more socially acceptable to this opposition than the previous coalition had been. Nationalists were still incensed by any suggestion of giving way to the Allies and pointed to the growing dependence of the German economy on foreign loans and to the oppressive presence of reparation agents and other restraints on the German economy because of the Dawes Plan. Above all, many lower-middle-class victims of the crisis of 1923 had not recovered from it and they helped to swell the growing ranks of the 'brown movement' whose energies Hitler so skilfully tapped later in the 1920s and whose disappointments were registered by their increasing desertion of the more moderate bourgeois parties like the DDP and DVP.[36]

Indeed, the more radical mood in the country at large among nationalists helps to explain why the promising impulses towards co-operation with the other moderate parties, which were beginning to come from the DNVP parliamentary delegation, did not fully develop. By 1924 the all-or-nothing anti-Republicanism of the DNVP was increasingly opposed by key groups in it and the professional, bureaucratic elements in its ranks. In part this reflected the disillusion with the failure of direct action against the government between 1919 and 1923, as well as a growing realisation of the material advantages to be derived from Stresemann's 'export-orientated' foreign policies and the economic reconstruction on the basis of the Dawes Plan. Then, too, there was the awareness of the need to influence domestic legislation, for example over food tariffs, by being represented in the government. Such motives explained the DNVP's presence in the governments of 1925 and 1927.[37]

Nevertheless, the fact that the DNVP actually split over the question of accepting the Dawes Plan and continued to resist the policies which Stresemann launched at Locarno, evidenced a fateful

[35] Hildebrand, op. cit., pp. 137–8.

[36] Cf. Heinrich Bennecke, *Wirtschaftliche Depression und politischer Radikalismus 1918–1938* (Munich, 1970), pp. 89–92.

[37] Stürmer, 'Parliamentary government', p. 67.

gap between the more realistic DNVP leadership and the party at large. It also emphasised that the progress of peaceful revisionism depended on the rightist–nationalist forces being restrained or at least kept within reasonable bounds. The participation of the DNVP in government has been described as the 'high-water mark' in the painful process of *rapprochement* between the parliamentary Right and the Republic, but the same event focussed the opposition of the anti-Republicans within the party against the state. By the end of 1927, the DNVP leader Graf Cuno Westarp was urging that outdated ideological formulae prevented a realistic outlook. In retrospect, however, the domination of the DNVP by such 'moderates' in the mid-1920s can be seen to have been 'only an interval in the history of the DNVP'.[38] This was confirmed by the events which took place after 1929.

With the onset of an even worse economic crisis than 1923, the latent class conflict in the Republic blossomed anew. The growth of political radicalism, present of course before 1928, became a matter of frightening record over the next few years. The 'Great Coalition' which came back into power under the SPD Chancellor Hermann Müller in the summer of 1928 was therefore certain to be subject to acute strains. Its members could agree on foreign policy and the Cabinet achieved a far-going revision of the reparations payments through the Young Plan, ready in early June 1929. It also moved a step nearer to complete evacuation of the Rhineland (p. 78). Nonetheless, the SPD and DVP members of the Cabinet in particular were subject to the strains imposed by the growing appeal of the extreme left (KPD) and extreme right (NSDAP). Facing a 'struggle against radical forces which threatened to steal their supporters', the parties therefore 'had to stand firm on their principles in order to keep their credibility'.[39] As in the crisis of 1919–23, the incompatibility between DVP and SPD principles proved the chief obstacle to tackling the economic crisis effectively. Even the limited working during the mid-1920s became more difficult to achieve, and the time-consuming interparty bargaining effectively paralysed Müller's government by the end of March 1930.[40]

[38] Stürmer, *Koalition und Opposition*, pp. 253–4.

[39] *Akten der Reichskanzlei: Kabinett Müller II*,**1** (Boppard am Rhein, 1970): xlv.

[40] Werner Conze, 'Die Krise des Parteienstaates in Deutschland 1929/1930', in Gotthard Jasper (ed.), *Von Weimar zu Hitler 1930–1933* (Cologne–Berlin, 1968), pp. 41–2.

FROM BRÜNING TO HITLER

Heinrich Brüning, who then became Chancellor, could hardly hope to succeed where Müller had failed. Although of the Centre Party, Brüning's appointment was very much on the sufferance of the traditional rightist sectors of German society, who favoured a broad-based but right-wing Cabinet which would also have room for the less extreme members of the DNVP. The 'above party' label attached to Brüning's Cabinet could not disguise where the realities of power lay. Significantly, the Army leaders had played a key role in advancing Brüning's candidacy for the chancellorship. Moreover, President Hindenburg, who had moved decisively to the right, gave to Brüning the emergency powers which he had refused to grant Müller. The political complexion of Brüning's Cabinet could be gauged, too, from his preferential treatment of the great landowners, though this was to some extent forced on him. In effect, Brüning's predicament appeared to preclude close co-operation with the SPD.[41] Thus, facing stalemate in the Reichstag, Brüning called for fresh elections at the end of 1930. At these elections the extreme, essentially anti-parliamentarian forces on the right and left, the KPD and NSDAP, broke through to a mass following for the first time. The blows dealt in these elections to the moderate bourgeois parties could not be offset by the relative success of the other two main pillars of the Republic, the Centre Party and the SPD, in holding their voters. As well as the collapse of its economy, therefore: 'So too the permanent structural crisis of parliamentary democracy in Germany had become acute.'[42]

It was important to Hitler's success in the 1930 elections that he had joined forces with the DVP, now under Hugenberg, and losing its less extreme parliamentary members as a result. The 'Alliance' gave Hitler growing access to the traditional centres of conservative power and assured him of a wider public hearing. Clearly, Hitler's cause was helped in proportion to the state of collapse of the discredited parliamentary institutions, but a resurgence of virulent nationalism played its part in the appeal of the Nazis. It was focused against the Western Powers and in particular against the Young Plan, which got through the Reichstag in May 1930 only with the greatest difficulty. It was an obvious ploy for the extreme Right to exaggerate

[41] Cf. Werner Conze, 'Brüning als Reichskanzler. Eine Zwischenbilanz', *Historische Zeitschrift*, **214** (1972): 310–34: M. Grubler, *Die Spitzenverbände der Wirtschaft und das erste Kabinett Brüning* (Düsseldorf, 1982).

[42] Werner Conze, 'Brünings Politik unter dem Druck der grossen Krise', *Historische Zeitschrift*, **199** (1964): 532.

the effects of outside restrictions on Germany's economic life in a time of continuing economic crisis and incendiary unemployment figures. With the Hugenberg–Hitler partnership cemented by the 'Anti-Young Front', revisionism was less a matter of long-term goals than one of immediate domestic necessity.

Brüning himself favoured a more forceful brand of revisionism, deliberately setting out to get rightist support for his actions and trying to ensure, above all, freedom of movement for German policy. His economic and financial policy during the crisis served this purpose. With the ending of foreign capital inflow and the withdrawal of credit from Germany during the economic crisis, the transfer payments for reparations under the Young Plan had to be met from a trade surplus. This could either be achieved through the draconian measures which Brüning imposed on the economy, deflating ruthlessly at the immediate cost of increasing domestic misery, or through the sort of international loan offered by France in 1931, as yet less damaged by the global crisis. Or Germany could have allowed the reparations payments to lapse. In fact, these last two alternatives threatened an increase in French controls and conditions which Brüning's domestic power base virtually precluded. Quite apart from the antipathy of the president and the *Reichswehr* to such a prospect, party support from the centre to the Right, and perhaps even from the right of the Centre Party itself, would have vanished overnight.[43]

In the last resort there was not enough time for Brüning's policy to be successful and the positive gains in the field of foreign policy were denied to him. Brüning did not alone create the dilemma in which he found himself, as his memoirs make apparent, but his espousal of the art of sabre-rattling on the international scene and the development of authoritarian government during his term of emergency rule made him a key figure in the transition from Stresemann to Hitler, irrespective of his claim that he was trying to defend democracy.[44] He failed in the last resort to counter the growing 'appeal to the irrational' in German society, while at the same time trying to capitalise on it in order to save his own government and restore Germany's full great-power status. Finally, Brüning could not appease his rightist critics by

[43] W.J. Helbich, 'Die Bedeutung der Reparationsfrage für die Wirtschaftspolitik der Regierung Brüning', in Jasper, op. cit., pp. 92–3. For an example of the growing extremism of prominent Centre Party politicians during the crisis see W. Ruge, 'Die Aussenpolitik der Weimarer Republik und das Problem der europäischen Sicherheit 1925–1932', *Zeitschrift für Geschichtswissenschaft*, **22** (1974): 273–90.

[44] Heinrich Brüning's, *Memoiren 1918–1934*, Bd 2 (Stuttgart, 1970, paperback), pp. 488–9. E. Kolb, *The Weimar Republic* (London, 1988), pp. 110–26.

foreign policy successes since the attacks by Hitler and others were but part of a general attempt to overthrow the government and to prepare the way for a regime free of the parliamentary swamp.

Thus, although there was by no means unequivocal support for the Hitler movement in the conservative ranks, their effort to brazen out the crisis in their own interests gave them ultimately little alternative other than to try to get behind them the mass support which the Nazis had built up so quickly. The traditional right in Germany shared Hitler's violent anti-Bolshevism – a threat all the more credible with the KPD gains after 1929 – as well as his belief in the need for a firmer policy towards the outside powers and the early restoration of Germany's great-power status. Together with the support of key economic groups, interested in 'firm' government, and that of some of the *Reichswehr* leaders, Hitler was in a good position to profit from the conspiratorial activity created at the centre of government by emergency rule. Such processes led to Hitler being installed 'legally' as Chancellor, after the interludes of government by Franz von Papen and Kurt von Schleicher. He was apparently safely harnessed by the powerful conservative forces in German society. This working partnership was no accident from Hitler's viewpoint. At no time could he have seized power by force alone. His ostentatious co-operation with the establishment perpetuated the illusion of continuity, particularly in foreign policy, but this was in reality a smoke-screen to conceal the transformation of Germany and its purpose, as can be seen when we turn now to the Third Reich.

Ideologically, the Hitler movement was rooted in expansionist doctrines. Some had affinities with other rightist aims in Germany's past and this was particularly true of those followed by certain key groups in the Nazi Party other than Hitler.[45] The latter's thoughts, however, went beyond anything that Wilhelmine Germany had had to offer – let alone the Weimer Republic with its 'peaceful revisionism' – by justifying expansion on the grounds of racial supremacy.[46] Central above all to Hitler's thought from the early 1920s was the belief that Germany's long-term economic and other problems could only be solved, in the first intance, by gaining territory in the east at

[45] Hildebrand, op. cit., pp. 13–19.

[46] See M. Michaelis, 'World power status or world dominion? A survey of the literature on Hitler's plan of world dominion' 1937–70', *Historical Journal*, **15**, No. 2 (1972): 331–60; E. Jäckel, *Hitlers Weltanschauung* (Tübingen, 1969), Chapter 2; T.W. Mason, 'Some origins of the Second World War', in E.M. Robertson (ed.), *The Origins of the Second World War* (London, 1971), p. 108; N. Rich, *Hitler's War Aims, Ideology, the Nazi State and the Course of Expansion* (London, 1973); G. Stoakes *Hitler and the Quest for World Dominion* (Leamington Spa, 1986).

the expense of Russia (p. 125). This ideal was reaffirmed in secret to the Army leaders immediately after Hitler's accession to power.[47] Exactly how and why Germany became involved in war with the West before Russia can be left to later sections. At this point all that needs to be stressed is that the pursuit of *Lebensraum* presupposed first and foremost the psychological and material preparation of Germany. The need for this can be most easily shown by glancing first at the state of the German armed forces when Hitler came to power.

Thanks in particular to the efforts of the German Chief of the Army High Command between 1920 and 1926, General Hans von Seeckt, the Republic had managed to make the most of the Army legally permitted by the Versailles Treaty. The forbidden General Staff and officer corps had been preserved in different guises and, because of Seeckt's exploitation of the loopholes left in the civilian control of the *Reichswehr*, the Army had developed along lines acceptable to the German officers. Advances had been made in training, and to some extent equipment, by means of German–Russian co-operation in the 1920s.[48] The potential for expansion of the *Reichswehr* was fair but, according to Walther Bernhardt's study of German rearmament, there was no dramatic increase in *Reichswehr* personnel beyond the 100,000-man limit set by Versailles before April 1933, in spite of rearmament programmes in 1930 and 1932.[49] Small advances had been made in the creation of an Air Force, while the Navy was largely outdated and had not even reached the numbers permitted by the Versailles Treaty.[50] The Germany of 1933 was manifestly unable to wage war on even one of its neighbours let alone a combination of them. This of course also helped to explain the pursuit of peaceful revisionism by Weimar governments. According to a recent study of the civil–military fabric of Weimar foreign policy, key military and naval leaders accepted the premise that Germany was too weak to risk war. Joint planning between the civilian and military authorities of the

[47] J. Noakes and G. Pridham, *Documents on Nazism 1919–1945* (London, 1974), pp. 508–9.

[48] The best overall account of the Republic and the Army remains F.L. Carsten's *Reichswehr und Politik* (translated as *Reichswehr and Politics*, London, 1966). For a different view of Seeckt see Claus Guske's, *Das politische Denken des Generals von Seeckt: Ein Beitrag zur Disckussion des Verhältnisses Seeckt–Reichswehr* (Lübeck, 1971), p. 273. See also K.-J. Müller *The Army, Politics and Society in Germany 1933–45*, (Manchester 1987).

[49] W. Bernhardt, *Die deutsche Aufrüstung 1934–9. Militärische und politische Konzeptionen und ihre Einschätzung durch die Allierten* (Frankfurt am Main, 1969), p. 38.

[50] W. Carr, *Arms, Autarky and Aggression. A Study in German Foreign Policy 1933–9* (London, 1972), pp. 26–7; D. Irving, *The Rise and Fall of the Luftwaffe. The Life of Luftwaffe Marshal Erhard Milch* (London, 1976, paper), pp. 29–35.

Weimar Republic evaluated at departmental level the state's power in relation to foreign forces and for national defence, as well as for exploiting any potentially favourable political situation such as that created by a possible Soviet–Polish conflict.[51]

There were, however, crucial differences of opinion between civilian and military leaders in Weimar Germany. The premise of Seeckt's policy was after all to make the most of the existing state form until such time as a revived German Army could fight if need be for the revision of Versailles, and the tensions between *Reichswehr* and Republic have been well enough described.[52] By the 1930s, for example, the AA feared, as a result of its experience of joint planning, that the Navy and Army commands could not be trusted to 'define the relationship between theoretical operational exercises and the actual international situation carefully and consistently'. By contrast, the crucial role of the *Reichswehr* in bringing Hitler into office and permitting him to stay there underlined the fact that Hitler and the generals had much in common in spite of a healthy mutual distrust and even distaste. Newer work on the nature of the German military suggests that its top leaders were strongly motivated by the inability of the Weimar system to guarantee the future material base for the expansion of the armed forces.[53] By contrast the priority given in Hitler's ideology to expansion put a premium on continued co-operation with the Army, whose power was certain to increase once the Republic was buried. This was made plain enough with the Röhm purge of 1934, when the long-standing tension between the Hitler movement's paramilitary arm, the SA and the *Reichswehr* was ended in favour of the latter.

THE ECONOMICS OF REARMAMENT

The purged ended, too, the hopes of the 'socialist' elements in the Hitler movement and thus opened the door to economic policies

[51] Post, op. cit., pp. 101ff.

[52] Apart from Carsten, see K. Demeter, *The German Officer Corps in Society and State, 1650–1945* (London, 1965); M. Kitchen, *A Military History of Germany; From the Eighteenth Century to the Present Day* (London, 1975).

[53] Post, op. cit., pp. 346–7. See Müller, op. cit., p. 20. For newer work emphasising the affinities between the armed forces and the regime see, O. Bartov, 'Soldiers, Nazis and War in the Third Reich'. *Journal of Modern History*, **63**, 1, (1991): 44–60; W. Deist, *The Wehrmacht and German Rearmament* (London, 1986); M. Messerschmidt, *Die Wehrmachtjustiz im Dienste des Nationalsozialismus, Zerstörung einer Legende* (Baden-Baden, 1987).

which were geared above all to rearmament. Rearmament, it was argued by Arthur Schweitzer, 'became the main goal and guiding principle for economic activity'.[54] Just as historians have been urging for some time the need to abandon the idea that there was a 'revisionist' then an 'expansionist' period of Nazi foreign policy, as opposed to the pursuit in a more open manner after 1936 of long-standing goals,[55] so economists point out the continuous economic developments between 1933 and 1939. The fact that the Nazi economic policies of 1934 made so much political capital of the determination to solve Germany's unemployment problem must not lead us to overlook the priority given to rearmament even at this stage. As one expert wrote recently:

> If the impression arises that the first year of National Socialist government were devoted to creating employment, that in the next years creating employment and rearmament went on side by side, this arose from the fact that the rearmament measures were at first kept secret and needed time before they made an economic impact, whereas the measures for creating work were broadcast loud and clear and had in fact already begun in 1932, so that their effects were obvious even by 1933/34.[56]

The solution to the unemployment problem was of course crucial in minimising internal opposition to the regime, just as its peaceful pose towards the outside world was intended to forestall hostile reactions from abroad in the risky early years of the Third Reich's existence. As the above quotation suggests, Hitler was helped by Brüning's legislation to solve unemployment, which he continued 'with the marked shift of emphasis towards quasi-military projects', such as the autobahn.[57] Hitler was also helped by the ease with which the relatively under-used German economy of the slump years was revitalised in the changed and purposeful atmosphere after 1933. Above all, the psychological impact of the depression conditioned all social groups to accept more readily the greater role played by rearmament in providing employment and to continue doing so after Hitler had thrown aside the veil of secrecy in 1935.[58] It also followed that political priorities intruded into economic policy on a scale which

[54] A. Schweitzer, 'On depression and war: Nazi phase', *Political Science Quarterly*, **62** (1947): 359. Cf. F. Blaich, *Wirtschaft und Rüstung im 'Dritten Reich'*, (Düsseldorf, 1987).

[55] Jacobsen, op. cit., p. 613.

[56] W. Fischer, op. cit., pp. 63–4.

[57] Carr, op. cit., p. 23. But cf. the reservations of R.J. Overy, 'Transportation and rearmament in the Third Reich', *Historical Journal*, **16** (1973): 390ff.

[58] Schweitzer, op. cit., pp. 347–8.

was not known in Germany before 1933,[59] although 'private enterprise' continued to be the basis of the German economy in the Third Reich.

There remains, however, some difficulty in describing precisely the relationship between Nazi economic policies and German foreign policy, 1933–39. The most obvious connections are easily disposed of. 'Autarchy' was not spelt out systematically until the introduction of the Four-Year Plan in 1936, but it was implicit in the regime's earliest legislation. The function of the President of the Reichsbank Hjalmar Schacht, was to provide the money for the government's rearmament plans. In practice, the extensive interference with the traditional banking and finance mechanisms which this required would have been impossible without the simultaneous attempt to seal off the German economy as far as possible from the economic forces of the outside world. Notably, the 'New Plan' of Schacht in 1934 dramatically extended the foreign exchange controls of Brüning's government. The Nazi regime acquired decisive influence over the extent and distribution of available reserves of foreign currency.[60] This could be rationalised by propaganda as a defensive step, designed to secure German jobs and to protect the German economy from the sort of outside influences which had harmed the Weimar Republic. However, the extent of Schacht's 'New Plan', which entailed 'the total regulation of foreign exchange',[61] sharply distinguished Germany's efforts from those of the other capitalist powers to protect their interests during the era of depression. Nor did the other powers give the prominence to the rearmaments industry which it received in Germany's reconstruction.[62] (See Table 1.)

Such measures did not exactly improve Germany's relations with other countries but they did not automatically commit Germany to war until 'Hitler's decisive intervention in the economic field in the

[59] Cf. T.W. Mason, 'The primacy of politics – politics and economics in National Socialist Germany', in S. J. Woolf (ed.), *The Nature of Fascism* (London, 1968), pp. 165–95.

[60] Otto Nathan, *The Nazi Economic System. Germany's Mobilization for War* (Durham, N. Carolina, 1944), pp. 107–36; C.W. Guillebaud, *The Economic Recovery of Germany 1933–8* (London, 1939), pp. 24ff; S. Dengg, *Deutschlands Austritt aus dem Völkerbund und Schachts Neuer Plan* (Frankfurt, 1986).

[61] Fischer, op. cit., p. 72.

[62] Cf. Mason, 'Some origins', pp. 116–19. After a discussion of the problems of estimating armaments expenditure, Mason decides that from March 1933 to March 1939 the Third Reich spent about half as much again as was spent on armaments in Britain and France put together in this period, cf. the discussion in the opening chapter of A. Milward, *The German Economy at War* (London, 1965). Finally, see Table 1 on arms expenditure at the end of this book.

summer of 1936 . . . ensured that autarchy would not be employed to protect living standards in Germany but simply to serve the Nazis' imperialist ambitions.'[63] By this time, on the other hand, it was fairly apparent that economic forces were not so much harnessed to political objectives as helping to determine them. Although the regime had managed to solve the unemployment problem and the economy was at near full stretch again, it was becoming increasingly difficult to see how to continue economic expansion on the present lines.

Not least important was the fact that notwithstanding its autarchic pretensions, Nazi Germany remained bound for the foreseeable future to try to improve its trading relations with the outside world. The vital foreign currency to purchase the raw materials necessary to keep German production moving along smartly had to come from an increase in foreign trade. By 1936, however, Germany's trade terms had worsened dramatically when compared with 1933. Rising import prices and falling export prices meant that German exports would have had to be increased in 1936 by some 20 per cent in order to pay for the same quantity of imports of raw materials as in 1933.[64] Obviously the international reactions prompted by Germany's autarchic policies helped to prevent the much-needed boost in trade. As yet this disappointing trend was not mitigated significantly by the shift of German trade towards dominating and exploiting the markets of South-East Europe (p. 159). In addition, German agriculture could not overcome the problem of declining food production. Scarce foreign exchange was being competed for by the demand for imported foodstuffs on the one hand, and the call for raw materials to keep the economy active and growing on the other.

In short, strains were arising from the regime's emphasis on armaments and 'heavy' industry at the expense of others part of the economy. The classic danger of overheating, the political menace of inflation and recession which had helped to bury the Weimar Republic, were looming for the thousand-year Reich. Contemporary economists suggested that it was possible to forestall the problem by moving the economy back to more normal lines; extra consumer goods could be made, helping to ensure in this way the increase in living standards which so many Germans had come to expect by

[63] Carr, op. cit., p. 60. A contemporary economist like Guillebaud warned about making facile deductions about war from the Nazi economy, op. cit., p. 260.

[64] *Documents on German Foreign Policy*, Series C, V, p. 902; S.H. Roberts, *The House that Hitler Built* (London, 1937), pp. 148ff.

1936.[65] As Schacht was beginning to argue, Germany could be reintegrated into the international capitalist community.

The fact that Hitler's 'decisive intervention' in 1936 ruled out this possibility by fixing more specifically the goal of autarchy confirmed the ultimate ambition of the Nazi regime. Hitler's secret memorandum on the Four-Year Plan dwelt again on the problem of living space in relation to Germany's economic problems. Since it was clear that autarchy was not attainable within the existing frontiers of Germany, its pursuit resolved itself into the familiar ideal of creating the conditions of successful expansion in due course. '(i) The German armed forces must be operational within four years. (ii) The German economy must be fit for war within four years.'[66] But although Göring was put in charge of the Four-Year Plan it did not resolve economic problems and did not herald the total mobilisation of the German economy for war – achieved only under the pressure of war itself.[67] Indeed, the Four-Year Plan itself was endangered by the habits and momentum of the traditional labour movement. Full employment and a shortage of skilled labour combined to make it difficult for the objectives of 1936 to be realised. This was a striking example of a general trend and, as others have pointed out, the Germany of 1939 had both a 'peace' and a 'war' economy – there were guns and butter.[68]

However, the information coming from the steadily growing number of studies on economic realities in the Third Reich has not in itself brought complete agreement on the relationship between economics and foreign policy. For some the apparent contradictions in the German economy during the 1930s are more easily explained by stressing that Hitler's concept of warfare was, initially at least, that of *Blitzkrieg*. Rapid victories, followed by the assimilation of new resources acquired in this way would hopefully obviate the need to

[65] Guillebaud, op. cit., pp. 256ff.

[66] Pridham and Noakes, op. cit., pp. 401–8. Cf. A.E. Simpson, 'The struggle for control of the German economy, 1936–7', *Journal of Modern History*, **31** (1959): 37–45; for a fuller study of the Four-Year Plan see D. Petzina, *Autarkie im Dritten Reich. Der nationalsozialistische Vierjahresplan* (Stuttgart, 1968).

[67] Overy, op. cit., pp. 408–9. Elsewhere Overy seems to believe that the Germans planned only limited warfare against their weaker neighbours, R.J. Overy, 'The German pre-war aircraft production plans: November 1936–April 1939', *English Historical Review* (Oct. 1975); 797.

[68] T. Mason, 'Labour in the Third Reich 1933–9', *Past and Present*, **33** (1966): 112–41; 'The legacy of 1918 for National Socialism', in Nicholls and Matthias (eds), op. cit., p. 231. Cf. the very good discussion of this issue in a chapter called 'How warlike a "war economy"?' in B.A. Carroll, *Design for Total war. Arms and Economics in the Third Reich* (The Hague, 1968), pp. 179–90.

mobilise the entire national energies; the price of war would be paid by the defeated and the Germans would not be asked to sacrifice too much, which would have been risky for the regime. Such a conception also made the most of Germany's limited resources and could even be reconciled with what has been termed the 'chaos of the leader state'.[69] Significantly, the staggering growth of the German armed forces came in the period 1937/38 to the autumn of 1939, which reflected the increase in manpower potential from the *Anschluss* and the annexation of the Sudentenland as well as the acquisition of the Czech armaments industry in the wake of Munich and Prague (see Chapter 5). However, other scholars refuse to accept such a neat explanation and, stressing the chaotic and difficult nature of Germany's economic development, prefer to see Hitler pushed by this at least as much as pushing it. From this vantage point, *Blitzkrieg* was at best an attempt to rationalise what was happening, at worst the expression of a desperate bid to shake off economic disaster, an enforced 'leap forward'. It only looked planned in retrospect.[70]

INSTITUTIONAL CONFLICTS

Although this idea is disputed it is at least in keeping with the results of the continuing exploration of the social realities of the Third Reich. The conflicting forces at work in the German state which had plagued Wilhelmine and Weimar Germany continued to do the same for Nazi Germany. This has become increasingly evident with the successful penetration by historians of the smoke-screen thrown up by the brilliant Nazi propaganda machine. The 'monolithic' aspect of the Nazi state was a façade. The fact that Hitler's rule ended the life of opposing political parties, imposed organisational structures and introduced machineries of government to create a uniformity of purpose did not mean that the historically conditioned state of affairs could be changed overnight. The very importance Hitler attached to

[69] See for example the conclusions of R. Bollmus, *Das Amt Rosenberg und seiner Gegner. Zum Machtkampf im nationalsozialistischen Herrschaftssystem* (Stuttgart, 1970).

[70] T.W. Mason, 'Innere Krise und Angriffskrieg 1938/9', in F. Forstmeier and H.-E. Volkmann (eds), *Wirtschaft und Rüstung am Vorabend des zweiten Weltkrieges* (Düsseldorf, 1975), pp. 158–88. Note the debate between Overy and Mason, R.J. Overy, 'Germany, domestic crisis and war in 1939', *Past and Present*, **110** (1987) and **122** (1989). See also R.J. Overy, *Goering. The 'Iron Man'* (London, 1984), pp. 76ff. For a wider discussion, J. Hiden, J. Farquharson, *Explaining Hitler's Germany. Historians and the Third Reich* (2nd edn, London, 1989), pp. 130–151.

expansion entailed, in the interests of speed, co-operation with and adaptation of the existing order of things, even if this meant dropping for the time being important ideological commitments, such as those to the farmer and to the small businessman.[71]

This explained why Hitler kept intact the structure of the state political machinery and bureaucracy, although they were penetrated at every point by the party machine and the 'leadership principle' was institutionalised; it explained why, in spite of proliferating controls and increased interference in the economy, Hitler sought above all the co-operation of business and industry. True, the strains in this 'partnership' increased after 1936 with the intensified drive towards autarchy, but private economic interests could prosper and flourish if they co-operated.[72] The structures which arose in Nazi Germany as a result of the marriage of party and state and party and industry almost defy analysis in their complexity. To describe the bewildering number of overlapping authorities within the Third Reich and to characterise them, the phrase 'institutional Darwinism' has been aptly coined.[73] Given the opportunites for confusion in the thicket of institutions, 'totalitarian' pretensions at control and manipulation must not be allowed to disguise actualities, which were very often quite different.

Such internal political and economic pressures were related to Hitler's readiness to take greater risks in 1938–39, but they do not suffice as an explanation of war origins without a study of the broader context of international relations. The state of Germany's armed forces alone compelled taking account of the realities of power on the international stage. The German Army was indeed tailored to the needs of Germany's geographical position and the sort of war this entailed; namely, an army that could fight a lightning campaign on one front while conducting a holding operation on the other.[74] Yet, while up-to-date equipment for key sectors of this army and the proper use of more highly trained units within it could give certain

[71] D. Schoenbaum, *Hitler's Social Revolution. Class and Status in Nazi Germany* (London, 1967), pp. 132, 160–1.

[72] The distinction is drawn between 'partial fascism' before 1936 and 'full fascism' after that year, by A. Schweitzer, *Big Business in the Third Reich* (Indiana, 1964); P. Hayes, *Industry and Ideology. IG Farben in the Nazi Era* (Cambridge, 1987). Cf. W. Sauer, 'National socialism: totalitarianism or fascism?', *American Historical Review*, **73** No. 2 (1967): 410.

[73] Schoenbaum, op. cit., pp. 202ff.; K.D. Bracher, *The German Dictatorship. The Origins, Structure and Consequences of National Socialism* (London, 1973, paperback), p. 291.

[74] Bernhardt, op. cit., pp. 125–30. Cf. comments of W. Murray, *The change in the European Balance of power 1938–9* (Princeton, 1984), pp. 3–49.

advantages to Germany, the extent of such advantage depended in large part on the reaction of the other powers. Much of Hitler's success during the crises of 1938–39 depended on convincing the opposing powers that the German armed forces were inherently superior to anything then existing. That this was believed to a great extent is self-evident from the Allied policies to Germany after 1937. In fact, the balance of forces between Germany on the one hand and that of its possible opponents in West and East Europe in 1939 was far closer than the subsequent German military victories suggested. Hitler himself was more aware than anyone that Germany's advantages on the military field would very soon be overtaken, as was apparent during his talk to key leaders in November 1937, recorded in the Hossbach memorandum (p. 96).

The relative closeness of the military balance of power of the opposing sides at the outbreak of the Second World War also makes it all the more important for us to understand how Hitler managed to conceal his ultimate intentions during the critical early years of his regime, when he could more easily have been stopped by preventive war. Again, to a large extent this resolves itself into a series of questions which are best answered with the framework of later chapters. However, if any general theme exists in this context, it is that too many European statesmen were ready to accept Hitler's plea that his policies followed on logically from Weimer revisionism. One essential ingredient in this recipe was the continued activity of the German Foreign Office in the service of the Hitler state, and it is worth returning briefly to the institutional context of policy-making. The fate of the AA after 1933 confirms how different were appearance and reality.

That the revisionist policies of the AA suited Hitler has been remarked upon often enough, and we cannot do better here than quote a student of the German Foreign Office after 1933:

> Until this time [1938] the German Foreign Office's functions and its personnel had remained substantially unaffected by five years of National Socialist rule. It's 'political' chief, Neurath, had been one of two pre-Nazi survivors in Hitler's cabinet. Under his amiable and comfortable stewardship the diplomatic bureaucrats had weathered the new era with singular good fortune, when compared with the other Reich agencies . . . The Foreign Office, which had not been 'democratised' by the Weimar Republic, did not expect to be *gleichgeschaltet* [integrated] by the Nazis.[75]

[75] P. Seabury, 'Ribbentrop and the German Foreign Office', *Political Science Quarterly*, **66** (1951): p. 553.

To accept this is not, however, to accept the deduction made by another expert, echoing the point made earlier in this chapter:

> Thus the German Foreign Office gave shape to German policy and even created it in so far as precise commitments and statements narrowed the range of opportunities and possibilities and implied certain future actions rather than others. Foreign policy is composed of discrete actions and commitments as much as it is made up of broad statements and grandiose aims. The Foreign Office had continued to make the former kind of policy in the Third Reich just as it had before, and its action gives little support to a general rule about weakened foreign offices in the twentieth century.[76]

The answer to this must be that it minimises the broader context of policy-making by placing too much emphasis on the higher executive apparatus. True, Hitlerian diplomacy made much use of the traditional power political approach. Equally, other 'para-diplomatic' agencies active in the Third Reich have not been shown to have had direct impact on Nazi diplomacy before 1939. However, as has been so persuasively argued in Jacobsen's study of Nazi foreign policy, diplomacy was only one aspect of that foreign policy and not the most important.[77]

This must be immediately clear by taking the longer perspective offered by Hitler's own ideological commitment to the goal of a racially pure, German-dominated Europe and, in the far future, perhaps the world. The AA, with its traditions and historic ties to the 'old' Reich could hardly be suited to the great task of the future new Germany. For that purpose, for the care and manipulation of Germans outside the Reich, the developing *völkisch* (*volk* – people, race) organisations were quite indispensable in the long run. Thus, if Rosenberg's *Aussenpolitische Amt* (APA) did not obviously influence diplomatic decisions, it did, for example, play a crucial role in preparing in secret for the carving up of Russia with the aid of the former Russian Germans, and it schooled the future national socialist élite for their tasks in dominating the Continent.[78] Hitler was careful not to let the work of the organisations caring for Germans abroad get in the way of more important tactical requirements before 1938, although from 1937 his interest in the German minorities outside the Reich appears to have quickened. In 1937 the *Volksdeutschen Mittelstelle* (VOMI) was put under SS control, giving Himmler and Heydrich

[76] L. Hill, op. cit., p. 570.
[77] Jacobsen, op. cit., pp. 599–600; Bracher, *German Dictatorship*, pp. 398ff.
[78] Jacobsen, op. cit., p. 600.

for the first time a foreign policy agency later to be exploited by them.

> Thus a radicalisation of the *Voltstumpolitik* (nationality policy) came about at the moment when Schacht's resignation signified the failure of the economic programme of gradually reintegrating Germany in the world markets and the new economic course made it plain that the Reich would follow the policy of autarchy until it won increased living space.[79]

If VOMI did not yet supplant the AA, its revolutionary implications cannot be ignored or minimised. Similarly, Ribbentrop's *Büro* or *Dienststelle*, set up in 1934, was not a substitute for the AA, but it assumed the function of an 'enlarged staff' for Hitler when Ribbentrop took over the AA in February 1938 and from this point Ribbentrop's office naturally mirrored Hitler's influence more.[80]

Although the AA therefore 'survived' it did so alongside the newer organs. As in internal politics, so these institutions provide further evidence of the 'dual state' created by Hitler. New and old coexisted, however uneasily.[81] For Hitler, intent on overturning and transforming the existing order, this had to be a transitionary phase. His self-appointed task was to strike at the alien forces ranged against the German state, which meant action both inside and outside the borders of the Reich.[82] Thus the interaction between domestic and external factors, always prickly in Germany's history after 1870, became more acute with Hitler's assumption of power. The consequences for Germany's foreign policy after 1933 can be seen as we trace the relations between the Third Reich and the other European powers in the interwar years.

[79] Ibid., p. 608.
[80] Ibid., pp. 610–11.
[81] Ernst Fraenkel, *The Dual State* (New York, 1941).
[82] Hildebrand, op. cit., pp. 139–40.

PART TWO

Germany and the European Powers, 1921–39

CHAPTER THREE
Germany, Britain and France

Germany's military weakness after the First World War precluded for the foreseeable future the forceful revision of Versailles, although German nationalists found this difficult to grasp. Those who felt that revision could only be attained through an understanding with France numbered a handful in the SPD and Democratic parties and was the official policy of neither.[1] By contrast, there was a widespread belief – apart from the German communists and a few others – that Germany should concentrate on securing Great Britain's goodwill and capitalise on the differences between the Allied Powers which had emerged during the Peace Conference (p. 14). Partly for this reason, Germany attempted to prevaricate over reparations payments and to obstruct the disarmament clauses of Versailles. The London Ultimatum of 5 May 1921 put a stop to this. Prompt action was demanded of Germany on disarmament and the trials of war criminals. The bill for reparations, which the Reparations Commission (REPKO) had finally worked out, was presented. The sum of 132 billion marks was to be payable by annual instalments of £100 million, as was a quarter of the value of Germany's exports. Milder than earlier schemes, these demands effectively rejected Germany's claim that its economic and financial crisis was caused primarily by reparations payments; that what was needed before any satisfactory solution to the reparations problem was a moratoriumn on payments and a foreign loan – as the German bankers had argued in 1919. When Wirth formed his government in May 1921, his policy of fulfilment

[1] H. Holborn, 'Diplomacy in the early Weimar Republic', in G. Craig and F. Gilbert (eds), *The Diplomats 1919–1939* (Princeton, 1953), pp. 160–1. Cf R.N. Hunt, *German Social Democracy 1918–1933* (Chicago, 1964), pp. 36f.

of the peace terms (p. 39) was necessary above all because Anglo-French differences had not in fact proved stronger than their shared desire to put an end to Germany's prevarications.

REPARATIONS

Between May 1921 and the French occupation of the Ruhr in 1923, the central concern of Germany's relations with the West, indeed the main problem of German foreign policy, was the reparations dispute. It cannot be understood solely in terms of economics. It has been calculated, for example, that the actual sums Germany was expected to pay under the London schedule of payments amounted to approximately 6 per cent of the Weimar Republic's national income. This was a significant charge on German resources, but it should not have been an impossible task for a country facing up to the need to limit domestic consumption to meet reparations payments.

The truth is that barely concealed beneath the arguments about the fairness or otherwise of reparations was the continuing antagonism between France and Germany, now enshrined in the Treaty of Versailles. As surely as the Germans sought its revision, so the French aimed to enforce it. Germany's concern with France's military superiority was matched by the French obsession with Germany's *potential* strength, both in terms of manpower and industrial weight. There was, as some French historians have recently stressed, nationalist fervour on both sides of the Rhine.[2] This imposed limits on the agreement possible between Germany and the Allies, but it makes rather more remarkable what steps were taken to achieve a *modus vivendi*, particularly those by Walther Rathenau, Wirth's Minister for Reconstruction.

Rathenau had been increasingly consulted on the intricacies of reparations problems by Wirth during the latter's term of office as Finance Minister in the summer of 1920. It was Rathenau who, together with other experts, prepared the plan for linking the rate with which reparations were to be paid to the current state of the economy and presented it for governmental consideration early in September 1920. In general, Rathenau recognised the importance of

[2] Cf E. Schulin, 'Rathenau et la France', *Revue Allemagne* (July–Sept., 1972), p. 556; On France's general position, A. Adamthwaite, *Grandeur and decline. France 1914–1940*, London, 1991; On reparations, S. Marks, 'The myths of reparations.' *Central European History*, 11 (1978): 231–55.

putting forward a scheme that would be both practicable for Germany and yet would 'make an honest impression on the nations of the world'.[3] Rathenau had already warned against defiance over the deliveries of coal required by the Peace Treaty, emphasising the dangers of any French occupation of the Ruhr.[4] He therefore regretted the German refusal to obey the Allied demands at the London Conference in January 1921 which led to the Allied occupation of the three Ruhr ports. His appointment to the Ministry of Reconstruction in Wirth's first government was therefore appropriate. After all, fulfilment set out to accomplish the dual task of convincing the Allies of Germany's goodwill and of lessening the resistance of domestic opposition inside Germany to the idea of co-operation.

Rathenau's position was an odd one in some respects. As 'crown prince' of the famous electricity company, the AEG, he was much interested in the economic *rapprochement* with Russia which was afoot in 1921 (p. 111) He, like Wirth, remained convinced of the importance of capitalising on Anglo-American concern for the economic problems of Central Europe and there has been growing recognition of his effort to rise above the inevitable postwar hostilities between Germany and France. Soon after taking office Rathenau set in motion secret personal contacts with his French counterpart, Louis Loucheur, an industrialist like Rathenau. Their meeting in Wiesbaden on 12 June was the first Franco-German ministerial confrontation since the war and eventually produced the Wiesbaden Agreement of 6 October 1921. This aimed to offset direct German aid in reconstructing the devastated areas of Northern France against the reparations payments, thus reducing some pressures on the German currency.

The Wiesbaden Agreement was part of a broader strategy to lift reparations out of the political arena. Yet, although Wirth took relatively prompt action over other parts of the London Ultimatum –

[3] D.G. Williams. 'Walther Rathenau: Realist, pedagogue and prophet, November 1918–May 1921', *European Studies Review*, **6** (1976): 115. For more detail consult D. Felix, *Walther Rathenau and the Weimar Republic. The Politics of Reparations* (Baltimore, 1971). For French impulses towards a *modus vivendi* see Georges Soutou, 'Die deutschen Reparationen und das Seydoux projekt 1920/21', *Vierteljahrshefte für Zeitgeschichte*, **23** (1975): 257–70. The standard work on reparations problems remains E. Weill-Reynal, *Les Réparations et la France 1918–1936* (Paris, 1948), 3 vols. The German viewpoint can be found of course in C. Bergman, *The History of Reparations* (Boston, 1927). See also B. Kent, *The Spoils of War. The Politics, Economics and Diplomacy of Reparations 1918–32* (Oxford, 1980); S. Schuker, *American 'Reparations' to Germany 1919–33*, (New Jersey, 1988), pp. 82ff.

[4] Williams, op cit., p. 114. On Rathenau, D.G. Williamson, 'Walther Rathenau. Patron Saint of the German liberal establishment,', *Leo Baeck Institute Year Book*. (London, 1975), pp. 207–22.

with a somewhat half-hearted beginning of war guilt trials and the belated disarming of the forbidden *Einwohnerwehren* (Home Guards) during 1921 – neither he nor Rathenau could solve the domestic/economic crisis in Germany and produce the sort of payments demanded by the French. The British and Americans, not to mention the Belgians, were uneasy about the separate deal between Germany and France and the Wiesbaden Agreement was not approved by REPKO until 31 May 1922. In any case the enduring hostility between French and German industrialists prevented France from exploiting the Rathenau–Loucheur agreement.[5] French industrialists preferred to reconstruct their damaged areas without Germany. Finally, the outcome of the partition of Upper Silesia in October 1921 hardened German attitudes towards the Allies, making even more difficult the policies of Rathenau and Wirth. Rathenau's office was left vacant in Wirth's second Cabinet. Thus, although Aristide Briand headed the government in France from January 1921 and sought to match Wirth's efforts at fulfilment with a policy of 'confidence in Wirth',[6] matters grew worse. It must be said that the narrowness of Wirth's domestic base for fulfilment (p. 39) was matched by that of French governments for any *rapprochement* with Germany or any real accommodation over reparations before the Ruhr crisis.

In the face of Germany's continuing economic crisis Wirth was compelled to plead on 14 December 1921, for a moratorium on payments – only six months after making the first instalments under the London Ultimatum. Britain remained sympathetic to Germany. Wirth's difficulties in 1921 had strengthened the growing British conviction that the economic recovery of Europe, and with it Britain's trade abroad, was dependent on German economic stability. Both Briand and Lloyd George had accepted the German agreement of December 1921 for a moratorium on reparations payments, conditional on Germany's readiness to accept Allied control of its finances.[7] At the Conference of Cannes in January 1922, the British concept of a more integrated European–world economy was developed further by the call for a world economic conference at Genoa,

[5] E. Laubach, *Die Politik der Kabinette Wirth* (Lübeck/Hamburg, 1968), pp. 78–9; J. Bariety, 'Industriels allemands et industriels français à l'époque de la République de Weimar', *Revue Allemagne*, **4**, No. 2 (April–June, 1974): 14–15.

[6] Schulin, op cit., p. 550.

[7] Lloyd George. *The Truth about Reparations and War Debts* (London, 1932), p. 65. In general, W.M. Jordan's, *Great Britain, France and the German Problem* (London, 1943), provides a very useful survey even today. The chapter in R.A.C. Parker, *Europe 1919–1945* (London, 1969), which has the same heading as Jordan's title, is balanced and full.

which would include Gemany and Russia. However, notwithstanding differences with Paris, London accepted that alongside efforts to return to economic normalcy, Paris's concern for security had to be given due regard.

This could be seen from Briand's parallel effort to tighten the Anglo-French relationship by finding a substitute for the lapsed Anglo-American guarantee of France's borders with Germany (p. 26). The British were still reluctant to extend their commitments in Europe and the French were not yet ready for the far-reaching accommodation with Germany, which Lloyd George's policy entailed. Ultimately, therefore, Briand was forced to resign in favour of Raymond Poincaré, a man pledged to uphold all the rights of France under the Treaty of Versailles. The Lloyd George–Briand scheme for a security agreement and the discussion of the reparations problem in the broader context of a settlement of Europe's economic problems at Genoa was aborted. From Germany's viewpoint, however, the very fact of such discussions was significant. Like the London Ultimatum and the Allied decision to partition Upper Silesia, the stillborn Briand–Lloyd George project confirmed the continuing community of interest between Britain and France which underlay their highly publicised differences.

Britain and France also shared the shocked reaction to the agreement signed between Germany and Russia at Rapallo on 16 April 1922, during the Genoa Conference. The timing and nature of this move could hardly fail to affect domestic opinion in France and Britain. The Rapallo Treaty was felt by the French to be a threat to their eastern allies and thus to France's security (p. 115). Poincaré could easily exploit this as he could the reactions in the West on 24 June 1922 when the German extremists murdered Walther Rathenau, whose name was associated with fulfilment. Wirth's efforts to achieve a full moratorium on reparations payments were blocked and his inevitable resignation came on 14 November 1922. Cuno's subsequent 'business Cabinet' had close links with the German nationalists through Cuno himself. The support of the SPD, essential to any policy of understanding with the West, was replaced by that of the DVP. The ensuing rapid development of the Franco-German publicity warfare made it clear that open and direct conflict was a matter of time. In Britain, the Genoa fiasco had strengthened Lloyd George's conservative opposition and this was at least likely to offer 'surly neutrality' if France acted. Notwithstanding the continuing British efforts to dissuade Poincaré from forcing a conflict with Germany over reparations, London shared the scepticism of Paris and Brussels at the new German plan presented at a conference in London on 9 December 1922.[8] The proposal coupled a five-year moratorium with a non-aggression pact over the Rhine for a generation. It made Poincaré no less desperate than he already was. On 9 January REPKO established technical faults in German coal deliveries, and shortly afterwards the French occupation of the Ruhr began. It was very much the last resort for the French premier.

In important respects, then, the Ruhr crisis is best understood as the outcome of a long-standing German–French nationalist conflict, rooted in the prewar and wartime experiences. At the same time the traumatic crisis of 1923 provided a check to those advocating extreme solutions in both Germany and France. In Germany, the policy of passive resistance cost the country more than it would have had to pay to finance the current reparations payments and it precipitated a social and economic crisis which opened the way for Stresemann's chancellorship and the return of the SPD to the government. The resulting economic reorganisation has been described already (p. 42). It was achieved before the foreign loans that Wirth had argued were essential, but this was less proof of German duplicity than of the salutary effects of the crisis itself. In France, dismay at its growing isolation, coupled with the cost to the French taxpayer of the Ruhr occupation, contributed to the fall of Poincaré. A large vote for a different policy was given in the elections bringing the radical socialist Edouard Herriot to power on 1 June 1924.[9] In Britain, the existence of the Labour government under MacDonald further favoured detente. Although Stresemann's chancellorship ended in 1923, as Foreign Minister thereafter he, too, could exploit the relatively favourable political balance in Marx's Cabinet (p. 46). The acceptance of the London Accords of 16 August 1924 was assured and this gave effect to the famous Dawes Plan.

Of paramount importance was the participation of the Americans, whose representatives on the committee of experts which presented its plan for reparations in April 1924 were Charles C. Dawes and Owen Young. The notion of US insistence on Allied debt repayments as a major cause of Europe's demand for German reparations is a popular one. It is also misleading. The Americans wished for merely token payments from their European allies in the decade following

[8] Laubach, op.cit., Parker, op cit., pp. 69–70. Further material can be found in D.G. Boadle, *Winston Churchill and the German Question in Foreign Policy* (The Hague, 1973).

[9] How propitious the situation seemed to Stresemann can be seen from H.A. Turner, *Stresemann and the Politics of the Weimar Republic* (Princeton, 1963), p. 170.

the US debt settlements of 1923–26. In Britain's case this amounted to little more than 0.8 per cent of its foreign investment portfolio.[10] The 800 million marks in loans which the Dawes Plan arranged were to come largely from the United States, It therefore, in effect, also accepted the burden of helping to finance German economic recovery, and with it the flow of payments. Additionally, the new scale of reparations payments was to be related to German economic recovery. Payments of 1,000 million gold marks in the first year of the plan were to rise to annual payments of 2,500 million in the five ensuing years. Built-in safeguards against the future danger of inflation included forbidding the new Reichsbank to discount treasury bills and ordering the retention of gold and foreign exchange to a minimum of 40 per cent of its note issue. Payments were guaranteed by assigning for security German railway revenues, the revenues of big German industries and some excise and customs duties. Equally important, foreign experts were to supervise the transfer of reparations payments abroad in such a way as to avoid undue strain on the external value of the mark.

The Dawes Plan was provisional, and for Stresemann, with his vision of full German economic freedom, necessarily imperfect. He remained committed to work for the decrease in reparations and their earliest disappearance. However, the new economic order provided the essential context for the next phase of Germany's revisionist strategy under Stresemann's guidance, which was analysed in general terms in Chapter 2. Contemporaries hoped that a more stable international order would quickly follow the economic one. France's unilateral action was excluded in future by the requirements of unanimity under the Dawes Plan in any finding of German default, and by the affirmation of the need for the economic and fiscal unity of the Reich. The artificial nature of French military superiority had been underlined in 1923 by its dependence in the last resort on Anglo-American support. This in itself was a major step forward in Stresemann's priorities.

It was no accident that the policy of conciliation between Germany and the Western Powers coincided with a new phase in France's own

[10] Felix, op cit., p. 38; cf. Weill-Reynal, op cit., Vol II, pp. 509, 517f., 522. S. Schuker, 'The end of Versailles' in G. Martel (ed), *The Origins of the Second World War Reconsidered, The A.J.P. Taylor Debate after Twenty-Five Years,* (London, 1986), p. 57. Cf. two important studies in this connection are W. Link, *Die amerikanische Stabilisierungspolitik in Deutschland 1921–32* (Düsseldorf, 1970); E. Wandell, *Die Bedeutung der Vereinigten Staaten von Amerika für den deutsche Reparationsproblem 1914–9* (Tübingen, 1971).

economic problems. The decline of the French franc, rooted in France's failure to reform its financial structure under the expectation of reparations, further committed France to the British and American orbit. The French were, however, reluctant converts to the appeasement of Germany. France's prime concern remained its own safety *vis-à-vis* Germany and this was not easily reconciled with Germany's view of her own security.[11] Thus, at the London Conference of 1924, Stresemann failed to secure the immediate evacuation of the Ruhr which was not completed until the following summer, between 1 July and 25 August 1925, prior to the Locarno Conference.

Part of the price of the London Accords was that the evacuation was made dependent on a satisfactory report of the Inter-Allied Military Control Commission (IMCC) on the progress of German disarmament. As a result of the findings of this inspection, which began on 8 September 1924, the conference of ambassadors decided on 27 December to postpone the evacuation of the Cologne zone of the Rhineland. This was due in 1925 under the Versailles terms if Germany behaved. Once again Britain demonstrated its unwillingness to sanction any new international order entirely at France's expense. That was true above all of the British Foreign Minister, Austen Chamberlain, although he was under considerable pressure from his imperialist critics in the Baldwin government to avoid any far-reaching guarantees in Europe.[12] The postponement of the Cologne evacuation reinforced Stresemann's concentration on placating France and was in part responsible for the timing of his famous memorandum to the Allies on 9 February 1925 which began the exchanges leading to Locarno.

LOCARNO AND ITS EFFECTS

The Locarno agreements, made on 16 October 1925, provided the pivot of German foreign policy in the 1920s. The central arrangement concerned the Rhineland. The so-called Rhineland Pact was signed by Germany, France, Belgium, Great Britain and Italy. It included a guarantee of the status quo of the German–French, German–Belgian borders, reciprocal renunciations of attack and the use of force and

[11] Cf. M. Salewski, 'Zur deutschen Sicherheitspolitik in der Spätzeit der Weimarer Rupublik', *Vierteljahrshefte für Zeitgeschichte*, **22** (1974): 123.

[12] J. Jacobson, *Locarno Diplomacy: Germany and the West 1925–1929* (Princeton, New Jersey, 1972), p. 19.

the submission of conflicts to the League, of which Germany was to become a member. For Stresemann, this part of the agreement was the all-important step to placate French fears of insecurity and thus to contribute towards the wider understanding from which the German revisionist cause was to benefit. It also removed the threat to Germany of a bilateral Anglo-French guarantee of the sort mooted at various times since 1919. It was inconceivable, given the British aversion to sweeping commitments in Europe, that such a bilateral pact would ever again be preferred to one including Germany.

For Germany the chief advantage lay in the weakening of the Versailles terms for its western borders. While the Peace Treaty regarded any violation of the demilitarised Rhineland as a 'hostile act', under the Locarno arrangements British and Italian aid for France was now only likely if a 'flagrant violation' took place. For the moment this was the best that could be achieved in view of Germany's military weakness. Nonetheless, at last British military help for France was to be forthcoming, if under unspecified circumstances. That this was impossible as yet to reconcile with Britian's world and imperial interests reflected the British hope that its influence could be asserted to avoid giving the military assistance it promised in the Rhineland Pact.[13] The significant feature of Locarno, from the German point of view, remains that the Anglo-French *entente* was preserved within it. The corollary to this was indeed the effective weakening of the ties between France and her eastern allies (p. 146). Dismay at this prospect explained in part the long French delay in responding to Stresemann's original note of February 1925.

How did the Locarno treaties relate to the progress of revision? An obvious yardstick is what Austen Chamberlain thought of as Stresemann's 'blueprint' for revision; the list of demands and unfinished business which Stresemann felt lay between Germany and the distant goal of a Reich restored to something like its original territorial status and full sovereignty; demands carried forward, as it were, from 1919 and systematically developed by Stresemann in the course of his tenure at the Wilhelmstrasse. These included, apart from reparations, the end of the Ruhr occupation and the earliest possible complete evacuation of the occupied Rhineland; the end of the IMCC; the dropping of the war guilt charges; the return of Eupen-Malmedy and

[13] Cf. M. Howard, *The Continental Commitment. The Dilemma of British Defence Policy in the Era of Two World Wars* (London, 1974, paper), p.95. For the texts see J.A.S. Grenville, *The Major International Treaties 1914–1973. A History and Guide with Texts* (London, 1974), pp. 95–8. A useful text is A. Orde, *British Policy & European Reconstruction after the First World War* (London, 1991).

the Saar, the latter before the plebiscite arranged by the Versailles Treaty for 1935; the *Anschluss*; the improved treatment of German minorities in Central Europe; and above all the revision of Germany's eastern frontiers and finally the question of colonies. Clearly, the revision of the eastern frontiers falls in a later chapter but it is sufficient to stress that Locarno pointed the way forward to this by its undermining of Franco-Polish/Czech ties. The need for British goodwill vindicated the official German line on colonies, as distinct from the Press campaigns for their return, that this question was not yet 'actual'. A policy of cautious preparation of the ground and of 'wait and see' was the appropriate response.[14] The question of minorities, again one more properly discussed in Chapter 5, was moved to a different plateau by Germany's entry to the League in 1926 as a consequence of the Locarno pacts.

The crucial and immediate questions concerned the implications of the Locarno agreement for Franco-German relations. Stresemann's domestic opposition was less impressed by the long-term advantages of Locarno for revising the settlement in East Europe or the possibilities for pressure which might follow from Germany's entry to the League, than it was struck by the renunciation of Alsace-Lorraine, the continued occupation of the Rhineland and the situation in the Saar. The evacuation of the Ruhr prior to Locarno was not regarded by nationalists as a concession but as a much-belated right. To secure his domestic basis, Stresemann was compelled by the political balance in Germany in the second half of the 1920s (p. 46) to promise that more would follow soon from the Locarno policy. In particular, Stresemann had to press for the rapid evacuation of the Rhineland (without which active revision in the east was impossible in any case) and satisfaction over the matter of disarmament, the state of which put Germany at a disadvantage.

Both of these matters Stresemann sought to tie to the notion of moral obligation implicit in Locarno, since no legal basis for either issue was given in the pacts, and to the assumption that evacuation was in order since French security had been achieved at Locarno.[15] But the language which Stresemann had to use at home did not make matters easier for Briand's own attempts to further Franco-German understanding. The French Ambassador to Berlin pointedly said to State Secretary Schubert in a talk of 20 January 1926, after yet another

[14] *Akten zur deutschen auswärtigen Politik 1918–1945*, Series B. (1925–33), Vol I, 1 (Göttingen, 1966–), pp. 464ff., 555ff. (Hereafter cited as ADAP.)

[15] Ibid., pp. 593ff. Cf. Jacobson, op cit., pp. 76–80.

German reference to domestic pressures as the reason for expecting prompt French action in the matter of the Rhineland occupation: 'Mr Briand does indeed recognise well enough the difficulties of the German government but urgently requests that consideration be given to his own great difficulties.'[16] In short, Locarno tended to be viewed by the French not as the beginning of a policy of concessions but as a poor substitute for the desired Anglo-French guarantee.

Stresemann's policies during the 'Locarno era', the description often applied to the years 1925–29, were met by a tantalising mixture of promise and frustration. This was high-lighted particularly by the much-vaunted 'personal diplomacy'. It had its roots in the postwar Allied conferences and conjured up the rosy picture of the big three, Briand, Stresemann and Austen Chamberlain, talking their way reasonably towards a more peaceful order, anticipating the more fateful face-to-face interviews of the next decade. The confrontation between Stresemann and Briand at Thoiry at the end of 1926 has often been seen, for example, as a landmark, a symbol of Franco-German *rapprochement* in the 1920s. Here was mooted a global settlement of the outstanding differences between the two countries. In particular, Briand sought to secure advance payment of German reparations in return for agreeing to the earlier evacuation of the Rhineland. Apart from his commitment to the cause of friendship between France and Germany, Briand was still obsessed by the need for France to escape from the currency crisis which had plagued it since the spring of 1925. However, international and domestic realities were bigger than personalities. Britain and America opposed the proposals regarding reparations deals. These were quite unacceptable before the full clarification of the debt between America and its European allies. It was also soon apparent to Stresemann that any attempt to advance the reparations schedule would prejudice his drive for the downward revision of the Dawes payments. That would have been unacceptable on domestic grounds alone. Poincaré's financial expertise – he was back in office in 1926 – helped resolve the French currency crisis and the projects of Thoiry were left for the time being.[17]

[16] Ibid., p. 130. For general consideration of the relationship between Stresemann's domestic difficulties and foreign policy cf. Turner, op cit., pp. 210–11, 218–19; M. Walsdorff, *Westorientierung und Ostpolitik. Stresemanns Russlandpolitik in der Locarno-Ära* (Bremen, 1971); L.E. Jones, 'Gustav Stresemann and the crisis of German liberalism', *European Studies Review,* **4**, No.2 (April, 1974): 141–63 (For further guidance see note 31 of Chapter 2.)

[17] Jacobson, op cit., pp. 84–90; J. Jacobson and J.T. Walker, 'The impulse for a Franco-German Entente: The origins of the Thoiry conference, 1926', *Journal of*

Nevertheless, the nexus between reparations and the evacuation of the Rhineland remained; the French tended to regard the occupation as the last guarantee of reparations payments, although Stresemann sought to persuade Briand that Germany's economic welfare provided better guarantees. In addition, French military leaders argued more strongly after Locarno for the need to keep the Rhineland under control, the most obvious sign of France's concern to secure its defences in the face of Germany's steady recovery. Their fears were reinforced by the IMCC reports. These left little doubt about Germany's continuous delays over disarmament. Ever aware of the promptings of President Hindenburg and other members of the Reichstag Foreign Affairs Committee who were calling for troop reductions in the occupied zones as a precondition of Germany's entry to the League in 1926, Stresemann continued to pester the French for specific details about the promised reduction in the occupying forces.[18] It says much for the impulses towards preserving the Locarno spirit that the German, British and French governments spent so much effort trying to ensure that this issue did not irreparably damage goodwill.

The British were interested in accommodating Stresemann over the issue of troop reduction and evacuation, but not at the cost of upsetting France too much. On 22 April 1926 Schubert, the State Secretary in the AA, complained to the British Ambassador to Berlin, D'Abernon, about France 'leading Germany by the nose' over the troop reduction issue; but even D'Abernon, who was personally very well disposed towards Germany, had 'a certain understanding for the attitude of the French'.[19] After the belated evacuation of the Cologne zone in January 1926, matters remained uneasy, but it was in keeping with the new spirit in international relations that in 1926 Germany was invited to join the preliminary preparations for a disarmament conference (which finally met in 1932). Stresemann was soon devel-

Contemporary History, **10**, 1 (Jan. 1975): 157–81. A more positive view of Thoiry is taken by H.-O. Sieburg, 'Das Gespräch zu Thoiry 1926', E. Schulin (ed.), *Gedenkschrift Martin Göhring. Studien zur europäischen Geschichte* (Wiesbaden, 1968), pp. 317–37.

18 On Stresemann's demands for troop reductions, *ADAP*, Series B, Vol. I, pp. 593ff. On France's celebrated defensive or 'Maginot mentality', see J.M. Hughes, *To the Maginot Line: The Politics of French Military Preparations in the 1920s* (Cambridge, Mass., 1971); D.C. Watt, *Too Serious a Business. European Armed Forces and the Approach to the Second World War* (London, 1975), pp. 36–7. For an example of someone on the German side cautioning patience over the Rhineland issues in the face of nationalist pressures, E. Geigenmüller, 'Botschafter von Hoesch und die Räumungsfrage', *Historische Zeitschrift*, **200** (1965): 606–20.

19 *ADAP*, Series B, Vol. I, p. 470.

oping the theme of 'equality of treatment' for Germany in the matter of armaments. Quite what was meant by this in practice was left unresolved for the moment. It did enable Germany to exploit more fully the inference in part V of the Peace Treaty that German disarmament was the prelude to more general disarmament in Europe. Those pressures increased when, with British help, the IMCC was withdrawn in January 1927, thus prolonging the Locarno partnerships by underwriting the fiction of German disarmament.[20]

Another nod in the direction of *rapprochement* between Germany and the Western Allies was made by their signature with the other powers of the Kellogg–Briand Pact on 27 August 1928. A pact to outlaw war, it omitted legitimate wars of defence from its operation and was hedged by other reservations on the part of the individual powers. Yet it provided the context for Stresemann to continue the discussion of immediate problems with Poincaré. By 16 September 1928, Stresemann had the satisfaction of getting Allied agreement to negotiations for an earlier evacuation of the Rhineland as well as explicit recognition of the need for a final solution of the reparations problems. The German Foreign Minister and the President of the Reichsbank, Hjalmar Schacht, felt strongly that the moment was right for such a settlement. German demands were in effect reinforced by the views of the agent who had supervised the reparations payments under the Dawes Plan, Parker Gilbert. He was well aware that the economic growth in Germany which made possible the prompt payment of reparations according to the Dawes plan, was dangerously dependent on short-term foreign loans, particularly American loans. Many other experts shared the fear that either Germany's continued economic welfare would lead to the Allies escalating their reparations demands or, worse, the Weimar Republic's economic collapse would cause a return of the controls and conditions of the early 1920s.

The continuing acrimony over these issues – less that of the experts than of the politicians, with their eyes over their shoulders to their electorates – was reflected in the time taken between the first report of the committee of experts under the American, Young, in December 1928 and the new plan's passage through the Reichstag in May 1930. The discussions continued through two conferences of governmental representatives at The Hague, in August 1929 and January 1930. They were accompanied by mounting cries of opposition inside

[20] Jacobson, *Locarno Diplomacy*, p. 96; *ADAP*, Series B, Vol. IV, pp. 476–7. Stresemann's memo of 6 March 1927 on his conversation with Briand.

Germany. Yet the Young Plan at last fixed the duration of payments, fifty-nine years. The final sum would total 37–40 milliard RM, as opposed to the 132 milliard demanded by the London Ultimatum of 1921. Germany's capacity to pay was taken for granted. The crucial difference between the Young and Dawes plans was the new provision for the ending of foreign controls. The responsibility for the transfer of payments was put on Germany's shoulders. The importance of America was additionally underlined by the provision for decreasing reparations payments in proportion to the possible decrease in Allied debts to America. Even Poincaré shared some of the anxiety for a timely settlement of the reparations issue. By 1929, France's reconstruction of her damaged areas was more or less complete and reparations were needed, strictly speaking, only to pay France's debts to her allies. From now on the debts of the Allies to the United States formed the largest part of the German debt.

The Young Plan therefore further limited the claim on German resources and shortly after, in 1932, the Lausanne Conference was to cancel reparations altogether. For the period 1919–31:

> Germany transferred to the Allies in cash and kind together an average of only 2.0 per cent of national income. At the same time Germany experienced a windfall profit resulting from the devaluation of foreign-owned mark dominated assets during the 1919–1923 inflation. Then, after 1931, it defaulted on most private foreign investments. These items combined yielded a unilateral transfer equal to a startling 5.3 per cent of German national income for 1919–31. On balance, the United States and to a lesser extent the European Allies subsidised Germany during the Weimar era.[21]

To Stresemann the acceptance of the German case for fixing the earlier date for evacuating the Rhineland to be completed by 30 June 1930, was a major success too. He could therefore say some eighteen hours before his death on 3 October 1929: 'We are again masters in our house.'[22] Viewed from outside, and from Paris especially, Stresemann's western policy was one of successive demands, built one upon the other and leading logically to a more powerful Germany than

[21] S. Schuker, 'End of Versailles', op. cit., p. 56. J. Néré, *The Foreign Policy of France from 1914 to 1945* (London, 1975), pp. 81–3; T. Lamont, 'The reparations settlement and economic peace in Europe', *Political Science Quarterly*, **45** (Sept. 1930): 321–6; E.W. Bennett, *Germany and the Diplomacy of the Financial Crisis* (Cambridge, Mass., 1962), pp. 1–14. For an example of German contacts with Parker Gilbert see M. Vogt (ed)., *Akten der Reichskanzlei. Das Kabinett Müller 11*, Bd I (Boppard am Rhein, 1970), pp. 140–2. The difficulties and passions raised on the German side can be found even in this dry record. See Documents 139, 173, 174, 175, 189.

[22] Cited by G. Castellan, *L'Allemagne de Weimar 1918–33* (Paris, 1969), p. 339.

France could ever have been comfortable with. Germany's attempt to give France 'security' along its borders with Germany was at the same time part of a broader strategy to create the preconditions for far-reaching revision of the East European settlement which Berlin regarded as essential to its 'security' (p. 145). By contrast, French policy demanded the maintenance of the East European status quo as necessary for its position *vis-à-vis* Germany. For France 'security' was not a divisible concept.[23]

In that sense at least, it is possible to look back to the 1920s and talk of the 'illusions of pactomania'.[24] Yet this does less than justice to Stresemann's effort to advance peace and international understanding through treaties. At the very least, the long-standing power-political quest of the German state was restrained at the centre of the policy-making apparatus, and especially in the German Foreign Office. State Secretary Schubert's work in reinforcing Stresemann's vision cannot be lightly dismissed. Their shared belief in balancing Germany's demands against those of European peace, exemplified by Schubert's interest in the Kellogg–Briand Pact, was an important factor in international relations.[25] Admittedly, there was little room as yet in Stresemann's policy for the not inconsiderable elements in Germany who believed in the need for a 'united Europe', although these extended their network of international contacts, including those with France, and they felt more hopeful because of Locarno.[26] So too did those industrialists and intellectuals in the 'Franco-German Committee of understanding', which laboured from 1926 to 1932.[27] Locarno has to be seen not simply for its importance to Germany's territorial revision. It also stands as an impressive attempt to define Germany's great-power status in a more realistic and pacific fashion. Although Stresemann's vision was rejected by important sectors of German society, a large body of opinion supported it before 1929,

[23] A. Hillgruber, *Kontinuität und Diskontinuität in der deutschen Aussenpolitik von Bismarck bis Hitler* (Düsseldorf, 1969), p. 20.

[24] J.B. Duroselle, 'The spirit of Locarno: Illusions of pactomania', *Foreign Affairs*, **50** (1971/72): 752–64.

[25] P. Krüger. 'Friedenssicherung und deutsche Revisionspolitik. Die deutsche Aussenpolitik und die Verhandlungen über den Kellog–Pakt', *Vierteljahrshefte für Zeitgeschichte*, **22** (1974): 236–7. 255; cf. P. Krüger, *Die Aussenpolitik der Republik von Weimar* (Darmstadt, 1985), pp. 389–93.

[26] K. Holl, 'Europapolitik im Vorfeld der deutschen Regierungspolitik. Zur Tätigkeit proeuropäischer Organisationen in der Weimarer Republik', *Historische Zeitschrift*, **219** (1974): 57; J. Freymond, *Le IIIe Reich et la Réorganisation économique de l'Europe 1940–2. Origines et Projets* (Leiden, 1974), p. 15.

[27] F.L'Huillier, *Dialogues franco-allemands 1925–33* (Paris, 1971). Cf. H. Lindner, 'Zur einigen Probleme der deutsch–französischen Verständigung nach dem ersten Weltkrieg', *Revue Allemagne*, **4** (April–June, 1974), pp. 29–37.

including the SPD, Democrats, Centre Party and substantial sections of the DVP and even some of the DNVP. Above all, Stresemann's policy was rooted in the belief of Europe's economic interdependence, although inevitably Germany's position was expected to be a commanding one.

In the last resort the ideal of international economic co-operation proved to be the biggest illusion of all. The edifice of international agreements erected in the 1920s existed in spite of rather than because of the economic policies pursued by the various European governments. That much was clear with the onset of the world economic crisis in 1929 and the differing reactions to it. There was an absence of international solidarity over economic issues which 'was almost as catastrophic for the world as the advent of Adolf Hitler'.[28] The balance between 'German' and 'European' interests which Stresemann's diplomacy was directed towards achieving was upset by the crisis. Popular pressures increased on German leaders to adopt a more active revisionist policy towards the Western Powers, as was evident during the life of the 'Great Coalition' under the social democrat Hermann Müller after 1928, even as the Young Plan was being prepared. The existence of the nationalist-inspired 'Anti-Young Front' confirmed the link between political radicalism at home and more dynamic policies abroad which became all the more apparent under Heinrich Brüning's government (p. 48). Nevertheless, domestic pressures were not the only cause of Brüning's policy towards the Western Powers, for he personally favoured a more determined effort to free German foreign policy from its remaining restrictions.

THE RADICALISATION OF FOREIGN POLICY

The change in emphasis was felt in the German Foreign Office, even though the Foreign Minister, Julius Curtius, from Stresemann's own party, was associated with his predecessor's policy. State Secretary Schubert gave way to von Bülow. The latter had been excluded from the preliminaries to the Kellogg–Briand Pact although at the time he had been the leader of the section in the German Foreign Office concerned with League of Nations matters (*Völkerbundsreferat*). The distinctly cooler reaction in the German Foreign Office to Briand's optimistic, certainly vastly premature scheme for a united Europe,

[28] Duroselle, op cit., p. 763.

put forward in his speech to the League on 5 September 1929 and in his formal memorandum of 17 May 1930, was a small sign of changing realities.[29] More unpleasant were the scenes which greeted the evacuation of the Rhineland – token of Briand's appeasement of Germany – in the summer of 1930. Apart from demonstrations by the *Stahlhelm*, President Hindenburg went so far as to question the continuing demilitarisation of the Rhineland, hardly calculated to placate the French.[30] It has been rightly said that: 'Around Bülow were gathered – particularly in the League and Disarmament sections (of the AA) the proponents of a distinct national great-power policy, if one admittedly grounded in a readiness for peace.'[31]

This might be applied to Brüning, who felt that Stresemann had not properly realised the potential for Germany's policy abroad. Critical in his memoirs of the price Germany paid for the earlier evacuation of the Rhineland – the Young Plan – Brüning 'was determined to forgo any prestige gain if it had to be tied to new conditions which could not be fulfilled'.[32] Justifying his efforts to secure the support of the Right in Germany in the face of inter-party quarrels, Brüning yet revealed a greater determination than Stresemann to take risks to secure Germany's objectives abroad. During a conversation with Hitler on 6 October 1930,[33] after the successes of the NSDAP in the September elections (p. 48), the Nazi leader was told of Brüning's expectations that the crisis would last for some five years, with little improvement likely before the summer of 1932. Nevertheless, the end of reparations and a simultaneous initiative in the matter of disarmament 'would be the prime aim of the foreign policy of the government'. Hitler was assured that the pursuit of these issues would lead, it was hoped, to a speedy undermining of the Versailles Treaty.

Although Brüning sought to ride the anti-Western currents in German nationalist circles, he made clear to Hitler that rightist opposition to his policy in its initial stage would be helpful since he

[29] W, Lipgens, 'Europäische Einigungsidee 1923–30 und Briands Europaplan im Urteil der deutschen Akten', *Historische Zeitschrift*, **203** (1966): 83–5.

[30] E. Eyck, *A History of the Weimar Republic* (New York, 1967, 2 vols, paperback), Vol 2, p. 263. See W.G. Ratliffe, *Faithful to the Fatherland. Julius Curtius and Weimar Foreign Policy* (New York, 1990), pp. 63–100.

[31] Krüger, 'Friedenssicherung', p. 241. Bülow's memorandum on Germany and the League of Nations, dated 27 Jan, 1926, gives a good indication of Bülow's approach. ADAP, Series B, Vol. I, pp. 160–2/

[32] H. Brüning, *Memoiren 1918–1934*, Bd 1 (Stuttgart, 1970, paperback), p. 180.

[33] Ibid., pp. 203–5. Cf. H. Graml, *Europa zwischen den Kriegen* (Munich, 1969), pp. 245ff.

could point to it to justify demanding concessions from the Allies. Of course, the world could not be told of Germany's aim to end reparations only half a year after the entry into operation of the Young Plan, since this would lead to a catastrophic withdrawal of foreign capital from Germany. But avoiding outside interference during Germany's economic crisis entailed the sort of harsh economic policy which increased the discontent on which the extremists could flourish. Similarly, while taking care not to antagonise France too much, there was no question of Brüning accepting the sort of loan offered by Paris in the summer of 1931, after the collapse of the Darmstadt Bank intensified the crisis in Germany. As we saw, the conditions of such a loan were not acceptable to the political forces on whose support Brüning was compelled to rely (p. 49). This was confirmed by Curtius's enforced resignation in October 1931. He was hounded by the nationalists for being too concilatory towards the Allies over the abandonment of the project for an Austro-German customs union (p. 152).

Germany was spared complete chaos by the standstill agreement on foreign debts and the Hoover moratorium on all international payments of reparations and related debts on 20 June 1931 – a useful enough answer to Brüning's demand a fortnight earlier for 'relief from the intolerable reparations burden'.[34] At the same time, Brüning's insistence on budgeting for Germany's second armoured cruiser confirmed the link between ending reparations and disarmament which he had indicated to Hitler. Both issues were vehicles to achieve the revision of Versailles. In 1932 the Disarmament Conference was looming and with it the prospect of clarifying what Germany meant by 'equality' of treatment. Some clue to this, and to the reality underlying Brüning's celebrated demands for international disarmament, was provided by genuine fears of insecurity in Germany among military and political circles in the face of the undoubted power of France and her ally Poland. These fears found expression in an Army memorandum written in 1925: 'The organizational basis for an increase in Armed Forces from 1931 onwards.'[35]

The document calculated that the recruitment situation for the German Army would be critical from 1931. Working on the assumption that 2.8 million men were needed for the eventuality of war, the memorandum observed that after 1931 it would no longer be possible to rely on First World War reserves. As yet, the numbers of reserves

[34] Eyck, op cit., Vol. 2, p. 313.
[35] Salewski, 'Zur deutschen Sicherheitspolitik', pp. 133ff.

built on the 100,000-man Army allowed by the Versailles Treaty would be too low. Since a lengthy rearmament period for the training of recruits was needed before any war, Germany had to step up rearmament by 1931 at the latest even to keep its security potential at the 1920s level. Alternatively, the other powers had to disarm. As Brüning said at the opening of the International Disarmament Conference in Geneva in February 1932: 'The German government and the German people, having been disarmed themselves, now challenge the whole world to join them in disarmament. Germany has a legal and moral claim to such a general disarmament, one that nobody can dispute.'[36] In fact, France could dispute over details, if not over moral rights. The British and American delegates to the Disarmament Conference were ready to compromise over Germany's claim to increase its rearmaments. The French insisted on their own security being assured before agreeing to abandon their existing superiority in land armaments and this provided the sticking point. Every British government had refused to accept further international obligations and without these France was understandably worried.

In mid-April 1932, Brüning exploited the presence at the Disarmament Conference of the British Prime Minister, Ramsey MacDonald, and the American Secretary of State, Henry Stimson, to get general approval of a scheme reducing the term of military service from twelve to six years. The proposals also envisaged training a further 100,000 men, either as additions to the *Reichswehr* or as auxiliary reserves; recognition of Germany's right to have the weapons denied by the Treaty of Versailles and the abrogation of part V of the Peace Treaty which limited Germany's military, naval and air strength. A new agreement was to replace these limitations. In fact, these demands gave expression to the sort of solution to German security which Army leaders like Generals Seeckt and Groener favoured: namely the creation of a larger professional strike force based on short-term military service and equipped with advanced weapons. The projected restructuring (*Umbau*) of Germany's military forces provides the vital context for Brüning's demands for 'equality of treatment'. To demand parity with France while undertaking such reforms would have given Germany decisive advantages; it would mean in effect, as the French said in a note on 11 September 1932, rearmament. Indeed, *Reichswehr* Minister Schleicher began Germany's secret rearmament in November 1932 by approving a scheme for the rebuilding of the peace-time Army, to be completed in three stages by March 1938. On 11

[36] Eyck, op cit, Vol 2, p. 348.

December 1932, after heated exchanges, and after Germany's threat to withdraw from the conference, the United States, Britain, Italy, France and Germany affirmed the German claim to 'equality of rights in a system which would provide security for all nations'. There was no practical scheme for disarmament. Since the French recognised what Germany was really trying to achieve in the disarmament and security talks, that is the redefinition of power positions, the acceptance of Germany's equality of right was not an impulse towards general peace in Europe, but the signal for further conflict.[37]

Not that it is helpful to see Brüning simply as part of an increasingly aggressive line on foreign policy linking Stresemann to Hitler. Brüning's western policies were pursued in a more forceful manner, but he remained wedded to the 'classic' peaceful revision policy. He was, however, deprived of personal victory by his enforced resignation at the hands of his rightist critics at the end of May 1932. Shortly afterwards the Lausanne Conference produced the agreement between Germany and the Western Powers. It was signed on 9 July and effectively buried the reparations problem. Neither did Brüning get the credit for the recognition of Germany's right to equality of treatment in the disarmament talks. But first Brüning then Schleicher forged the diplomatic–military instruments which Hitler was able to exploit in the early stages of his regime. In that sense at least Brüning's success in moving Germany's revisionist policy forward made it easier for Hitler to convince the outside world that he was simply continuing the process. In effect, Hitler used his advantage to launch a policy with which neither Brüning nor his successors nor the military leaders identified themselves.[38] To perceive this, some account must be taken of the ideas which Hitler had been developing about the Western Powers since the 1920s.

HITLER AND THE WESTERN POWERS

Of central importance was the wish he expressed in *Mein Kampf* – generally agreed to have been reinforced by the Ruhr crisis of 1923 – to achieve an alliance with England (as he generally termed Britain). The crisis of 1923 encouraged Hitler to modify his hitherto typically nationalist antipathy towards any co-operation with the Versailles

[37] Salewski, 'Zur deutschen Sicherheitspolitik', p. 138.

[38] Ibid., pp. 138ff; Lee and Michalka, *German Foreign Policy 1917–1933. Continuity or break?* (Leamington Spa, 1987), pp. 120–3.

victors. He became convinced that it was possible to separate Britain and France, a mistake which neither Wirth nor Stresemann had ever made.[39] The British alliance would further Hitler's planned war of revenge against France, for which Italy, too, was already marked in Hitler's thoughts (p. 175). One most striking difference between Hitler and Weimar policy-makers was this acceptance of war, not simply as an unavoidable evil, but as an integral feature of a nation's struggle to survive and to grow; an essential part of his 'Darwinian' belief in the survival of the fittest. Above all, Hitler believed that an alliance with Britain would give him the freedom of movement he needed to carry out the first stage of German expansion into East Europe and Russia; the quest for *Lebensraum* which became such a central feature of his 'programme' from 1924 onwards at the very latest.[40] In short, and at least partly through his reflection on the failure of German Imperial policies in the First World War, Hitler rejected decisively in the early 1920s the view that Germany could be a great continental and Imperial power at the same time. Hitler hoped that as long as Britain's naval and colonial supremacy was unchallenged, it would tolerate his defeat of France and the conquest of European Russia, as he argued in his *Second Book*. Those historians who stress the global rather than European preoccupations of Hitler's foreign policy strategy, point out that even in *Mein Kampf*, and certainly in his *Second Book*, the idea of colonial expansion at a very much later stage, after the European phase of his 'programme', was marked. In this phase a breach with Britain was possible, especially if it chose the wrong side in the distant and ultimate clash between Germany and America.[41] If it chose correctly, as Hitler hoped, Britain

[39] A. Hitler, *Mein Kampf*, translated by R. Manheim, introduced by D.C. Watt (London, 1969), p. 564.

[40] For the argument that Hitler came to his decisions on *Lebensraum* in the east after he had conceived of a partnership with Britain see A. Kuhn, *Hitlers aussenpolitisches Programm. Entstehung und Entwicklung 1919–39* (Stuttgart, 1970), pp. 95, 99, 100ff.

[41] A. Hillgruber, 'England's place in Hitler's plans for world domination', *Journal of Contemporary History*, **9**, No. 1 (Jan. 1974): 11; A. Hillgruber, *Deutschlands Rolle in der Vorgeschichte der beiden Weltkriege* (Göttingen, 1967), pp. 68ff; K. Hildebrand, *The Foreign Policy of the Third Reich* (London, 1973), p. 21. Hitler's belief in an eventual struggle between Germany and America persisted, although by the end of the 1920s he was less impressed by America's racial strength and less troubled by the fear of immediate opposition from it, G.L. Weinberg, 'Hitler's image of the United States', *American Historical Review*, **69** (1964): 1006–111. While America's role is not covered in this book its importance to the Allies was self-evident as Weinberg has argued in *The Foreign Policy of Hitler's Germany. Diplomatic Revolution in Europe 1933–6* (Chicago/London, 1970), p. 133. Cf. Hans-Jürgen Schröder's fine study, *Deutschland und die Vereinigten Staaten 1933–9. Wirtschaft und Politik in der Entwicklung des deutsch-amerikanischen Gegensatzes* (Wiesbaden, 1970).

would be a sort of junior partner to Germany, with what exact results even Hitler had not quite worked out in the 1920s.

Doubts may well arise about the *extent* of this 'elaborate theorising', but the concept of 'opportunism' does not satisfactorily explain Hitler's foreign policy, any more than it does his ideology, which, like it or not, had a consistency about it.[42] It is impossible to overlook the importance atached to 'England' in Hitler's world of ideas even if, as in other areas, the actual course of Hitler's foreign policy in the 1930s differed in details from his vision of the 1920s. As soon as he came to power he affirmed in private the intimate connection between his plans for *Lebensraum* in the east and the policy to be followed towards Britain, in a talk of 3 February 1933 professing his explicit intention of securing an alliance with that country. Some remarkably diligent German historians went so far as to see no less than ten stages in Hitler's policy towards Britain between 1933 and 1945, in the first of which, 1933–35, 'Hitler tried all possible ways and means, conventional or otherwise, of reaching an alliance with England at the expense of his colonial and maritime ambitions.'[43] Since this effort was accompanied by a steady rate of decline in German–Russian relations, such a protracted attempt to woo Britain was itself a decisive break from the foreign policy of the Weimar Republic, with its emphasis on co-existing with East and West and with its greater awareness of the susceptibilities of France.[44]

In 1933 very obvious power-political realities reinforced Hitler's desire to come to agreement with Britain, quite apart from its central place in his long-term ambitions. The combined weight of France and her East European allies – above all Poland – forced Hitler to be cautious in his western policies. Hitler said in 1932, when contemplating the risky period needed to transform the principle of equality of treatment in armaments to the reality of German forces which would make possible more active policies: 'If ever there are grounds for preventive war, there are in this case for an attack by France

[42] E. Jäckel, *Hitlers Weltanschauung* (Tübingen, 1969), pp. 9–23; H. Holborn, 'Origins and political character of Nazi ideology', *Political Science Quarterly*, **79** (Dec. 1964): 542–54; E. Matthias, 'The western powers in Hitler's world of ideas', in Nicholls and Matthias (eds), *German Democracy and The Triumph of Hitler* (London, 1971), p. 162; N. Rich, 'Hitler's foreign policy', in G. Martel, (ed.), *Origins*, pp. 119ff; G. Stoakes, *Hitler and the Quest for World Dominion* (Leamington Spa, 1986), pp. 64ff; J. Hiden, 'National Socialism and foreign policy 1919–1933', in P.D. Stachura (ed.), *The Nazi Machtergreifung* (London, 1983), pp. 146–61.

[43] Hillgruber, 'England's place', p. 13; cf. Josef Hencke, *England in Hitlers politischen Kalkül, 1935–9* (Boppard am Rhein, 1973), p. 27.

[44] Kuhn op. cit., pp. 145–6.

against Germany.' The implication was that the existence of such forces *would* be a threat to France, a not surprising conclusion, even in view of his intention to throw off the chains of Versailles[45] let alone his documented aims in East Europe. Hitler naturally played these down in order to emphasis his continuation of Germany's established revisionist policy. Indeed the presence of his conservative allies in the Cabinet, not to mention the influence of the German Foreign Office, also made this essential. It was equally obvious, however, that the French remained implacably opposed to giving up their advantages in armaments over Germany once Hitler was in power, and certainly not before new guarantees of France's security were forthcoming.

The prospects of success at the Disarmament Conference when it reconvened on 31 January 1933 were therefore virtually nil. Hitler could not simply reject out of hand the draft disarmament convention, worked out by Anthony Eden and Alexander Cadogan, which Ramsay MacDonald put to the conference on 16 March. It proposed specific figures for the first time. These would give Germany the same strength as the other European powers – apart from Russia – and after five years the same weapons. A standing disarmament commission was envisaged. Nothing was said about Germany's future air and sea forces. The French countered by pointing to the existing reserves in the SA and SS and to the suspected 'remilitarisation' of German youth already under way. While admitting the general need for disarmament and Germany's parity, France demanded that the process last eight years. Only in the last four years could the Eden plan be implemented, after the first four had given proof of Berlin's good intentions. Germany was to be allowed to have short-term service, but not to be permitted any real increase in troop numbers or modernisation of weapons. Bitterly disappointed, the British nonetheless put forward the French proposals on 14 October 1933.[46]

Thus Hitler was given the golden opportunity to leave the conference and the League on the same day, professing his own peaceful intentions and ostensibly upset by the clear failure of the conference to achieve disarmament and by its obvious aim to discriminate against Germany. In fact, Hitler had told his Cabinet meeting on 8 February 1933 that rearmament was to have the first priority for the next four to five years.[47] As the impasse was approaching at the Disarmament

[45] C.B. Burdick, 'German military planning and France, 1930–8', *World Affairs Quarterly*, **30** (1959/60); 299–313.

[46] Earl of Avon, *The Eden memoirs. Facing the Dictators* (London, 1962), pp. 43–7.

[47] *Documents on German Foreign Policy, 1918–1945*, Series C, Vol. I (London, 1957–), Document No. 16. (Hereafter referred to as DGFP).

Conference, the *Reichswehr* was pressing for the discussions to be broken off, and General Werner von Blomberg, the Defence Minister, had little difficulty in convincing Hitler of the need for this step when they spoke on 4 October 1933. It was already impossible to reconcile Germany's secret rearmament and military planning with the talks with the Western Powers.[48] For this reason little can be gained by examining the detail of the schemes which continued to be discussed until the Disarmament Conference was finally ended in May 1934. Hitler viewed it merely in terms of how best it could benefit his own plans for rearmament, and the protracted negotiations bought Germany valuable time.[49] According to the Reich budget for 1934/35, the military expenditure of the Reich was to rise by some 90 per cent and there were provisions for an Air Force, still strictly forbidden. The *Luftwaffe* was already being secretly 'reborn' under the guidance of State Secretary for Air, Erhard Milch, and by the end of 1933 was employing two million workers on airfield and factory construction.[50]

Historians still emphasise the diplomatic skill of Hitler in the early years of his regime, and his success in avoiding multilateral pacts such as that suggested at the Disarmament Conference. Equally, the proposal by Mussolini on 18 March 1933 for an agreement between Britain, France, Germany and Italy on how best to revise the status quo – naturally in a way which best suited Italy – put no restraint on Germany's international position. By the time it was signed on 7 June 1933, the French had removed everything from the text that offended them and the British remained keen, like Hitler, for separate agreements. The European powers wanted to believe in Hitler's 'pacific' foreign policy. The plain fact of the matter is that Hitler's early successes were founded in the harsh realities of the Western Powers' predicament and in the untried nature of the Anglo-French relationship. The French were obsessed with defence, not attack; no sooner was the Rhineland free of foreign occupation than the French were building their fortified Maginot Line.[51] With France increasingly dependent on Great Britain since the 1920s, the latter's contribution towards a Franco-German conflict had never been spelled out. The

[48] G. Wollstein, *Vom Weimarer Revisionismus zu Hitler. Das deutsche Reich und die europäische Grossmächte in der Anfangsphase der nationalsozialistischen Herrschaft* (Bonn, 1973), pp. 292–4.

[49] Weinberg, *Foreign Policy*, pp. 43–4.

[50] D. Irving, *The Rise and Fall of the Luftwaffe. The Life of Luftwaffe Marshall Erhard Milch* (London, 1976, paperback), p. 33.

[51] Watt, *Too Serious a Business*, pp. 35–7.

extent of Britain's 'continental commitment' was still uncertain, to say the least.

On this uncertainty Hitler continued for some time to found his hope for an alliance with Great Britain, which would also reduce anxieties about what France might do. Paradoxically, that same uncertainty obscured the hard core of mutual self-interest in the Anglo-French relationship which we have stressed underlay their disagreements over the 'German problem' in the 1920s. The fund of British goodwill on which Hitler could draw was hardly inexhaustible, even in the British Foreign Office, let alone in large sectors of British public life. The disappointing outcome of Alfred Rosenberg's efforts to work for an Anglo-German understanding during his stay in Britain in 1933 showed as much. The British distrust of Nazism and hostility towards its ideology, deepened by the domestic excesses in Germany, co-existed from the start with the impulses to placate reasonable German grievances.[52] There were never any grounds in Britain for a bilateral alliance with Hitler, let alone one directed against France's interests.

The British did not, however, make this clear beyond reasonable doubt. Hitler continued to misread the signs, although Prime Minister Baldwin was to say in 1934 that the British frontier was on the Rhine. His White Paper on Britain's proposed rearmament on 4 March 1935 justified it by reference to Germany's own provocative armaments policy. Yet Hitler exploited the fitful exchanges with the Western Powers as a useful smoke screen. Thus he welcomed the Anglo-French communiqué of 3 February 1935, for a limited general settlement involving regional security pacts, Germany's return to the League and a reciprocal regional agreement against air attack, shortly before the German Cabinet approved a secret decree on the Air Force on 26 February.[53]

Hitler had sounded reactions on German rearmament by letting Goering refer on 9 March 1935 to the fact that the German Air Force was being built up. The virtual absence of formal protest from the Western Powers helped to encourage the announcement on 16 March 1935.[54] On this date Hitler proclaimed the reintroduction of conscrip-

[52] Kuhn, op. cit., pp. 149–50; D.C. Watt, *Personalities and Policies. Studies in the Formulation of British Foreign Policy in the Twentieth Century* (London, 1965), p. 118. DGFP, Series C, Vol I, No. 237, Hoesch's report on Rosenberg in England; cf. D.C. Watt, *How War Came* (London, 1990), p. 77.

[53] Cf. A. Crozier, 'Prelude to Munich. British foreign policy and Germany', *European Studies Review*, **6** (1976): 358; W. Carr, *Arms, Autarky and Aggression. A Study in German Foreign Policy 1933–9* (London, 1972), p. 45.

[54] Ibid., pp. 45–6.

tion in Germany, six days after the French decision to extend compulsory service from one to two years and to reduce the age of enlistment to offset the effects of France's declining birth-rate.

In reality, introducing conscription and the affirmation of Germany no longer being bound by the Versailles limitations had long been regarded by the Nazis as the prerequisite for recovering Germany's freedom of movement in foreign policy. The British and French moves on rearmament, on 4 and 10 March 1935, respectively, simply provided a convenient justification for Hitler. Since rearmament made Germany more 'alliance-worthy' in Hitler's eyes, he saw no reason why it should prevent agreement with Britain.[55] This in spite of the fact that in response to Germany's proclamation on armaments Britain, France and Italy met in Stresa, and on 14 April expressed collective regret as well as reaffirming their loyalty to the Locarno treaties and their belief in the need for maintaining Austria's independence (p. 179).

In retrospect it is not difficult to see why Hitler refused initially to be too daunted by the prospect of a more concerted Anglo-French response to his diplomacy; nor that he failed to grasp 'the not immediately tangible and largely indirect nature of the British interest in Europe',[56] as he had failed so to do in his reflections in the 1920s. On the one hand France, beset by domestic upheaval, lacked the leadership ready to march against Hitler – a failure not so surprising in view of the bitter memories in Paris of what happened when they took unilateral action in 1923. Admittedly, the French did attempt to reactivate their eastern alliances, in addition to intensifying their own rearmament. After becoming Foreign Minister in Februaary 1934, Louis Barthou made a strenuous bid to achieve an *Ostlocarno* and to strengthen France's relations with the Little *Entente* in the spring and summer of 1934. Later there was the direct alliance with Soviet Russia, concluded by his successor, Laval, on 2 May 1935. Such efforts showed France reverting to its 1920s policy of encircling Germany. As will be seen, however, the realities of East Europe, the continuing gap between West and East and Hitler's success in signing a German–Polish Non-Aggression Pact on 20 January 1934, combined to relieve the Nazi regime from pressure here (p. 156). And with Britain, the Third Reich was able to conclude a naval pact by 18 June 1935.

For Hitler this seemed to be a considerable triumph, coming as it did so soon after his flouting of the Versailles restrictions on arma-

[55] *Mein Kampf*, pp. 566–7.
[56] Hillgruber, 'England's place', p. 10.

ments. In effect it legitimised this step, as Hitler realised it would when he suggested to Foreign Minister Simon and Eden during their Berlin visit in March 1935, that Germany voluntarily limit its naval tonnage to 35 per cent of that of Britain. The pact eventually specified this figure. It also gave Germany the right to equal submarine tonnage with the Commonwealth, although the Germans agreed not to go above 45 per cent without giving notice. These figures promised Hitler superiority over the French Navy and provided more than enough scope for what Germany could actually build in the immediate future. It was a body blow to the 'Stresa Front' and it also removed for Hitler some of the menace in the French policy of encirclement and containment of Germany. Hitler had already assured Admiral Raeder in March 1935 that the Navy would be systematically rebuilt, irrespective of the coming negotiations with Britain.[57] Above all, Hitler considered the Anglo-German naval agreement as a step towards his desired alliance with Britain. Joachim von Ribbentrop, whose office was then preoccupied with working for the co-operation of Britain, saw the pact as of 'world historical importance'.[58]

Not surprisingly the judgement on Britain's policy here has been harsh indeed.[59] Nevertheless, it was hardly the intention of the British government to work with Hitler against France, as the Führer hoped. For Britain, the Anglo-German Naval Agreement was in part the expression of its well-established policy of making concessions in order to win Germany back to the concert of European powers and to persuade it to honour its international obligations. Reluctant wholly to endorse France's intransigent attitude towards Nazi Germany, Britain's co-operation with Germany was represented as the only alternative short of war. War was inconceivable both in terms of British public opinion, notwithstanding the critics of Baldwin and Simon, and in terms of Britain's strategic predicament – a point to which we shall shortly return when discussing appeasement.[60] Beset by financial difficulties and the sort of institutionalised

[57] M. Salewski, *Die deutsche Seekriegsleitung 1935–45*, Vol. I (Frankfurt am Main, 1970), pp. 15–16. Major expansion plans were in progress April 1934 – March 1936, Weinberg, *Foreign Policy*, p. 176.

[58] *DGFP*, Series C, Vol. IV, No. 131.

[59] D.C. Watt, 'The Anglo-German Naval Agreement of 1935: An interim judgement', *Journal of Modern History*, **28**, No. 2 (June 1956): 155–75; K.D. Bracher, 'Das Anfangsstadium der Hitlerschen Aussenpolitik' in G. Jasper (ed.), *Von Weimar zu Hitler 1930–33* (Cologne–Berlin, 1968), p. 492.

[60] A convenient survey is provided by J.P.D. Dunbabin, 'British rearmament in the 1930s: A chronology and review', *Historical Journal*, **18**, No. 3 (1975): 587–609. See, too, W.N. Medlicott's balanced, *Britain and Germany: The Search for Agreement 1930–1937* (London, 1969).

parliamentary political opposition that was absent in Nazi Germany, there was still painful progress towards defining and countering the likely threat from Hitler – notably in Britain's growing obsession with matching German air power. This found its expression in the conclusions of the Defence Requirements Committee in the autumn of 1935.

The report suggested a two-power standard for the naval fleet, to defend and deter in the Far East as well as to meet the needs for possible war against Germany; a field force of five divisions to be ready for action on the Continent, backed up by twelve Territorial Army divisions and arrangements for industrial production to be geared to the needs of war in a limited period. In addition the Air Ministry scheme proposed the building of 1,736 first-line aircraft, including 1,000 bombers, by 1939. Together, these proposals 'constituted the first serious programme to enable the British armed forces to take part in a major war against their most probable adversaries'[61] The struggle to implement such policies was of course by no means over, but an awareness of this broader perspective confirms that Hitler and Britain were pursuing diametrically opposed policies. Thus it has been said of the Anglo-German Naval Agreement: 'For Hitler it was supposed to be the means towards a German–English alliance, for England a step towards a worldwide naval agreement with Japan and America.' Or, as another German historian put it: 'Hitler's blueprint on bilateral lines and the multilateral policy of the British stood in irreconcilable opposition.'[62]

It is at any rate of considerable interest that meticulous studies of

[61] M. Howard. op. cit., p. 115. An extremely interesting attempt to relate the Anglo-German Naval Agreement of 1935 to such broader strategic requirements in Britain and indeed to many other factors bearing on British foreign policy is H.H. Hall III's, 'The foreign policy-making process in Britain, 1934–5 and the origins of the Anglo-German Naval Agreement', *Historical Journal*, **19**, No.2 (1976): 477–99. This conveniently discusses recent literature on the Anglo-German Naval Agreement, including E.H. Haraszti's, *Treaty-breakers or 'Realpolitiker'? The Anglo-German Naval Agreement of June 1935* (Boppard am Rhein, 1974).

[62] The first quote from Kuhn, op. cit., p. 175, the second from Hildebrand, op. cit., p. 39. The C-in-C of the German Navy, Raeder, discussed with Hitler in June 1934 the progress of the fleet, originally designed with mainly Poland and France in mind, and talked about the prospects for its use against Britain. For the suggestion that this showed that the possibility of war against Britain was already being seriously considered, Weinberg, *Foreign Policy*, pp. 176–7, although such a conflict did not dominate naval planning until early 1938. Hillgruber, *Deutschlands Rolle*, p. 83 stresses the concern of Hitler and Raeder to avoid risk of conflict with Britain until the fleet was ready. Cf. Salewski, op. cit., pp. 13–14. See, too, Jost Dülfer, *Weimar, Hitler und die Marine. Reichspolitik und Flottenbau 1920–1939* (Düsseldorf, 1973); C.-A. Gemzell, *Organisation, Conflict and Innovation. A Study of German Naval Strategy and Planning 1888–1940* (Lund, 1973).

Hitler's attitudes towards Britain show that in spite of his success with the Naval Agreement, he began to entertain increasing doubts from 1935 as to whether England could in fact be either wooed into an alliance or pushed into one by the application of pressure.[63] These doubts were certainly reinforced by the events of 1936, a year of crucial importance in Germany's relations with the Western Powers. The outbreak of war between Italy and Abyssinia in the winter of 1935/36, culminating in the Italian King Victor Immanuel being proclaimed Emperor of Abyssinia on 5 May 1936, helped finally to bury the Stresa Front. It also increasingly affected the nature of any four-power pact approach to diplomacy by making impossible thereafter any protracted co-operation between Italy, Britain and France *against* Hitler's Germany. By contrast, the renewed Italian–French tensions brought Hitler a step nearer to his alliance with Italy, which he had also conceived in the 1920s. Additional links were forged between the Germans and Italians through their shared interest in the outcome of the Spanish Civil War. In all, the situation in the Mediterranean, with its prospect of protracted warfare in an area of vital interest to Britain and France, offered Hitler the chance of greater freedom of movement in Europe (Chapter 6). Hitler's remilitarisation of the Rhineland on 7 March 1936 was thus made less risky than it might otherwise have been.

In the context of the 'revisionist' policy which Hitler professed to be following, the remilitarisation of the Rhineland was the next logical step. Its timing – Hitler did not intend to seize the Rhineland before the spring of 1937 – was occasioned both by the unexpectedly favourable international situation as well as, perhaps, by Hitler's desire to revive the waning enthusiasm for his regime by a popular success.[64] Publicly, Hitler justified this destruction of Locarno by referring to the pending ratification by France of its pact with Soviet Russia, which Hitler argued was in itself incompatible with the Locarno treaties. The risk, Hitler felt, was considerable. The forty-eight hours after remilitarisation were, as he said later, the most worrying time in his life.[65] The Rhineland action dealt a body blow to France's system of eastern alliances and, by opening up for Hitler the prospect of properly defended western borders, was the essential

[63] Hencke, op. cit., p. 38.

[64] Weinberg, *Foreign Policy*, pp. 241ff; see also E.H. Haraszti, *The Invaders. Hitler Occupies the Rhineland* (Budapest, 1983).

[65] Joachim Fest, *Hitler* (London, 1974), p. 497. Hitler was worried but not bluffing – D.C. Watt, 'German plans for the reoccupation of the Rhineland', *Journal of Contemporary History*, **1**, No. 4 (Oct. 1966): 193–9.

precondition for the eventual expansion into Eastern Europe, especially when Belgium shielded the Ruhr by her declaration of neutrality a year later. Yet Hitler had said in 1934 that he was prepared to accept Locarno providing the Saar dispute was removed. Since the Saar had returned to Germany at the beginning of 1935 after a plebiscite, the Rhineland occupation robbed of any credibility Hitler's pronouncements on foreign policy to the outside world.[66]

Hitler capitalised on the growing *rapprochement* with Italy to try to make sure of Mussolini's goodwill before marching troops into the Rhineland. His policy towards Britain could hardly remain unaffected by the evolution of the Rome–Berlin Axis, to which the Italians referred at the close of 1936 (p. 186). Britain's imperial connections were touched in a most sensitive point by Italian activities in the Mediterranean and in Africa. For Hitler the problem of reconciling in his policies the interests of his two would-be 'allies' was bound to grow more intractable. Hitler could hardly continue to maintain that war over colonies was impossible for Germany, given the action of Italy. Although Hitler's strategy towards Britain entailed playing down German colonial demands in the early years of the Nazi regime, their acquisition in the distant future was an essential part of his overall scheme, when a racially regenerated Germany, already dominant in Europe, would make its bid for world power. That this would then involve possible conflict with Great Britain at least lay in the logic of his ideas on Germany's future, as was suggested earlier. The concern of German propaganda at the close of 1935 with German colonial claims was expressed on 7 March 1936 by Hitler's first public demand as Chancellor for colonial revisions. If the colonial demands were indeed made to divert attention from his policies in Europe and to pressurise Britain, they were also an indication of the later 'stage' of Nazi Germany's expansion and helped Hitler to integrate those important political and economic groups in Germany who, through their colonial associations, were demanding territories abroad.[67]

Other areas of Nazi foreign policy added to the strain of German–British relations. The more pronounced anti-Bolshevik line of Hitler in 1936 and the mounting fervour of Nazi efforts to portray Germany as a vital bulwark against Communism – the better to justify action in East Europe (p. 129) – tied in with Hitler's interest in

[66] H. Graml, *Europa zwischen den Kriegen* (Munich, 1969), p. 334.

[67] In the summer of 1935 Ribbentrop was ordered to set up the Reich Colonial Association which, it has been argued, gave Hitler a tool to be used later against Britain, K. Hildebrand, *Vom Reich zum Weltreich. Hitler, NSDAP und koloniale Fragen 1919–1945* (Munich, 1969), pp. 343.

exploiting the Russo-Japanese conflict and enlisting the aid of the Japanese, his third would-be ally. While it had certainly been part of Britain's policy to involve the Western Powers with Germany in a defensive block against the communist threat,[68] its imperial position was even more at risk from Japan.[69] As Rosenberg warned Hitler in 1934: 'Even if the English are unsure, an open *rapprochement* with Japan, already troublesome for them, could drive them right into the arms of the French. England regards Tokyo as more dangerous than Moscow.'[70] Such considerations alone, never mind the Anglo-French relationship, frustrated Hitler's effort to include Britain along with Germany, Italy and Japan in what has been described as a worldwide quadrilateral in 1936–37.[71] As it dawned on Hitler that Britain might not after all give him a free hand to take action in East Europe, he inevitably considered turning Rosenberg's maxim to his own advantage. He told Ciano on 24 October 1936, that, should Britain refuse to tolerate German action in East Europe as part of Germany's effort to erect an anti-Bolshevik bulwark, it might be forced to by the superior weight of Germany, Italy and Japan.[72]

That Hitler was still attracted by the idea of an alliance was confirmed by the appointment of Ribbentrop in August 1936 as Ambassador to London. He was told to 'bring back' Britain. At the same time, the passivity of Britain and France during the Abyssinian and Spanish crises and in 1937 the Sino-Japanese War, tended to reinforce the notion that was forming in Hitler's mind that he might be able to start Germany's expansion on the Continent without Britain's backing.[73] All that was needed was for British policy to remain passive. Yet, when Ribbentrop had failed by the summer of 1937 to achieve his master's aims in London, his influence was exerted increasingly on Hitler to regard Britain as an enemy and to transform the tripartite pact of 1937 between Italy, Germany and Japan (p. 188) into a military alliance directed against Britain.[74]

The only obvious conclusion to be drawn from such considerations is that the Nazi leaders could not be sure of Britain's intentions by 1937. Hitler's first public departure from the vision of *Mein Kampf* was made in a speech of 13 September 1937 when he observed that

[68] G. Niedhart. *Grossbritannien und die Sowjetunion 1934–9. Studien zur britischen Politik der Friedenssicherung zwischen den beiden Weltkriegen* (Munich, 1972).

[69] Howard, op. cit., pp. 99, 101–3.

[70] Kuhn, op. cit., p. 188.

[71] Ibid., pp. 191ff.

[72] Ibid., pp. 198–201.

[73] Hencke, op. cit., pp. 77ff.

[74] Ibid., p. 96.

'England and France do not want to see in Europe any readjustment of the balance of power in Germany's or Italy's favour.'[75] In spite of this, Nazi foreign policy moved to a more overtly expansionist phase between 1936 and 1938, the pivotal point being the winter of 1937/38. Apart from the exigencies of the international scene, this development can hardly have been unrelated to the progress of Germany's internal consolidation. As was suggested in Chapter 2, the intensified rearmaments drive not only expressed Hitler's determination to expand Germany's frontiers in due course but also reflected the mounting domestic/economic pressures on the regime. A more adventurous foreign policy raised in more acute form the need to consider the question of immediate objectives, tactics and priorities.

One controversial piece of evidence that this was going on was the talk which Hitler held with a select audience on 5 November 1937. Present were Fritsch and Raeder, respectively Commanders-in-Chief of the Army and Navy, Foreign Minister Neurath, Blomberg, the Commander-in-chief of the *Wehrmacht*, Göring and Friedrich Hossbach, Hitler's adjutant and the man whose name has been given to the memorandum of the meeting. There is dispute about the value of Hossbach's evidence and about the ultimate meaning of Hitler's monologue at the meeting.[76] Few would want to see it by itself as evidence of a meticulously worked-out blueprint for aggression. However, the intention of Hitler to use force in the pursuit of the concept of *Lebensraum* in the East was more openly emphasised at the meeting, as was his readiness to contemplate the ensuing hazards. Also notable, was Hitler's stress on the need for Germany to capitalise on its progress in rearmament before the rest of the world caught up or German weapons became obsolescent. All of which convinced him that, come what may, Germany could not wait longer than 1943–45 to solve her problems – a date referred to on other occasions.[77]

And of Hitler's opponents? After the occupation of the Rhineland and the collapse of the Locarno system, Anthony Eden, Britain's Foreign Minister since December 1935, offered France a guarantee in November 1936, but this did not include France's allies in East Europe. At any rate, Hitler was at pains to assure his listeners on 5 November 1937 that action against Austria and Czechoslovakia (vital

[75] Kuhn, op. cit., p. 209.

[76] Cf. H.W. Koch, 'Hitler and the origins of the Second World War: Second thoughts on the status of some of the documents', in E.M. Robertson (ed.), *The Origins of the Second World War* (London, 1971), pp. 168–71; A.J.P. Taylor, *The Origins of the Second World War* (London, 1964), pp. 168–72.

[77] Hillgruber, *Deutschlands Rolle*, p. 83.

to ensure his continental base for later action against Russia) could probably be achieved without active resistance from Britain or France. He even suggested that Britain had probably 'already quietly written Czechoslovakia off'. Should Britain and France be heavily involved elsewhere, notably in the Mediterranean, or should France lapse into civil war, he was ready, he said, to fall on Austria and Czechoslovakia immediately, and not to wait until Germany was fully prepared. Yet in the same meeting not only France but Britain too were seen as 'our enemies, who both hate us.'

Many have seen this as the turning point, when Hitler abandoned the idea of a deal with Britain or even made it a target.[78] Others argue that, while moving ahead in 1937–39 with the first phase of his continental expansion, Hitler continued to hope for an alliance.[79] Be that as it may, it must be repeated: he appeared ready to take greater risks in East Europe without British acquiescence. Perhaps he continued to believe that England would say much and do little, but since this could not be absolutely guaranteed, any further step towards expansion in East Europe always contained the threat of conflict with the West. Given this spectre of a two-front war, the various German military directives and planning exercises of the 1930s have also been used to shed further light on the crucial shift in Hitler's foreign policy, 1937–38.

The directives do not reveal that Hitler had fixed any specific time for military action. Seen in conjunction with the political evidence and giving due weight to Hitler's ideology they are, however, revealing. Until the middle of 1937 Germany's strategic planning had been largely defensive, following on from its exposed position between France and her eastern allies and from its initial military unpreparedness. By the end of 1935, France was still regarded as the most likely source of a major attack. Plans for deployment in this eventuality (*Plan Red*) assumed only that Czechoslovakia would help her French ally, but not in an offensive role. General Beck, Chief of the General Staff, at first would have nothing to do with the military exercise launched on Blomberg's instructions in late May 1935, to

[78] Cf. E.M. Robertson, *Hitler's Prewar Policy and Military Plans, 1933–9* (London, 1963), p. 113. Recent detailed studies of Hitler and England make it more difficult to accept the idea that Britain was already a target for Hitler in November 1937. Cf. D.C. Watt's deft 'Appeasement. The rise of a revisionist school?', *Political Quarterly*, **36** (1965): 206.

[79] Kuhn, op. cit., pp. 214–19. Admittedly Kuhn thinks that Hitler was now wanting to compel Britain towards an alliance and Hencke, op. cit., pp. 99ff., stresses that Hitler had definitely seen by late 1937 that he would not be able to get the alliance on his terms.

consider in detail the feasibility of a surprise attack on Czechoslovakia. Beck did agree by 1937 to the preparation of *Plan Green*, an alternative deployment plan postulating a lightning pre-emptive strike against Czechoslovakia to prevent it attacking Germany while she was engaged in a war on the West. Yet the directive of 24 June 1937, formalizing the existing strategic planning, still put *Plan Red* before *Plan Green*.[80]

By contrast, the amendment to Blomberg's directive of June 1937, made by Jodl on 7 December 1937, dramatically changed the picture. It was based in part on reports from the Hossbach conference and in part on the need for the Army to keep pace with Göring's changes in Air Force directives after the conference. There was the same concern to avoid a two-front war when carrying out an offensive against Czechoslovakia. There was the same readiness, not to say desire, to execute it before Germany was fully prepared for conflict, should international conditions favour it – that is if France and Italy were at war, Britain neutral and only Russia likely to aid the Czechs. Now, however, *Plan Green* had top priority. War against Czechoslovakia was necessary at the right moment, ideally when Germany was fully armed, 'so that the solution of the German problem of living space can be carried to a victorious end even if one of the other Great Powers intervene against us.' *Plan Green* was transformed 'from a defensive strategy into the keystone of an offensive plan inspired by Hitler and designed to serve the ends of National Socialist Imperialism'.[81]

From the winter of 1937/38 Hitler's western policy was at the very least more determinedly directed at preventing Britain and France from interfering in his policies towards East Europe as he prepared to accelerate the pace of his foreign policy. A recent study of Germany's rearmament 1933–38 concluded of the forces which were to back up Hitler's diplomacy in this hazardous phase that, even if the Army had not been as fully prepared and equipped as planned, and if its fighting strength was not as great as its numbers suggested, it fulfilled its purpose at that stage of rearmament. It was strong enough to end Germany's defencelessness and, because the outside world overesti-

[80] Robertson, *Hitler's Prewar Policy*, p. 92, tends to think it was the expression of planned aggression; not so Carr, op. cit., p. 79.

[81] Ibid., p. 80; Watt, 'Appeasement', pp. 205–6. See the discussion in W. Bernhardt, *Die deutsche Aufrüstung 1934–9. Militärische und politische Konzeptionen und ihre Einschätzung durch die Allierten* (Frankfurt am Main, 1969), pp. 84–8.

mated its strength, credibility was given to Hitler's threat to use force if need be to secure his aims in East Europe.[82]

APPEASEMENT

It is ironic that as Hitler was moving into higher gear, Chamberlain (who abhorred war as much as Hitler appeared to welcome it) arrived at the head of the British government with his policy of 'appeasement'. Public discussion of that policy has been coloured ever since by the all too familiar newsreel image of an ageing Chamberlain, waving his, ultimately worthless, piece of paper on his return from the Munich Conference. Yet research in the archives has long since modified the largely negative picture of appeasement. Hindsight has grossly simplified the choices facing the Chamberlain government, and it is misleading, in the first place, to reduce the discussion of appeasement to the actions and motives of one British premier. Cabinet records have long since made it clear that the opening months of Chamberlain's government and 'at an extension, even Munich itself', was the final stage of a phase of British policy that began well before Neville Chamberlain became prime minister; that this policy can be traced back to Eden's efforts as Foreign Minister from the end of 1935 to achieve a comprehensive settlement of outstanding problems with Germany, when he abandoned the piecemeal approach which had characterised Anglo-German exchanges after 1933. Both Eden and Chamberlain found room in their policies for the simultaneous development of Britain's armed strength, although playing this down to avoid provoking Hitler to greater extremes.

The earliest studies using Chamberlain's papers already indicated his grave doubts as to whether, in the long run, Hitler would understand any language other than that of force. Applying that, however, appeared fraught with problems. Not the least of these was financial.

> The great increase in government expenditures [by the 1930s] and the large defense loans, did cause inflation; the many orders abroad for the machine-tools, steel, aircraft and instruments which a weak British industry could not produce itself, drastically raised the amount of imports; yet the transition of the economy from a peacetime to a wartime basis meant that the proportion of manufactures devoted to exports was

[82] Ibid., p. 91. It was nonetheless heavily outnumbered by its probable opponents. Cf. B. Mueller-Hillebrand, *Das Heer, 1933–45, Vol. 1* (Darmstadt, 1954), p. 61.

> falling rapidly. The balance of payments was worsening, the standard rate of income-tax was higher than at any time since 1919, and the floating of government loans to pay for defence was weakening Britain's credit and leading to a run on sterling.[83]

It was in 1937 after all, that a British White Paper for the first time gave a public estimate of the total costs of rearmament, the magnitude of which (not much less than £1,500 million over the next five years) confirmed the seriousness of the mood in Britain. By 1939 the treasury believed that defence spending at the current rate would so weaken Britain's overall stability that ultimately it would not be able to stand the strain of war.[84]

As well as the growing commitment in relation to Europe, Britain was compelled to continue with the burden of maintaining its imperial defences. The sorry catalogue of British financial and economic problems and of its extended strategic commitments has therefore increased our understanding of appeasement. This is not to say that personal factors can ever be eliminated from judgements on the nature and duration of appeasement policy. Equally, many might be offended by the evidence that Chamberlain required agreement with Germany not only to maintain peace, but also to preserve his own political position, and that of the Conservatives over Labour.[85] Whether in spite of or because of 'appeasement', the British rearmament plans, for all their mistakes, eventually proved adequate in war.[86]

Reflection on Britain and on the Anglo-French relationship 1937–38, was not likely to give Hitler any conclusive answer to how his future policies in East Europe would be received. Nor, in the event, did the Anglo-French responses to the actions themselves. On the one hand, there was further proof of the continuing passivity of Britain and France as Hitler took over Austria in March and then proceeded to enforce a settlement of the Czech question at Munich in

[83] P. Kennedy, 'Appeasement', in G. Martel (ed.), *Origins*, p. 152. No attempt can be made here to offer a systematic guide to the literature on appeasement. A masterly survey is Watt's 'Appeasement' article already cited, and this is updated by his essay on this theme in A. Sked (ed.), *Crisis and Controversy. Essays in honour of A.J.P. Taylor* (London, 1976). W.R. Rock, *British Appeasement in the 1930s* (London, 1976). See, too, C.A. MacDonald, *The United States, Britain and Appeasement 1936–1939*, (London, 1981); A. Thorpe, *Britain in the 1930s* (London, 1992); W.J. Mommsen, L. Kettenacker (eds), *The Fascist Challenge and the Policy of Appeasement* (London, 1983).

[84] See M. Cowling, *The Impact of Hitler* (Cambridge, 1975).

[85] Dunbabin, op. cit., pp. 600–1.

[86] Ibid., p. 608; N.H. Gibbs. 'Das britische Aufrüstungsprogramm 1933 bis 1939 und das Ausmass seiner Abhängigkeit von der Entwicklung in Deutschland', in F. Forstmeier and H.-E. Volkmann (eds), *Wirtschaft und Rüstung am Vorabend des zweiten Weltkrieges* (Düsseldorf, 1975), pp. 245–63.

September 1938 (Chapter 5). At the same time, although a great deal of the literature on the Second World War origins lovingly catalogues the British efforts throughout 1938 to pressure the Czechs into giving Hitler what he wanted, it does not sufficiently emphasise that in this process Britain was not only taking more initiative in East Europe, but was also undergoing with France a painful readjustment.[87] Hitler was therefore at the very least heightening the risk of conflict with the West by persisting in expanding German territory. Indeed, his military directives after the May crisis in Czechoslovakia (p. 163) spoke now in terms of clearing up the Czech issue the better to deal with the hostile powers in the west. It would hardly have sufficed to call his bluff at Munich as the 'anti-appeasers' argued to Chamberlain's exasperation.[88] Precisely Hitler's acceptance of the risk of an earlier general conflict suggests that – given the state of British–French preparedness – Munich was inescapable, or even 'massively over-determined'.[89] Our knowledge today of the nearness of the military balance cannot alter the problem as it appeared to the men of 1938.

That Hitler alarmed others in Nazi Germany by his willingness to prosecute such a 'forward policy' after 1937 is well known. It is convenient here to make more explicit our assumption that, within the limits imposed by the international situation and the domestic context, Hitler decided major foreign policy issues in the last resort. This was not immediately apparent after 1933, when Hitler's internal and external predicament necessitated co-operating with the conservative forces in Germany's political, military and economic establishment. As we saw in Chapter 2, that was, however, inevitably a transitional phase. The conference of 5 November 1937 marked a break, revealing mutual disillusionment between Hitler and his conservative allies. Neurath, Blomberg and Fritsch were seriously alarmed and warned Hitler of the dangers of the war with the West

[87] For a survey based on cabinet records see K. Middlemas, *Diplomacy of Illusion. The British Government and Germany 1937–9* (London, 1972). On the painful experience of coming to terms with the changed order in East Europe after the First World War, P.W. Schroeder, 'Munich and the British tradition', *Historical Journal*, **19**, No. 1 (1976): 223–43. On France's reaction to Germany and the Munich crisis, R.J. Young, 'French policy and the Munich crisis: A reappraisal', *Historical Papers*, Canadian Historical Association (Ottawa, 1970): 186–206; 'The aftermath of Munich: The course of French diplomacy October 1938 – March 1939', *French Historical Studies*, **8** No. 2 (1973): 305–22.

Two good general accounts to set alongside A.J.P. Taylor's book, still to be valued in many respects, are those by R. Parkinson, *Peace in Our Time* (London, 1971) and C. Thorne, *The Approach of War 1938–9* (London/Melbourne/Toronto, 1968).

[88] K. Feiling, *Life of Neville Chamberlain* (London, 1946), p. 347.

[89] Schroeder, op. cit., p. 242.

over East Europe, just as Schacht was arguing in 1937 for a return to economic normalcy. To an important extent, however, such objections had already been settled by the fateful collaboration of German conservatism with the Third Reich in its initial stages. This applied in particular to the German Foreign Office and the Army. Their revisionist ambitions conveniently overlapped at many points with Hitler's expansionist plans, and by the time the differences became obvious it was a little late in the day.

The broad consensus behind Hitler in the early days of the regime suggested that Hitler's conservative opponents welcomed the prospect of gains but deplored the risks. Yet arguments over means were settled by the success of Hitlerian diplomacy 1933–38, which in turn reinforced Hitler's domestic standing. Nazi ideology had also made its converts in the citadels of the establishment. These were themselves flanked by numerous para-diplomatic and other bodies (p. 60). Logically, by 4 February 1938, the last Cabinet meeting of the regime, Hitler was able to remove the last major centres of opposition to an expansionist policy. Army leaders Blomberg, Fritsch and Foreign Minister von Neurath were displaced. In the reshuffle sixteen older generals were retired and forty-four transferred. The dissolution of the War Ministry and the substitution of the Higher Command of Armed Forces (OKW) under the complaisant General Wilhelm Keitel, placed the Army neatly under Hitler, now also Commander-in-Chief of the Armed Forces. Ribbentrop, whose 'Notice for the Führer' of 2 January 1938 urged that Britain was Germany's most dangerous enemy, swept into the Foreign Office. Walter Funk, who replaced Schacht as Minister of Economics, was to report for further instructions about his post to Göring, head of the office for the Four-Year Plan (p. 56).[90]

These moves were not without risk for Hitler. The ensuing *Anschluss* (p. 162) was a diversion from internal politics as well as the expression of long-held desires by Hitler, but the crucial factor was the submission of those voices who were either convinced that Britain would go to war to stop Germany in East Europe or who argued the need for Germany's economic policies to be changed (p. 56). Importantly, the hopes of the small but active group of would-be resisters to Hitler in the Army, Foreign Office and political life, pinned their hopes for restraining Hitler in 1938 on the assistance of the Allied

[90] Fest, op. cit., pp. 541–3. For further details on the Army see H.C. Deutsch, *Hitler and his Generals. The Hidden Crisis January – June 1938* (Minneapolis, 1974); K.J. Müller, *Das Heer und Hitler: Armee und Nationalsozialistisches Regime 1933–40* (Stuttgart, 1969); R.O'Neill, *The German Army and the Nazi Party* (London, 1966).

Powers. It was held to be essential to concert internal resistance with the hoped-for opposition of Britain and France to Hitlerian diplomacy.[91] However, when Hitler heard of the efforts of his top Army leaders in their conference of 4 August 1938 to gain support for their resistance to conflict with the West, he subsequently announced at a conference of his own in Jüterborg that he would solve the Sudeten question by force in the next few weeks. Chief of Staff Ludwig Beck, whose memorandum had formed the basis for the discussion of 4 August, resigned. Although his successor General Halder also rejected Hitler's war plans, any hope of successful action against Hitler was ended dramatically with the Allied agreement to hold the conference at Munich. In the last resort, the Allies chose to disregard the overtures from the opponents of Hitler in 1938 because they did not provide credible alternatives to the Führer; they could not be seen to represent the sort of mass following offering hope of a negotiated general settlement between Germany and the Western Powers, which was the goal of appeasement.

In spite of the criticism of Chamberlain[92] other work on the German resistance to Hitler has indicated that even the vision of these opponents expanded with Hitler's successive achievements; that they continued to reveal that ambiguity towards the question of Germany's power and position in Europe which had put many of them in the Nazi camp in the first place.[93] By contrast, the British continued to nurse their contacts with German 'moderates' like Funk and Schacht and, of all people, Göring. Chamberlain was vitally interested (in view of Britain's own economic problems) in 'economic appeasement'. However, large sectors of Germany's business community were in hot pursuit of the gains accruing from rearmaments and the prospects of new territory. Hitler, therefore, had little difficulty in keeping exchanges on the subject of economic appeasement from interfering with his political priorities, although they provided a useful smoke-screen. In addition, the steady penetration by Germany of the economic life of South-East Europe (p. 159) stood in opposition to French interests in the Balkans and to Britain's desire to keep an 'open door' in this area.[94] Germany was still importing British goods

[91] Fest, op. cit., pp. 559ff.

[92] Cf. G. Ritter, *Carl Goerdeler und die deutsche Widerstandsbewegung* (Stuttgart, 1954), pp. 198f.

[93] Cf. H. Graml, *et al.*, *The German Resistance to Hitler* (London, 1970), pp. 18–19, 24. Perhaps the best book on the resistance remains P. Hoffmann, *Widerstand, Staatsstreich, Attentat. Der Kampf der Opposition gegen Hitler* (Munich, 1969).

[94] C.A. MacDonald, 'Economic appeasement and the German "moderates"', *Past and Present*, **56** (Aug. 1972): 105–35.

to the tune of £20.6 million in 1938, but economic appeasement was hardly likely to dissuade Hitler from his autarchic policies any more than political appeasement could prevent him from pushing ahead in the diplomatic arena.

This was confirmed by Hitler's pointed attacks on the 'anti-appeasers' after Munich; by his hard-line policy towards Britain at the close of 1938; by Germany's cynical disregard for the Western members of the mixed commission which was set up at the Munich conference to arrange the Czech borders (p. 165). Hitler's own disappointment at being deprived of a military solution to the Czech crisis is well known. He informed Mussolini on 29 September 1938, that he intended to fight Britain and France in due course.[95] Persevering with his continental expansion in spite of the growing confirmation after Munich that Britain and France were concerting their policies to oppose him, 'compelled [Hitler] to insert an intermediate link in his continental strategy; the forcible expulsion of England from the Continent, coupled with the overthrow of France, before embarking on the great campaign in the East'.[96] Ideally Poland was to play its part by co-operating with Nazi Germany as a client state in Hitler's expansionist plans. There was no prospect of that after the Rape of Prague in March 1939, when the rump Czech state was finally invaded (p. 165), because the British and French determination to call a halt to further German territorial expansion by force, resulted in a provisional Anglo-French guarantee of Poland. It was announced by Chamberlain on 31 March 1939, and was eventually given a definitive form by the Anglo-Polish Agreement of Mutual Assistance of 25 August 1939. On 13 April 1939, after Italy's attack on Albania (p. 166), Anglo-French guarantees of Greece and Romania were also proclaimed.

The guarantees had, it has been suggested, 'almost no discernible foundation in recent Foreign Office thinking',[97] but they had surely some foundation in the growing concern of Chamberlain and French Premier Daladier since the summer of 1938 to clarify their armaments position, in the vastly changed public mood after Munich, and in 'the all-sufficiency of this Anglo-French link in the eyes of both govern-

[95] According to Italian sources Hitler brought a map to his meeting with Mussolini before the conference and discussed his plans for a lightening attack on Czechoslovakia followed by a campaign against France, A. Bullock, *Hitler. A Study in Tyranny* (London, 1960 printing), p. 428.

[96] Hillgruber, 'England's Place', p. 15.

[97] D. Lammers, 'From Whitehall after Munich: The Foreign Office and the future course of British policy', *Historical Journal*, **16** No. 4 (1973): 856.

ments'.[98] One study of the guarantee to Poland even advanced the startling argument that it was a deliberate challenge by Britain, intended to provoke Hitler; the expression of Britain's determination to fight for its interests in Europe.[99] Yet most historians argue that the guarantee was to deter Hitler rather than threaten him, and Anglo-French initiatives after the Rape of Prague continued the aim of binding Hitler to an agreed settlement. But, in keeping with the belief that had informed British rearmament in the 1930s, such negotiations were considered better conducted from a position of strength. Such a position was being achieved, painfully it is true, by the time the British and French reached agreement to act together in February 1939, a date roughly coinciding with that which the Chiefs of Staff had warned the British Cabinet in 1935 would be the earliest possible date to fight a war.[100] The 'Thirty-niners', as these pessimists have been called, might well have noted the large gaps remaining in Britain's preparations after the Prague invasion, particularly in the all-important air defences. The formidable problem of training the masses after the introduction of conscription remained but the 'continental commitment' was to be irrevocable.

The details were not of course known to Hitler, but the military directive on Poland had already been drafted on 3 April (p.166). He was determined to press on with his forward policy even though he was on the verge of achieving the opposite of what he had claimed to want in *Mein Kampf*. The Anglo-French guarantees simply clarified Hitler's immediate objectives, namely to isolate Poland and to make sure that the *Blitzkrieg* against her did not produce a premature general war with the West. He found it difficult to believe in the Anglo-French guarantees because of his conviction that Munich had demonstrated the bankruptcy of Allied policies in East Europe. Clearly, there was even less prospect of anything coming from the renewed British contacts with the German 'moderates' in the spring and summer of 1939 or from the brief resurgence of economic appeasement when Wohltat, of the German Ministry of Economics, visited London in July.[101] Hitler's course began to converge with that

[98] W.N. Medlicott, 'The coming of war in 1939', in W.N. Medlicott (ed.), *From Metternich to Hitler. Aspects of British and Foreign History, 1814–1939* (London, 1963), p. 247.

[99] S. Newman, *March 1939: The British Guarantee to Poland* (London, 1976). Cf. Newman's book with that of A. Prazmowska, *Britain, Poland and the Eastern Front, 1939* (Cambridge, 1987).

[100] Dunbabin, op. cit., p. 597.

[101] MacDonald, op. cit., pp. 128–30.

of the 'extremist' Ribbentrop as the British had feared. In fact, this was the logical outcome of Hitler's changing views on Britain.

The continuing uncertainties which Hitler felt stemmed less from any uncertainty of intention towards Poland than from the changing constellation of international forces, as was evident from the somewhat contradictory statements on Britain recorded in the Schmundt protocol of 23 May 1939.[102] By then it was becoming apparent to Hitler and Ribbentrop that the prospects for converting the tripartite pact to a military alliance against the Allies were not bright. The Japanese politicians were less concerned in the immediate future with Britain than they were with their conflict with Russia. Although the Italian–German alliance was converted to the 'Pact of Steel' in May, the Nazi leaders were left in no doubt about Italy's desire to keep out of an early conflict with the West (p. 188). Ribbentrop's 'policy' was in tatters.

In the face of this, Hitler's commitment to action against Poland finally resulted in a '180-degree turn' in his policy towards Great Britain.[103] Instead of achieving his original idea of an alliance with the British against Russia, he chose in 1939 to make a deal with the USSR and thus to convince Great Britain of the futility of trying to stop action against Poland. His offer of 25 August 1939, of a worldwide deal with Britain and its Empire, was conditional on German action first in Poland. As ever, the 'alliance' was to be on Hitler's terms. By way of explanation Hitler said to Burkhardt on 11 August 1939: 'Everything I do is directed against Russia; if the West is too stupid and blind to grasp this, I shall be forced to reach agreement with the Russians, to attack the West and then, after its defeat, turn against the Soviet Union with my combined forces.'[104] That this was possible, in spite of the ideological enmity between the Nazi and Soviet systems, reflected the enormous gulf which had opened between the West and the USSR, compounded as this was by Soviet–Eastern European disputes (p. 166). As it happened, the West's low opinion of Soviet military power meant that Hitler's effort to deter Britain and France by his pact with the Soviet Union was wasted in London. The Italian declaration of non-belligerence had more impact on the Western Powers.[105]

Hitler's western policy during the final crisis was certain to fail. Britain's natural concern for its own defence and that of its empire

[102] *DGFP*, Series D, Vol. VI, No. 433.
[103] Hillgruber, *Deutschlands Rolle*, p. 90.
[104] C.J. Burckhardt, *Meine Danziger Mission* (Munich, 1960), p. 348.
[105] But cf. C. Thorne, op. cit., pp. 179–80.

did not obscure the truth in the end that, as in 1914, British and French security were inseparable. The Anglo-French declarations of war on 3 September 1939 brought Hitler into conflict with the Western Powers at a time not of his choice although his own policies had made it certain.

CHAPTER FOUR

Germany and Russia

The keynote of German–Soviet relations in the 1920s was one of hesitancy. This derived from uncertainty about the eventual outcome of the upheaval in Russia following the Bolshevik revolution of 1917 and from the ambivalent Allied policies towards the Soviet leaders during the period of intervention and civil war. Germany's 'wait and see' line on Russia expressed its continuing need to relate its policies to those of the Allies. This helps to account for the patchiness of German–Soviet relations between 1918 and 1921 when contacts were even maintained between German officials and White Russians in Berlin. In March 1921 the Treaty of Riga brought to an end the Soviet–Polish war and intervention was at an end. Soviet power was manifestly established. Faced with this fact the Allied Powers, France above all, resorted more to unholding the 'barbed wire' fence of border states around Russia (p. 137) while they simultaneously intensified their preparations to penetrate the vast new markets of the Soviet state. At the same time, Lenin was compelled by events to adjust his hopes for imminent world revolution and to accept the need for temporary compromises with the capitalist world in the interests of the survival of the new regime in Russia. The New Economic Policy (NEP), introduced by Lenin in March 1921, was at least in part an expression of this need. It provided some incentives for foreign business in Russia, and Britain, the chief rival of Germany for Russia's business, was not slow to sign a temporary trade agreement with Moscow on 16 March 1921.[1]

[1] Cf. E.H. Carr, *The Bolshevik Revolution 1917–1923*, Vol. 2 (London, 1952), p. 278; Vol. 3 (London, 1953), pp. 276–7; M.V. Glenny, 'The Anglo–Soviet Trade Agreement, March 1921', *Journal of Contemporary History*, **5** No. 2 (1970): 63–82; R.H. Ullman, *The Anglo-Soviet Accord*, (New Jersey, 1973).

These factors together made it impossible for Germany to hesitate any longer about normalising its own relations with the Soviets, as Foreign Minister Simons had already urged at the end of 1920.[2] On 6 May 1921, the German–Russian Provisional Agreement was signed. It virtually expressed Germany's *de jure* recognition of the Soviet regime. The agreement also improved prospects for the protection of private German business in Russia by effectively converting the existing POW relief agencies under Gustav Hilger and Viktor Kopp into consular missions.[3] It has often been suggested that the timing of this agreement was intended by the Germans as a gesture of defiance to the Western Powers, who had delivered the London Ultimatum on the previous day.[4] In fact, it is plausible to see the German–Russian Provisional Agreement as an attempt by German officials to secure what had been painfully achieved with the Soviets at a particularly difficult moment for German foreign policy.[5] The 1921 agreement was not in itself irreconcilable with fulfilment in view of the parallel effort being made by the Allies to secure a foothold in the Russian economy. Nevertheless there were difficulties because of the political implications of closer economic ties with the first-ever Communist state.

This became clearer during the continuing debate about Russia inside Germany, which was intensified by the events of 1921. Most political parties shared with German commerce a desire to partake of business with Russia in view of Germany' enormous wartime losses and the general disruption of its long-established trading patterns in East Europe. However, within this general aim were differing conceptions. German heavy industry counted on gaining access to the desperately needy Russian market and on defeating as far as possible the competitive efforts of the West to supply industrial machinery and expertise to the Bolsheviks. The political conclusion was obvious and had already been drawn by key industrialists such as Felix Deutsch and Hugo Stinnes: ultimately, closer political ties were indispensable for better German–Soviet economic relations, because even under NEP the Communists controlled the 'commanding heights' of the economy and there was a Soviet monopoly of foreign trade: therefore

[2] H. Helbig, *Die Träger der Rapallo-Politik* (Göttingen, 1958), p. 45; H. Linke, *Deutsch–sowjetische Beziehungen bis Rapallo* (Cologne, 1970), pp 122ff.

[3] G. Hilger and A.G. Meyer, *The Incompatible Allies* (1971 edn, New York), p. 67.

[4] Cf. G. Freund, *Unholy Alliance. Russian–German relations from the Treaty of Brest-Litovsk to the Treaty of Berlin* (London, 1957), p. 88.

[5] E. Laubach, *Die Politik der Kabinette Wirth* (Lübeck/Hamburg, 1968), pp. 110–11.

have political ties, even at the cost of upsetting the Allied Powers.[6] Such pressures grew considerably between late 1921 and early 1922, when the coming World Economic Conference at Genoa threw up the prospect of Germany simply having to take its due share of Russia's business as a member of Lloyd George's projected international consortium, (p. 69).

The representatives of heavy industry, the DVP, and of the nationalists, the DNVP, brought out still more clearly the anti-Western implications of aggressive economic policies towards Russia by their determination to put a stop to fulfilment. Closer ties with Russia could effectively block any suggestion of integration with the Allied Powers. Even elements in the Centre Party and the DDP were sympathetic to this idea.[7] It was in the context of this broad band of support in German public and private life for closer ties with Russia, that in 1921 certain political and military figures continued to work for an eastern bias to German foreign policy as the best way to combat the Versailles order.[8] Of particular significance were the growing links between the *Reichswehr* and heavy industry in 1921. The already shaky vision of a German–Russian 'alliance' to destroy Poland in 1920 during the Soviet–Polish War had vanished with the military defeat of the Red Army. Nonetheless, the intermittent contacts between the German and Russian military leaders from 1919 to 1920 left General von Seeckt, chief of the *Reichswehr*, with the basis on which to build more long-term schemes. Seeckt's aim was to restore Germany's military power with the illicit aid of the Russians and to prepare for the distant day when Poland could be punished and Versailles overthrown.[9]

[6] On German heavy industry and Russia see E.H. Carr's useful sketch, *German–Soviet Relations Between the Two Wars, 1919–1939* (Baltimore, 1951), pp. 52–3. There is much of use in G. Rosenfeld's *Sowjetrussland und Deutschland 1917–1922* (East Berlin, 1960), pp. 260–2, and in his *Sowjetunion und Deutschland 1922–1933* (Berlin, 1984). By contrast, J. Freymond stresses that there was considerable interest in German industrial circles generally for wider European economic co-operation, although the *Reichsverband der deutschen Industrie* remained sceptical of the prospects of such co-operation, Le IIIe *Reich et la Réorganisation Economique de l'Europe 1940–2. Origines et Projets* (Leiden, 1974), pp. 19–23. Other important studies of German–Soviet economic relations in the 1920s are H.J. Perrey, *Der Russlandauschuss der deutschen Wirtschaft Die deutsch–Sowjetischen Wirtschaftsbeziehungen der Zwischenkriegszeit* (Munich, 1985); M. Pohl, *Geschaft und Politik. Deutsch–russisch/sowjetische Wirtschaftsbeziehunngen 1850–1988* (Mainz, 1989).

[7] Cf. the thesis developed by H. Graml, 'Die Rapallo-Politik im Urteil der westdeutschen Forschung', *Vierteljahrshefte für Zeitgeschichte* (Oct. 1970), pp. 366–91, especially p. 382.

[8] Cf. T. Schieder, 'Die Entstehungsgeschichte des Rapallo–Vertrags', *Hitorische Zeitschrift*, **204**, No.3. (June 1967): 551ff.

[9] F.L. Carsten. *Reichswehr und Politik* (Cologne/Berlin, 1964), p. 78.

In practical terms this resolved itself in 1921 into the task of beginning industrial production in Russia for military purposes, with Germany supplying financial and technical aid and even establishing German firms on Russian soil. Early in 1921, a special section had been set up in the *Reichswehr* Ministry devoted to Russian affairs, the *Sondergruppe R*. By the spring, *Reichswehr* officers were in discussion with Russian representatives and links were made with German firms, Albatroswerke, Blohm and Voss and Krupp.[10]

RAPALLO – ITS ORIGINS AND ITS SIGNIFICANCE

The impression of a purposeful and co-ordinated development of Germany's policy towards Russia between the Provisional Agreement of 1921 and the Treaty of Rapallo in 1922, which this bald record appears to show is, however, a misleading one. In neither the economic nor the military field was progress other than hesitant and marked with reservations on both sides. Restraints on a too active Russian policy were imposed by Wirth's coalition (Centre–DDP–SPD) and by key personalities such as President Ebert and Friedrich Rosen, Foreign Minister in Wirth's first government, as well as by Behrendt in the Eastern Department of the *Auswärtiges Amt*. These were extremely worried about the possible effects on German–Allied relations of closer ties with the Soviets. Nor could the ideological gulf be forgotten. The existence of the international organisation of the Communist parties, the Comintern, was a constant reminder of the Bolshevik interest in future world revolution. That Soviet policy towards the capitalist West was conducted on different levels was confirmed by the Comintern's involvement in the KPD's 'uprising' on March 1921, even as Narkomindel, the Soviet Commissariat for Foreign Affairs, was seeking to normalise relations with the Weimar Republic.[11] Although the rabid anti-Communism of German nationalist–rightist circles in the 1920s did not prevent co-operation with Soviet Russia on the international scene,[12] the SPD

[10] Ibid., pp. 141ff.; An earlier but still usefully compact survey is H.W. Gatske's Russo–German military collaboration during the Weimar Republic', *American Historical Review*, **63** (1957/58): 565–97.

[11] F.A. Krummacher and H. Lange, *Krieg und Frieden. Geschichte der deutsch–sowjetische Beziehungen von Brest–Litovsk bis zum Unternehmen Barbarossa* (Munich, 1970), pp. 114–15.

[12] Cf. Walter Laqueur, *Russia and Germany. A Century of Conflict* (London, 1965), pp. 134–5.

remained opposed to any step which increased the weight of the KPD, their ideological offspring but bitter enemy and rival for radical working-class support after 1918.[13]

In the summer of 1921, the emphasis on placating the Western Powers necessarily meant publicly trying to restrict the German–Soviet exchanges to the economic field. This was in accordance with moderate party views and indeed those of German light industry, not nearly so dependent on Russian markets.[14] Conversely, Wirth was bound to react to the setback to fulfilment after the vastly unpopular Allied decision in October 1921 to partition Upper Silesia. In shifting the emphasis in his policies towards the Soviets, Wirth was also expressing his own liking for co-operation between Berlin and Moscow. It is well known that in his second administration he appointed so-called 'easterners' such as Ago von Maltzan, head of the Eastern Department of the AA, to key positions. Wirth himself became Foreign Minister for a while as well as Chancellor. He had been kept informed about the secret military contacts with Russia in 1921 and Maltzan also heard of these, before his appointment.[15] When Wirth took a more active line on Russia the military negotiations also moved forward. In Berlin there were various exchanges, the most important being those between General Hasse, Victor Kopp, the Soviet plenipotentiary in Berlin, and the Soviet Commissar for Foreign Trade, Leonid Krassin. The discussions took place largely in General Schleicher's flat and again included contacts with heavy industry, notably with the Junkers concern in Dessau.[16] In the autumn of 1921 the first German–Russian mixed undertakings were also being founded. It was through Wirth's intermediary action that early in 1922 some 150 million marks were made available to the German High Command to help resolve the financial difficulties arising in the military talks with the Russians.[17]

Undoubtedly, the 'Rapallo lobby' made the agreement with Russia seem unavoidable.[18] One of the central assumptions of West German

[13] On this hostility, thoroughly reciprocated by the Bolsheviks and founded in Russian distrust of the SDP before the war, see D. Geyer, 'Sowjetrussland und die deutsche Arbeiterbewegung 1918–32', *Vierteljahrshefte für Zeitgeschichte*, **24**, No. 1 (1976): 14–16. More generally see E. Matthias, *Die deutsche Sozialdemokratie und der Osten* (Tübingen, 1954).

[14] Laubach, op. cit., p. 113.

[15] Cf. Schieder, op. cit., pp. 551–2.

[16] Carsten, op. cit., pp. 141–2.

[17] Ibid., p. 143. On the German–Russian undertakings see Hilger, op. cit., pp. 165ff.

[18] Krummache and Lange, op. cit., pp. 133–4

historical writing on Rapallo, that Germany's worsening international situation in the winter of 1921/22 itself made inevitable a 'knock on the eastern gate', has rightly been questioned in view of the longstanding interest of Wirth in closer relations with the Soviets.[19] In truth, however, there was considerable domestic opposition in France to any *rapprochement* with Germany or any deal over reparations, and Poincaré's arrival at the head of the French government prior to the Genoa Conference confirmed this (p. 69). The French hard line on reparations undoubtedly encouraged Wirth and Maltzan to respond by exploiting the spectre of a separate Russian–Allied deal over reparations on the basis of Article 116 of the Versailles Treaty, which reserved for Russia the right to claim reparations from Germany. The article had in fact been drawn up very much with the idea of a restored 'White' Russia in mind. Although it was barely conceivable that Lenin would exploit in this way what he called the 'robber peace' of Versailles, the Soviets were not averse to raising the bogey of a separate reparations deal with the West prior to Genoa. Maltzan was able to use the situation to reinforce his own arguments about the need for a German–Russian agreement.[20]

At the same time, neither Wirth nor Maltzan shared the preferences of Seeckt and other 'easterners' for an exclusive reliance on the Russian connection,[21] although the activation of German–Soviet relations necessarily increased the influence on policy-making of the *Reichswehr* and heavy industry. Drafts of the later Rapallo Treaty were drawn up during the German–Soviet exchanges in Berlin prior to Genoa, but Wirth was not prepared to accept the suggestion made, first by Karl Radek at the beginning of 1922 and then in early April by the Soviet Commissar for Foreign Affairs, Chicherin, that an agreement be concluded before the Genoa Conference met and that Germany and Russia co-ordinate their strategy during the conference. Wirth's Foreign Minister from early 1922, Walther Rathenau, would not have permitted this either. He expressed most forcefully the anxieties of moderate German opinion not to damage relations with the Western Powers prior to the Genoa Conference.[22]

[19] Graml, 'Die Rapallo-Politik', p. 377.

[20] On Russia and reparations see W. Eichwede in D. Geyer (ed.), *Osteuropa Handbuch. Sowjetunion, Aussenpolitik* (Cologne/Vienna, 1972), p. 162; cf. Laubach, op. cit., pp. 184–9; see too, Laubach, 'Maltzans Aufzeichnungen über die letzten Vorgänge vor dem Abschluss des Rapallo-Vertrages', *Jahrbücher für Geschichte Osteuropas*, Neue Folge, **22**, No. 4 (1975): 572–3.

[21] Cf. M. Walsdorff, *Westorientierung und Ospolitik. Stresemanns Russlandpolitik in der Locarno-Ära* (Bremen, 1971), pp. 42–5.

[22] Schieder, op. cit., pp. 568–9. Of course Rathenau was pessimistic since America

For Rathenau, the proposed international consortium offered Germany the most obvious way to reconcile its interests in Russia with its policy of fulfilment towards the Western Powers. His concern, therefore, was not to avoid agreements with the Soviets, but rather to make sure that they were not concluded prematurely. His overriding concern for Germany's economic welfare, not to mention his position at the head of the great electricity company, the AEG (p. 67), made him as concerned as anyone not to risk Germany losing out in the economic race for Russia. The colourful descriptions of Rathenau staggering out of bed to be rushed into finally signing the agreement at Rapallo on 16 April 1922, so much a part of the early Rapallo literature, rather miss this point.[23] Those who have argued that Germany's economic prospects would not have been damaged without the Rapallo agreement, on the grounds that Russia needed Germany more than Germany needed Russia, have overlooked the enormous importance which Western economic experts then attached to the opening of the Soviet markets. One thing was quite clear. It was felt to be a matter of political survival to the Bolshevik leaders to break up the Western plans for a consortium. They therefore insisted on a separate treaty with Germany, which in addition could serve as a precedent for later separate agreements with the capitalist powers.[24]

It would therefore have demanded epic self-denial by the German leaders to turn down the agreement with Russia, even if it had not been desired by influential sectors of the Republic's establishment. As Rathenau, President Ebert and others had feared, the timing of the agreement during the conference at Genoa could hardly have been worse in terms of its immediate effects on Germany's relations with the West. For a long time there was much dispute about the wider implications of the Rapallo agreement, and it has not quite disappeared even today. Historians of the former German Federal Republic tended to portray the agreement as a justifiable attempt to recover some freedom of movement in foreign policy. They played down the aggressive implications of the Rapallo Treaty for Poland (p. 141) by

was to be absent from the conference and reparations were not on the agenda, K.D. Erdmann, 'Deutschland, Rapallo und der Westen' *Vierteljahrshefte für Zeitgeschichte*, **11**, No.2 (1963): 115.

[23] Cf. Laubach, 'Maltzans Aufzeichnungen', pp.577–9; Rosenfeld, op. cit., p. 262; E. Kollmann, 'Walter Rathenau and German foreign policy. Thought and action', *Journal of Modern History*, **24** (1952): 138.

[24] Eichwede, in Geyer, op. cit., p. 163. On the enormous importance of foreign trade to Germany after 1919, J. Freymond, op. cit., pp. 13–14.

stressing that it was not accompanied by a secret military alliance.[25] These arguments have been supported by reference to the innocuous nature of the treaty's text. Both governments renounced their mutual war debts, resumed normal diplomatic relations, stipulated that the principle of most-favoured-nation treatment was to govern their relations and promised each other mutual assistance 'in the most benevolent spirit' for the alleviation of their economic difficulties. The Soviets were spared any future threat of a combined onslaught on their economy by the capitalist West by the German–Russian undertaking to have a preliminary exchange of views if such schemes were mooted again. This was made more explicit in a secret exchange of notes.[26]

Predictably, French, Anglo-Saxon and *emigré* East European historians were far more critical of the treaty, arguing that the German–Russian military collaboration was as good as a military alliance and urging that the 'spirit' of the Rapallo Treaty was more important than its text. They agreed that it reflected the German–Soviet reaction to their outcast status after Versailles, but brought out more the threatening implications of the treaty for the border states lying between Germany and Russia, Poland above all. Rapallo was therefore additional proof of Germany's tendency after 1919 to exploit the 'Russian card' to bring additional pressure to bear on the Western Powers to revise Versailles.[27]

Under the impetus of the debate on continuities in German foreign policy such arguments were also strongly supported by a number of historians of the then West Germany. For these, Rapallo seemed to be the expression of forces in German politics which had traditionally followed policies aimed at furthering Germany's own power and at making Germany 'alliance worthy', even at the expense of inter-

[25] Graml, 'Die Rapallo-Politik', brings this out very clearly in his discussion of the major West German writers on Germany's Rapallo policy.

[26] The text of the treaty can be found in J.A.S. Grenville (ed), *The Major International Treaties 1914–1973. A History and Guide with Texts* (London, 1974), pp. 139–40.

[27] Freund, op. cit., p. 118, refers to Germany gaining 'an alliance against the Versailles powers': this interpretation is shared by C. Fink, *The Genoa Conference. European Diplomacy, 1921–1922* (Chapel Hill/London, 1984), p. 176: Cf. Josef Korbel, *Poland Between East and West. Soviet and German Diplomacy Towards Poland* (Princeton, 1963), pp. 116–17; Oscar Halecki saw it as an 'open threat against the nations which separated the two partners', *Borderlands of Western Civilisation. A History of Eastern-Central Europe* (New York, 1952), p. 432. The implications of Rapallo for East Europe are followed in the next chapter. On Wirth's strong anti-Polish line and Rapallo, Carsten, op. cit., p. 145. An interesting French study is R. Bournazel, *Rapallo: Naissance d'un Mythe. La Politique de la Peur dans la France du bloc national* (Paris, 1974).

national understanding.[28] Indeed, as has been argued, the Rapallo Treaty *did* give expression to such forces.

In the last resort, however, this was not all it expressed. Wirth's own political future remained tied up with the outcome of fulfilment. That in itself makes it difficult to see Rapallo simply in terms of German playing off East and West. On the contrary, the fact that the Rapallo Treaty made Wirth's policy towards the Western Powers more difficult – but just as essential – was in part the result of the early difficulties on the path to peaceful co-existence. This aspect of Rapallo was most emphasised by the historians of the Communist-controlled states of Eastern Europe and the Soviet Union after the Second World War.[29] From this viewpoint, the Rapallo agreement becomes a 'belated peace treaty'. This does also accord with other findings on East Europe (cf. p. 141) and it was important for Germany to have the threat of Article 116 removed. Franco-Polish efforts to substantiate the claims of the small East European states to reparations from Germany were thereby undermined and a contrast was made to the impasse over reparations in the West.[30] Finally it was only two years later that the other West European powers recognised the Soviet regime. The gulf between capitalism and Communism made the early German recognition of Soviet Russia at Rapallo as upsetting to the Western Powers as it seems understandable from today's vantage point, when peaceful co-existence is accepted as axiomatic, and when, indeed, the 'Common European Home' is painfully reappearing.

It was, moreover, a matter of record that the German–Soviet agreement did not commit German foreign policy to an excessive reliance on the Soviet Union. True, the KPD welcomed the Rapallo Treaty for obvious reasons, and both the military leaders and German nationalists, together with heavy industry, continued to make sure that the link with Russia was maintained. So, too, did Count Brockdorff-Rantzau, German Ambassador to Moscow 1922–29,[31] although he was

[28] Graml, 'Die Rapallo-Politik', p. 374.

[29] Cf. A. Anderle (ed.), *Rapallo und die friedliche Koexistenz* (East Berlin, 1963); G. Rosenfeld, 'Die sowjetisch–deutschen Beziehungen und der Kampf der Sowjetunion für Frieden und Sicherheit in Europa in den Jahren 1922–32', *Jahrbuch für Geschichte der UdSSR und der volksdemokratischen Länder Europas*, **12** (1968): 171–91.

[30] F. Epstein, 'The question of Polish reparations claims, 1919–22. A contribution to the interpretation of the Treaty of Versailles', in R.F. Byrnes (ed.), *Germany and the East. Selected Essays*, (Bloomington/London, 1973), pp. 89-97. Cf. Schieder, op. cit., p. 599; J. Hiden, 'The "Baltic problem" in Weimar's Ostpolitik', in V.R. Berghahn, M. Kitchen (eds), *Germany in the Age of Total War* (London, 1981), pp. 156–7.

[31] Walsdorff, op. cit., pp. 29–39; Cf. T.K. Koblyakov, 'Nachalo Rapall'skogo perioda v sovetsko–germanskikh otnosheniyakh (1922–3)', *Istoriya SSSR* (Nov./Dec. 1973): 19–20.

uneasy about the independence of the *Reichswehr* leaders in their dealings with the Soviets and his quarrels with Seeckt almost kept him out of the Moscow post. In general the other parties, excepting the SPD, welcomed the treaty in the Reichstag as a step towards a more 'active' foreign policy (cf. p. 139). While compromised by their antipathy towards Poland, which even moderate and realistic German leaders shared with nationalist circles, those who opposed exclusive ties with Russia before Rapallo continued to do so afterwards. No more did the Soviet leaders regard the relationship as an exclusive one.

According to Lenin, the treaty was an essential step in a policy which aimed to exploit the divisions within the capitalist camp and to increase the room for movement of Soviet policies until the conditions were ripe in due course for the spread of revolution. The German–Soviet relationship was inevitably affected by the contradictions inherent in the Leninist theses. Interested in supporting Germany against Anglo-French dominance, the better to preserve a balance of power in Europe more favourable to the Soviet Union, the Bolshevik leaders regarded the German working classes as the key to the future spread of revolution and continued to try to influence these accordingly. Inevitably, Narkomindel and the Comintern were not always happy bedfellows.[32] In addition, it was clear after 1922 that Stresemann was pursuing a more concerted attempt to integrate Germany's political, military and economic relations with the Soviets and to relate them more appropriately to Germany's relations with the Western Powers. Thus the path of the German–Soviet 'partnership' was no smoother after Rapallo than before.

The force of these arguments was demonstrated by the events of 1923, a crucial year in Weimar–Soviet relations as it was for Germany's Western policies. Germany benefited from Russia's support of its passive resistance, to the extent that Soviet warnings to France and Poland during the Ruhr crisis helped to keep East Europe neutralised, thus reducing the threat of combined pressure from France and Poland. Moreover, with the bourgeois–military interest groups more solidly behind Cuno's 'business' government and happy with the defiance of the Allies, (p. 42) advances were made both in military and economic relations between Germany and Russia. By the summer of 1923 an agreement was reached which ensured that German participation in Russian armaments industries was properly

[32] Eichwede, in Geyer, op. cit., pp. 167ff; T.H. von Laue, 'Soviet diplomacy: G.V. Chicherin, People's Commissar for Foreign Affairs', in G.A. Craig and F. Gilbert (eds), *The Diplomats 1919–1939* (Princeton, 1953), pp. 234–81.

under way.[33] In June negotiations were reopened for a full economic treaty. In general, 1923 witnessed the continuing recovery of Germany's lead in Russia's foreign trade which had begun with the Provisional Agreement of May 1921, at which time Britain had occupied the top position. The value of this has been questioned, since the overall decline in Russia's total trade after 1917 also meant a drastic reduction in Germany's share of Russian markets, when compared with the situation before the First World War.[34] In 1923, however, a time of grave economic crisis for Germany, any advance was important, and with the re-opening of economic negotiations the possibility at least existed of greater gains. Nonetheless, the arrival of Stresemann to head the government in August and the abandonment of passive resistance soon disposed of what was left of the spectre of a Soviet–German bloc united against the Versailles Powers. The year ended instead on a low point in the Rapallo 'partnership'.

The logic of Germany's position in post-Versailles Europe compelled agreement with the Western Powers if it were to survive, and in any event there were inherent contradictions in Soviet policy towards Germany. At the outset of the crisis Karl Radek and the Comintern had, notwithstanding Narkomindel's diplomatic support of Berlin, worked to convince the German bourgeoisie that its interests lay in combining with the proletariat in a 'revolutionary' resistance to France. This was a tactical attempt to foster the alliance of German nationalism and Communism for the purposes of revolution – the 'Schlageter line', after the name of the German thug killed in the Ruhr. It gave way after August, under the pressure of mounting crisis inside Germany, to the Comintern attempt to restore a combined front between the KPD and SPD. By October 1923, KPD–SPD coalition governments in Saxony and Thuringia were to provide a basis from which to organise the revolution.[35] This belated and ill-organised policy was to mark a turning point in the Comintern's activity in Germany, the last in a line of disastrous failures by the KPD to seize power after 1918. The brutal suppression of the rebellion in Saxony by the Stresemann government underlined the continuing

[33] Carsten, op. cit., pp. 153–4. also T. Uldricks 'The Soviet diplomatic corps in the Chicherin era', *Jahrbücher für die Geschichte Osteuropas*, **23, 2** (1975): 213–24.

[34] Laqueur, op. cit., pp. 132–3; R.P. Morgan, 'The political significance of German–Soviet trade negotiations, 1922–5', *The Historical Journal*, **6**, No. 2 (1963): 253–4.

[35] E.H. Carr. *A History of Soviet Russia. The Interregnum, 1923–4* (Penguin, London, 1969), pp. 182–97; W.T. Angress, *Stillborn Revolution. The Communist Bid for Power in Germany 1921–3* (Princeton, 1963); M. Ruck, *Die freien Gewerkschaften im Ruhrkampf, 1923* (Cologne, 1986).

ideological hostility towards Bolshevism in Germany, in spite of the normalisation of diplomatic relations after Rapallo. The blow given to Bolshevik hopes for revolution in Germany contributed decisively to the painful shift inside Russia from Lenin to Stalin, towards the idea of 'socialism in one country' between 1924 and 1929.

Preoccupied increasingly with consolidating the revolution at home, nonetheless it remained important to the Bolsheviks to preserve their ties with Germany in the face of hostile world capitalism. The 'year of recognition', 1924, did little to dispel Soviet fears, particularly since the inauguration of the Dawes Plan seemed likely to turn Germany more towards the Western Powers. The Soviet leaders therefore, spent considerable effort placating Berlin (who refused to believe in the fiction of a Comintern independent from the Soviet government) and promised early in 1924 that no further attempts would be made to interfere in German internal affairs.[36] Indeed, after 1923 the Comintern line was steadily made subservient to that of Narkomindel as the goal of world revolution became still more distant. The 'Stalinisation' of foreign Communist parties was reflected in the KPD. Under Ernst Thälmann's leadership from 1925, the KPD faithfully toed the Moscow line. There were no more ill-co-ordinated uprisings. Until 1928 the KPD sought practical co-operation with the socialist parties in Germany. The task was not easy but, apart from a couple of later incidents, one source of immediate friction between Germany and Russia was at least reduced.[37] The difficulties in German–Soviet relations after 1923 stemmed far more from the changing international scene. Just as Stresemann was attempting to achieve a more lasting and profitable *rapprochement* with the West (in 1924–25), so the Russians, more aware than ever of their vulnerability after the German fiasco in 1923 and engaged in a growing conflict with Britain in the Near East, were even more anxious to prevent precisely such a *rapprochement*.

WEIMAR-SOVIET RELATIONS UNDER STRESEMANN

Far from being able to play the 'Russian card' to wrest concessions from the West, the connections with Moscow which Stresemann

[36] Eichwede, in Geyer, op. cit., p. 168.

[37] Cf. Ossip K. Flechtheim, 'The role of the communist party', *The Road to Dictatorship. Germany 1918–1933. A Symposium by German Historians* (London, 1970), p. 106.

inherited made his western policies more rather than less difficult. Not that Stresemann wanted to abandon the Soviet Union, in spite of his antipathy to that country.[38] The events of 1923 demonstrated conclusively the benefits to Germany of ties with East and West, and those in Germany in favour of continuing contacts with Russia were too influential to ignore. The Locarno strategy did, however, bring Germany nearer to the West and to the League of Nations, which the Soviets detested and reviled as an organ of the capitalist world. The constant German assurances to Russia during the 'Locarno era' could not still Soviet doubts. Stressmann's untiring effort to explain and justify his western policy to the Soviet leaders never entirely convinced them. Economic and military co-operation helped of course to keep the two powers in some degree of harmony. There is some force to the suggestion that economic policies were used by Germany in the mid-1920s to preserve the political link. The clutch of trade treaties signed between Germany and the Soviet Union on the eve of Locarno were meant to reassure the Russians of Germany's continuing friendship without endangering the coming security pact, which Moscow wanted to frustrate.[39] But the economic prospects remained desirable in themselves, particularly to German heavy industry, which did not benefit so greatly from the increased financial dependence of Germany on the Western Powers after the Dawes Plan. The percentage of German exports going to Russia in 1925 was a mere 2.5 per cent of the overall total and German heavy industry, still hungry for export markets, could hardly be happy as, in 1924–25, America and Britain exceeded Germany's share of Russian trade.[40]

As to the Soviet–German military relations, Brockdorff-Rantzau attempted in February 1924 to restrict these to a minimum and to divert German credits to the broader economic purposes of German undertakings on Soviet soil. Yet he subsequently developed better relations with Seeckt and, despite the worried reservations of German political leaders, Russo-German military collaboration in 1924–25 began to move into a new phase, 'concerned not so much with production but with the testing of war materials and with the training of German military personnel in the use of weapons and equipment

[38] Walsdorff, op. cit., p. 29, emphasises Stresemann's antipathy to Russia. Apart from the general studies already cited on Stresemann, see H.W. Gatske, 'Von Rapallo nach Berlin. Stresemann und die deutsche Russland-Politik', *Vierteljahrshefte für Zeitgeschichte*, **4**, No. 1 (1956): 1–29; Z.J. Gasiorowski, 'The Russian overtures to Germany of December 1924', *Journal of Modern History*, **30** (1958): 99–117

[39] R.P. Morgan, op. cit., p. 262.

[40] Ibid., p. 262.

forbidden under the Treaty of Versailles'.[41] If anything, this might be taken as evidence of ambivalence in Stresemann's Soviet policies for it was not unconnected with Germany's desire to restrict Poland. This aim alone gave Stresemann an additional interest in mending his Russian fences after the Locarno settlement, quite apart from Brockdorff-Rantzau's support of Soviet initiatives for a political agreement with Germany which would remove some of their worries about the Locarno treaties. The Soviets were not satisfied with Stresemann's achievement at Locarno; namely in exploiting the argument about Germany's exposed geographical position to relieve Berlin of the obligations of League members to impose sanctions against aggressors under Article 16 of the League covenant. In effect Germany's special relationship with Russia was accepted by the West as part of the price of Locarno.

In this respect it was safer for Stresemann to proceed with the Treaty of Berlin, which was concluded on 24 April 1926. The delay in Germany's League entry early in 1926 advanced the timetable of German–Soviet negotiations, which pleased those forces in German politics who were primarily interested in a more forceful foreign policy. But this must not be allowed to obscure the fact that Stresemann was moving nearer to that balance between East and West which had escaped Wirth. The proof of this was the relatively calm response of the Western Powers to the Treaty of Berlin when compared with their earlier reactions to Rapallo.[42] The Berlin Treaty firmly underlined Germany's neutrality and its aversion to sanctions against the Soviet Union. A note exchange committed Germany to a policy of friendship with the Soviet Union when joining the League, and reaffirmed that Germany alone was to decide who was the aggressor in any conflict.[43]

If due account is taken of the reservations in both Germany and Russia about their mutual relations during the 1920s, the Treaty of

[41] Gatske, 'Russo-German military collaboration', pp. 576, 578; cf. Carsten, op. cit., pp. 253ff.

[42] Our thesis makes unacceptable the contention that the Berlin Treaty 'was intended as a standing threat to the Western Powers that it would be transformed into an alliance if Germany were not accommodated in such matters as the evacuation of the Rhineland, reparations, armaments and political equality', H.L.Dyck, *Weimar Germany and Soviet Russia, 1926–33. A Study in Diplomatic Instability* (London, 1966). Cf. the memorandum by von Bülow of the German Foreign Ministry of 27 Jan. 1926: 'The agreements under discussion with the Soviet government are only conceivable on the basis created by Locarno and (Germany's) entry to the League.' *ADAP*, Series B, Vol. I, p. 162.

[43] Texts in Grenville, op. cit., pp. 142–3.

Berlin was no more a 'high-water mark'[44] than it was part of a steady decline in the German–Soviet friendship after Rapallo.[45] Both powers continued to profit for some time on the economic and military level from their co-operation and their cultural relations were quite extraordinarily resilient.[46] In the late 1920s, it is true, the record of the mixed German–Soviet companies which had been set up after 1921 to exploit the concessions made by the Russians was a rather stormy one. This was due partly to Soviet prevarications and obstructiveness in the face of foreign economic activity and partly to capital shortages in Germany in the early 1920s, as well as to the tendency of Weimar businessmen to look for quick profits and early withdrawal from Russia.[47] Even so, some of the concessions survived and Germany's importance to Russia's economic development was recognised by the formation in August 1928 by German firms, trading companies and banks of the *Russlandausschuss der deutschen Wirtschaft*. This committee was a rough counterpart to the Soviet monopoly of trade. A German section of the Soviet *Handelskammer* in Moscow was also erected, composed of representatives from German firms and the Soviet Commissariat for Foreign Trade.[48] Difficult as it was for German governments to arrange credits in the face of their own financial difficulties during the early 1920s, a credit fund was raised by leading German banks in 1925 of 75 million RM, later 100 million. By 1926, as a consequence of the Berlin Treaty, a 300 million RM credit was arranged for Russia to purchase German goods. It was guaranteed by up to 70 per cent by the German government in co-operation with various German *Lands* (*Länder – provinces*). These essentially short-term credits were in effect made revolving in due course and by 1930–31, the then German Ambassador to Moscow, Dirksen, finally negotiated long-term loans for Russia. Under the stimulus too, of Soviet needs for its Five-Year Plan, German exports to Russia had risen by 1932 to some 47 per cent of total Russian imports. Indeed, as the economic crisis unfolded in Germany after 1929, the very survival of important German manufacturers depended on Soviet orders,

[44] Carr. *German–Soviet relations*, p. 91.

[45] Laqueur, op. cit., p. 133. A stimulating short essay to set alongside Laqueur's book is W. Conze, *Das deutsch–russische Verhältnis im Wandel der modernen Welt* (Göttingen, 1967).

[46] Laqueur, op. cit., p. 143.

[47] Hilger, op cit., p. 175.

[48] Krummacher and Lange, op. cit., p. 207. For the then East German writers the *Russlandausschuss* was 'an operations staff of German monopoly capital against the USSR', K. Laser, 'Der Russlandausschuss der deutschen Wirtschaft, 1928–41, *Zeitschrift für Geschichtswissenschaft*, **20**, No. 1 (1972): 1384.

notably tool machinery firms. The Soviet Five-Year Plans employed large numbers of German technicians and engineers.[49] Similarly, German–Soviet military co-operation reached its high point by the opening of the 1930s and there was an impressive record of joint training and experiments with weapons forbidden to Germany – notably aircraft, tanks and gas.[50]

It is when the political ties are examined in this same period that the changing nature of German–Soviet relations can be seen at its clearest. Again, this was not a sudden event and is perhaps best conceived as part of a gradual process throughout the 1920s, a consequence of the evolving international climate, of the momentous internal changes going on in Russia as Stalin's ascendancy took place, and finally of the radicalisation in German politics after 1928. Clearly, Stresemann was interested in continuing co-operation with the Soviet Union over East Europe and over Poland. Since the use of force against Poland was excluded for the foreseeable future, the combined diplomatic and economic pressures of Germany and the Soviet Union were of the utmost importance in keeping open the options in East Europe. At the same time the question was being raised as to how far Soviet–German policies and aims in East Europe were compatible (see Chapter 5). Although vitally concerned to retain their friendship with Germany and to prevent the Locarno policy leading to an anti-Soviet configuration, Germany's entry to the League and the very existence of the Locarno pacts were compelling the Soviets to reconsider their own tactics. Not only were there clear signs in 1925/26 of the Soviets trying to improve their relationship with France (not to put more pressure on Germany but, somewhat unrealistically, on Britain), but in October 1925 Chicherin expressed his country's readiness to send an observer to Geneva. In January 1926, the Soviet leaders agreed to take part in the disarmament committee.[51] There was indeed a continuing gap between the League's concept of security and Russia's attempts in the second half of the 1920s to surround itself by a series of bilateral non-aggression treaties with its western and eastern neighbours (p. 152). In such a context, however, the German–Soviet relationship was a potential force for European peace and no longer (if it had ever been) an exclusive 'partnership'. Germany

[49] Cf. Hilger, op, cit., pp. 238ff.; A.I. Stepanov, Die sowjetisch–deutschen Beziehungen 1928–1932 im Lichte diplomatischer Dokumente', *Zeitschrift für Geschichtswissenschaft*, **18** (1970): 1474–5.

[50] For an assessment of Germany's military strength, including that derived from aid from Russia, Carsten, op. cit., pp. 401ff.

[51] Eichwede, in Geyer, op. cit., p. 195.

wished to act, for example, as a mediator in the Soviet–British dispute of 1927, when relations between London and Moscow were severed after the British raid on Arcos, the Soviet trading company in London, and again in the Sino-Soviet dispute of the same year.[52]

In retrospect Russia was moving along the line which led via Chicherin's displacement by Maxim Litvinov (whose work in the League and its organisation after 1927 identified him with collective security and who formally replaced Chicherin in July 1930) to the attempts to co-operate with the Western Powers in the 1930s. Whether this would have been achieved at the same speed without the changes wrought in German policies and politics after 1928, with the onset of the world economic crisis, is a matter for speculation. What was certain was that – in direct contrast to the rise in economic and military collaboration between Russia and Germany 1928–1931/32 – political relations between the two former 'outcasts' of Versailles went downhill with a rapidity which was barely concealed by the outwardly formally correct diplomatic ties.

The temporal coincidence of Germany's internal crisis with that in the Soviet Union, as Stalin prepared to collectivise and drag Russian industry into the twentieth century, made this inevitable. Stalin's own struggle to remove the 'rightist' opponents inside Russia to his economic plans necessarily brought a 'leftist' swing in the activity of the Comintern and therefore the KPD.[53] Early in 1928 the new Comintern line was announced, and until 1933 the KPD reverted to its attack on the SPD as the enemy of the working class. It was not a coincidence that this was also an attempt to block the danger of Franco-German conciliation, espoused by Stresemann and Briand, and which the SPD above all supported, a menace which Moscow found too much as it strained its resources to the utmost at home. It was unfortunate, to say the least, that Stalin's attempt to divert attention from home to the danger abroad should have also precluded any forceful attack until too late on the Nazis, since these were only too determined to put paid to any prospect of Franco-German understanding.[54] The Comintern line, which labelled the Social Democrats as 'social fascists', played its part in ensuring the paralysis of left-wing reaction against Hitler by preventing co-operation between

[52] Krummacher and Lange, op. cit., pp. 199–200; Dyck, op. cit., pp. 99–100.

[53] Jacobsen, 'Primat der Sicherheit, 1928–1938', in Geyer, op. cit., p. 228.

[54] In general, see Th. Weingartner, *Stalin und der Aufstieg Hitlers. Die Deutschlandpolitik der Sowjetunion und Hitlers Machtergreifung* (Bonn, 1966). An interesting insight into KPD/SPD conflicts is provided by T. Kurz, '*Blutmai*'. *Sozialdemokraten und Kommunisten im Brennpunkt der Berliner Ereignisse von 1929* (Berlin/Bonn, 1988).

the KPD and SPD. In turn, the rapid growth of the KPD as a result of the crisis in Germany made it impossible any longer for German governments to perpetuate the convenient but fictional distinction between 'Bolshevism' and 'Russia', which had made possible the 'Rapallo partnership' in the first place. The conservative Right reverted rapidly to type by the end of the 1920s.[55] How deep was the hostility to Bolshevism was made only too clear by the explosion of support for the Nazi Party as Hitler reawakened German fears of the red menace and the memory of 'November 1918'.

HITLER'S QUEST FOR *LEBENSRAUM*

With German–Soviet political relations formally correct but strained as a result of the growth of Germany's militant revisionism under Brüning and Schleicher, Hitler's arrival to power did not immediately change much on the surface of things. Once again, however, it is necessary to bear in mind Hitler's own thoughts on Russia which had been developing since the war. Those views were indeed rooted in Germany's eastern policies during the First World War. They looked back to the enticing prospect of German expansion and the dismemberment of European Russia at the time of the Treaties of Brest-Litovsk and Berlin in March and August 1918 (p. 10). The new elements appeared in Hitler's developing thought on Russia between the end of the war and the publication of *Mein Kampf*. By then, the question as to whether Germany should be either a great sea power or a great land power had been answered decisively in his own mind. First, war had to be waged at some date for *Lebensraum* in the east at Russia's expense. The dismemberment and conquest of Russia would provide the basis for Germany's later bid for world power (cf. p. 11).[56]

The economic, political and strategic rationale behind this was not new, given what happened in the First World War, but the underpinning of it by reference to racial theories most certainly was. There is agreement as over nothing else about the importance to Hitler of the ideological drive against Bolshevism, portrayed by the Führer as dominated by Jewish influences and incompatible with the existence

[55] Laqueur, op. cit., p. 136.

[56] A. Kuhn, *Hitlers aussenpolitischen Programm. Enstehung und Entwicklung 1919–1939* (Stuttgart, 1970), pp. 99ff.; *Mein Kampf*, pp. 586–609; cf. A. Hillgruber, *Deutschlands Rolle in der Vorgeschichte der beiden Weltkriege* (Göttingen, 1967), p. 66 for the influence of 1918 on Hitler's views on Russia; G. Stoakes, *Hitler and the Quest for World Dominion* (Leamington Spa, 1986), pp. 110ff.

of National Socialism.[57] This was confirmed by Hitler's determined resistance to the pressures coming from within the Nazi movement for different emphases on foreign policy. The nearest to Hitler's views, perhaps, were those of Walther Darré, the party expert on peasant and agrarian problems and Hitler's later Minister for Food and Agriculture. He, too, emphasised the need for racial policies in the east and the need to redress the urban/rural imbalance of industrialised Germany by gaining land in the east, but he neglected the questions about Germany's imperial, worldwide future which preoccupied Hitler even in the 1920s.[58] By contrast, Gregor Strasser's 'wing' of the movement allowed its revolutionary socialism to express itself in a pro-Russian anti-British stance, which was not acceptable to Hitler to say the least (p. 85). The strand of the movement most closely related to Wilhelmine imperialism aimed at the restoration of the borders of 1914, and was therefore similar in this respect to the views of the conservative Right, the DNVP and DVP, who advocated the need for a working partnership with Russia.[59] Hitler, however, was against the policy leading to Rapallo. Indeed, some of Hitler's associates in the National Socialist movement, notably Scheubner-Richter, were then actively trying to foster closer relations with those Russian *émigrés* in Germany who were still dreaming of the struggle for a new Russia and the overthrow of Lenin's regime.[60]

The fact that the 'Rapallo line' was not discontinued at once when Hitler became Chancellor was in part a consequence of Germany's general weakness, as well as a necessary concession to prevailing international realities, and to the views of Hitler's conservative allies in the AA and the *Reichswehr*. Few European statesmen had yet digested the ideological arguments advanced in *Mein Kampf* for Germany's drive to the east. The outwardly normal diplomatic relations between Germany and the Soviet Union in 1933, taken in conjunction with Hitler's cautious stance to the West (p. 87), again helped to convey the illusion of continuity with Weimar foreign policy, with its concern to strike a balance between East and West. In

[57] A. Hillgruber, 'Die "Endlösung" und das deutsche Ostimperium als Kernstück des rassenideologischen Programms des Nationalsozialismus', *Vierteljahrshefte für Zeitgeschichte*, **20** (1972): 133–53.

[58] K. Hildebrand, *The Foreign Policy of the Third Reich* (London, 1973), p. 18.

[59] Ibid, p. 14.

[60] H.-A. Jacobsen, *Nationalsozialistische Aussenpolitik 1933–8* (Frankfurt am Main, 1968), pp. 48–54, on Russian influences; Laqueur, op, cit., pp. 50–78; R.C. Williams, *Culture in Exile. Russian Emigrés in Germany, 1881–1941* (Ithaca/London, 1972), pp. 167ff; cf. J. Hiden, 'National Socialism and foreign policy 1919–1933' in P. D. Stachura (ed.), *The Nazi Machtergreifung* (London, 1983), p. 151.

reality, the underlying tensions in German–Soviet relations in the period 1929–33 had already prepared the ground for Hitler to change German policy towards Russia. In addition, the progress made by the new regime in consolidating its internal position in 1933/34, shifted the balance in favour of Hitler's diplomacy at the expense of the AA. The severity of Hitler's drive against German Communists and the elimination of the KPD finally ended the Weimar Republic's uneasy compromise between anti-Bolshevism at home and friendship with Russia abroad. At the same time German–Soviet economic ties continued, as will be seen.[61]

Exactly how far Hitler judged both the internal and external situations to have improved may be seen from the Non-aggression Pact between Germany and Poland in 1934 (p. 157), which was a dramatic and decisive break with the Weimar Republic's Russian policy. It marked the virtual close of normal diplomatic and political exchanges between Berlin and Moscow. The resignation of the German Ambassador, Nadolny, over the new German line of hostility towards the Soviet Union was one of the more demonstrative expressions of resentment in the German establishment.[62]

The limited resistance of Hitler's conservative allies in the AA and *Reichswehr* reflected the fact that they were already compromised to some degree by their espousal of more militant revisionism (p. 50). Potentially valuable as was Soviet–German military collaboration in the Weimar Republic, it was founded on the premise of long-term preparations. As we saw, advances had been made in experiments with a range of weaponry from poison gas to tanks and above all flying training; valuable experience had been gained in officer training. These were hardly germane to the massive expansion of Germany's armed forces envisaged by Hitler. The commitment of the *Reichswehr* leaders to the expansion of military forces compelled them, if reluctantly in many cases, to give up the military link with Russia. By the end of September 1933, all German military undertakings in Russia had been liquidated. The gathering momentum of Germany's

[61] G. Wollstein, *Vom Weimarer Revisionismus zu Hitler. Das deutsche Reich und die europäische Grossmächte in der Anfangsphase der nationalsozialistischen Herrschaft* (Bonn, 1973), p. 291; G.L. Weinberg, *The Foreign Policy of Hitler's Germany. Diplomatic Revolution in Europe 1933–36* (Chicago/London, 1970), p.75.

[62] Weinberg, op. cit., p.75, argues, on the basis of decisions taken in Berlin on German–Russian relations 1933–9, that Hitler, unlike his diplomats, was not particularly worried by Soviet hostility because of his low estimates of Soviet strength. On the exclusion of other views on Russia in the 1930s, see Jacobsen, *Nationalsozialistische Aussenpolitik*, p.447. K. D. Bracher, *'Das Anfangsstadium der Hitlerschen Aussenpolitik'*, in G. Jasper (ed.), *Von Weimar zu Hitler 1930–33* (Cologne–Berlin, 1968), p. 491, also stresses the break in German–Russian relations.

rearmament policy on the international stage after 1929, crowned by Germany's departure from the Disarmament Conference and the open proclamation of German rearmament in 1935 (p. 89), removed the need in any case for the illegal co-operation with Russia. By 1936, when Hitler's anti-Soviet line was being vented more publicly, the *Reichswehr* was already too involved with the cause of continuing rearmament to exercise any decisive influence on the strategic deployment of the armed forces. Their overwhelming concern remained the prevention of a two-front war.[63] The Navy and Air Force had always been less preoccupied with the link with Russia. In the Navy, in particular, account had been taken of Russia's enmity in strategic planning exercises long before the Army moved beyond its preoccupation with Poland and France.[64]

The treaty with Poland appeared at first to have improved the Soviet prospects for reaching an understanding with the Western Powers. In September 1934 Russia entered the League and in the following year the Soviet–French and Soviet–Czech mutual assistance pacts were signed with Nazi Germany. Soviet policies to the West reflected Stalin's growing fear of war with Germany, particularly after the Third Reich's announcement of rearmament in 1935. If and when war came it had to be on grounds most favourable to the Soviet Union. Above all, the situation had to be avoided where the Western Powers turned Germany against Russia to save themselves.[65] The gulf between Russia and the West was still enormous and the legacy of Soviet–Western distrust from the period of intervention and the 1920s made itself felt.

In fact Hitler could not be ready for war against Russia until much later, (p. 96), and certainly not before the situation in East Europe was changed in Germany's favour. Yet, whereas the Weimar Republic's policy of co-operating with both East and West had prevented any systematic exploitation of the gulf between Russia and the Allied Powers, Hitler's policies demanded and even thrived on Soviet–Western antagonisms. Without these Hitler would have had much less room for manœuvre in East Europe. It was not by chance that in 1935, when Hitler appeared to move nearer to Britain with the

[63] On German military relations at this time see G.H. Stein, 'Russo-German military collaboration. The last phase 1933', *Political Science Quarterly*, **77** (1962): 54–71; K. Niclauss, *Die Sowjetunion und Hitlers Machtergreifung* (Bonn, 1966), Chapter IX.

[64] M. Salewski, *Die deutsche Seekriegsleitung*, Vol I (Frankfurt am Main, 1970), pp. 1–3.

[65] Carr, *German–Soviet Relations*, p. 123; H.-A. Jacobsen, in Geyer, op cit., p.234, emphasises the defensive line of Soviet policy 1934–38. Cf. W.W. Scott, *Alliance Against Hitler. The Origins of the Franco-Soviet Pact* (Durham, N. Carolina, 1962), pp. 158ff.

Anglo-German Naval Treaty (p. 91), his anti-Bolshevik drive began to show itself more clearly on the international stage.[66] How seriously Stalin viewed the situation was confirmed by the inauguration at the seventh and final congress of the Comintern in the summer of 1935 of the policy leading to the 'Popular Front' idea. Belatedly, Moscow supported the united front of all Left parties against fascism. This could, however, do little to offset the burden of existing distrust between East and West.[67]

The years 1936 and 1937 proved as crucial to the Third Reich's relations with the Soviet Union as they were to the state of Anglo-German and Franco-German relations. The worsening of Western–Soviet relations during the Spanish Civil War became more marked as a result of foreign reactions to the purges inside the Soviet Union. The slaughter reinforced the existing doubts of Britain and France about the effectiveness of Russia's contribution to any collective front to oppose Hitler. Conversely, the weak reaction of the Western Powers to Hitler's remilitarisation of the Rhineland and the Anglo-French policy of non-intervention in Spain, increased Soviet fears about the ultimate intentions of the West, particularly at a time when Russia was pre-occupied with Japan's threat to the Soviet position in Asia. On this Germany capitalised with its Anti-Comintern Pact with Japan, formally signed on 25 November 1936 (p. 187). On one level, the climaxing of Hitler's anti-Bolshevik propaganda in these years and the louder pleas for Nazi Germany to be regarded by the free world as a bulwark against Bolshevism were designed as much as anything to confuse the Western Powers and to increase Germany's room for movement. Moreover, the Anti-Comintern Pact had anti-Western and particularly anti-British implications (p. 95). But its threat to Russia cannot be played down in view of Hitler's talk with Oshima on 22 July 1936, when reference was made to splitting Russia into its historic parts. Additional evidence for Hitler's enduring hostility to the Soviet Union was to be found in his private remarks on the Four-Year Plan of 1936, and his renewed emphasis on *Lebensraum* in the east (p. 96).[68]

While the Western Powers were not exactly displeased by the anti-Soviet sentiments of Hitler's regime, it should have been obvious to

[66] Jacobsen, *Nationalsozialistische Aussenpolitik*, p. 342.

[67] B. Jelavich, *St Petersburg and Moscow. Tsarist and Soviet Foreign Policy, 1814–1974* (Bloomington/London, 1974), pp. 340ff.

[68] Cf. Weinberg, *Foreign Policy*, pp. 342–8. For more on Japan and Germany in this context. Th. Sommer, *Deutschland und Japan zwischen den Mächten, 1935–40. Vom Antikomminternpakt zum Dreimächtpakt* (Tübingen, 1962).

the German leader that this did not give him *carte blanche* in East Europe. In spite of this he ultimately gambled on non-intervention by the West as he prepared to increase Germany's territory eastwards in 1937/38. Inevitably, therefore, both Soviet–German and Soviet–Western relations entered a crucial phase after Hitler's dramatic successes over the *Anschluss* in March 1938 and the Munich settlement in September (p. 104).

Munich brought the collapse of Stalin's and Litvinov's attempt to maintain peace by means of collective security. The Comintern policy after 1935, of encouraging socialists and Communists to combine in 'Popular Front' coalitions against Fascism, was also ended. There remains doubt about the extent of Russia's readiness to support Czechoslovakia, as it repeatedly said it would in 1938 during the Czech crisis. The tensions in the Far East added to the desire of Soviet leaders to avoid a possible war on two fronts in the future, which in any event would have been beyond the resources of the Soviet state at that stage.[69] Perhaps after all the Russians were trying to reinforce the will of the Western Powers to resist Hitler. The fact remained that the Soviet leaders were kept on the sidelines at Munich, and Soviet fears that the West was trying to turn Hitler against Russia were intensified. Since the consolidation and defence of the Soviet state remained the primary concern of Stalin, one obvious way to overcome the isolation of Russia after Munich – in the face of Western passivity on the one hand and Germany's growing power on the other – was to come to some arrangement with Hitler. Although the public speeches of Soviet leaders in the autumn of 1938 stressed the need for the Soviet Union to resist fascism and Stalin even spoke in November of a 'second imperialist war', cold realities compelled him to reconsider relations with Germany. Thus Deputy Foreign Commissar Vladimir Potemkin said, while discussing Munich with the French Ambassador in Moscow: 'My poor friend, what have you done? As for us I do not see any other outcome than a fourth partition of Poland.'[70]

THE NAZI-SOVIET PACT, 1939

Conversely, Hitler's own disillusionment with the Western Powers, and Britain in particular, began to colour his attitude to the Soviet

[69] H.A. Jacobsen, in Geyer, op. cit., p. 254.

[70] Cited in T. Uldricks, 'A.J.P. Taylor and the Russians', in G. Martel (ed.), *Origins of the Second World War Reconsidered. The A.J.P. Taylor Debate after Twenty-Five Years* (London, 1986), p. 166.

Union. After Munich, 'Hitler's increasingly bitter references to the West were matched by a corresponding diminution of acrimony, qualitative and quantitative, in regard to Soviet Russia.'[71] The intimate connection made in Hitler's thought between his British and his Russian policies (p. 85) remained, although the emphasis was changed. Just as the relationship to Russia during 1934–37 reflected Hitler's concentrated effort to secure Britain's acquiescence for a free hand for Germany in East and Central Europe, so the mounting resistance of the West in 1938/39 determined the tactical shifts in Hitler's policy which ultimately brought the Nazi–Soviet pact of 1939.

Decisive in bringing the shift about was the reaction of Poland and the place given to Poland in the British and French guarantees in East Europe after the rape of Prague in March 1939. Poland's resistance to becoming a junior partner of Hitler's Germany was strengthened but not caused by the Anglo-French guarantees.[72] By 3 April, Hitler recognised that the exchanges between Lipski and Ribbentrop would not produce an acceptable solution to outstanding German–Polish problems and he ordered the preparation of military directives for the invasion of Poland (p. 166). Meanwhile the West continued to be sceptical about the value of the Soviet Union as an ally, and refused to accept Soviet suggestions after the Rape of Prague for a conference of anti-fascist powers to concert military measures.[73] This simply reinforced Stalin's readiness to consider abandoning the option of collective agreement with the West in favour of a timely agreement with Germany, giving the Soviet Union more time at least to build up its own strength.[74] Poland, therefore, again became a bond between Germany and Russia with the signal difference that now a German government was actually planning aggression against its enemy in Warsaw.

The Anglo-French guarantees of Poland then Romania, Greece and Turkey in April/May 1939 dramatically improved the Soviet bargaining position by supporting a ring of buffer states between Germany and Russia. Stalin could now chose either to co-operate with the West against the 'aggressor' envisaged in the Allied guarantees or he could allow any conflict to be confined to Central and West Europe, so long

[71] Carr, *Soviet–German Relations*, p. 125.

[72] Cf. A.N. Cienciala, *Poland and the Western Powers, 1938–9. A study in the Interdependence of Eastern and Western Europe* (London/Toronto, 1968), pp. 190, 224.

[73] *DBFP* 3rd Series, Vol IV, No. 421.

[74] Cf. A.B. Ulam, *Expansion and Coexistence. The History of Soviet Foreign Policy, 1917–1967* (London, 1968), p. 267.

as the Soviet nightmare of a German–British agreement failed to materialise.[75] Whereas the Allies at last took the initiative in April (France on the 14th for a military alliance pursuant to the Soviet–French pact of 1935, Britain on the 15th with a request for the Soviet Union to declare its readiness to give support to its East European neighbours in the event of a German attack on Poland or Romania, if they so wished), it was from Moscow that overtures were made to Berlin.

On 17 April the Soviet Ambassador to Berlin, Merekalov, told the State Secretary in the AA, Weizsäcker, that 'there exists for Russia no reason why she should not live with Germany on a normal footing. And from normal the relations might become better and better.'[76] In view of the continuing exchanges between Russia and the Allies from April, it might be hasty to argue that Stalin had already made his mind up irretrievably for an agreement with Germany. However, some things were quite clear. Firstly, the British–French–Russian exchanges were more widely publicised. As they progressed obstacles to agreement multiplied and Britain, in spite of increasing pressure from France, finally stuck fast in its refusal to allow the Soviets to apply the blanket formula of 'indirect aggression' to the Baltic states, which was felt to entail the risk of Soviet action against these without any properly founded excuse.[77] Secondly, the German–Soviet exchanges were secret and obstacles diminished in almost direct proportion to the rate at which they appeared in the discussions with the West.

They developed against a background of long-standing economic negotiations. Many have stressed the decline of German–Soviet economic relations after 1933, but fewer have emphasised the fact that they declined at a slower pace than political relations. They provided the vital link for Hitler to exploit in 1939. No doubt self-interest on both sides explained the continuing economic contacts after Hitler came to power. The acute need in Germany for raw materials and food staples under Nazi economic planning (p. 55) could be offset to some extent by supplies from Russia, whose own requirement was for industrial and ready-made goods, which German heavy industry,

[75] Cf. Stalin's celebrated speech of 10 March 1939 to the Eighteenth Congress of All-Union Communist Party, and on this, J.E. Davies, *Mission to Moscow* (London, 1942), pp. 279–80

[76] *DGFP*, Series D, Vol VI, No. 215.

[77] Cf. *DBFP*, 3rd Series, Vol. VI, No. 414. On the subject of non-aggression treaties in Soviet and German policy, see R. Ahmann's important book, *Nichtangriffspakte: Entwicklung und operative Nutzung in Europa, 1922–1939* (Baden-Baden, 1988).

exerting considerable pressure through the *Russlandausschuss* was determined to meet.[78] In the last resort there was not the expected growth in this two-way traffic, as the trade figures indicate (Table 3), because political priorities in both states precluded it. Still, a series of trade and credit agreements testified to the undoubted appeal of making the German and Soviet economies more complementary to each other.

The Nazi regime did not break off the negotiations to refinance the Soviet debt to Germany in 1933 and such arrangements were 'almost routine' in subsequent years, according to the head of the economic department of the German Embassy in Moscow, Gustav Hilger.[79] The amounts of credit involved tended to rise. The treaty of 9 April 1935, arranged for a 200 million RM credit for Russia to buy German goods. In addition, a series of short-term clearing agreements were concluded to circumvent the currency restrictions in Germany after Schacht's 'New Plan' (cf. p. 54), the first one on 29 August 1936. It was with the prospect of negotiating an extra 200 million RM credit (in the air since early 1938 although the preliminaries were conducted fitfully) that early in February 1939 – notably, after the German failure to secure an agreement with the Poles – the People's Commissar for Foreign Trade, Mikoyan, handed over to Hilger the draft of a new commodity agreement. In the ensuing phase of the economic negotiations political priorities intruded more obviously. After 22 May 1939 the Soviet leaders coupled the positive outcome of the economic talks with a demand for the clarification of German–Russian political relations.[80]

Litvinov's replacement by Molotov on 3 May 1939, had already removed the anomaly of a People's Commissar for Foreign Affairs who was so publicly linked with collective security at a time when Soviet diplomacy was seeking the maximum room for manœuvre. The length of time between May and the conclusion of a German–Soviet agreement in August tends to confirm the Soviet interest in exploring the limits of what could be gained from either the Western Powers or Germany. Yet the chances of Stalin joining any conlict with the West against Hitler in 1939 were becoming increasingly remote. The undeclared frontier war between Japan and the Soviet Union from May 1939 gave Stalin an additional reason for avoiding war with Germany. For his part, Hitler may not yet have

[78] Laser, op. cit., pp. 1398ff.
[79] Hilger, op cit., p. 284.
[80] *DGFP*, Series D, Vol. VI, No. 424.

decided finally in favour of a German–Soviet understanding, but soon the pressures of military planning were making themselves felt in Berlin.[81] The weather prospects for a successful campaign against Poland determined that it should begin by the end of August 1939. When *Case White* (attack against Poland) was worked out by mid-June it gave 20 August as the date for preparations to be completed for the surprise attack.[82]

The growing urgency imposed by military planning was reflected in the comments which Schnurre, of the German Foreign Office, made on 26 July 1939 to the Soviet chargé in Berlin, on the need for Germany and Russia to rearrange their relationship to take account of their respective vital interest. This was accompanied by the suggestion that there were no real foreign policy conflicts from the Baltic to the Black Sea and the Far East. By 29 July, on Ribbentrop's instructions, the German Ambassador in Moscow, Count Schulenburg, put the matter more unequivocally by telling Molotov that Germany was ready to take account of 'all Soviet interest' in the Polish question and, in the case of the Baltic states, of Russia's vital Baltic interests.[83]

Against the background of the Anglo–French–Soviet negotiations (which had reached the stage where on 31 July Chamberlain announced the proposal for an Allied military delegation to go to Russia to conclude the military convention foreseen in the draft political agreement of the 24 July), the German initiative was a dramatic attempt to sway the Russians to Hitler's side. The Allied military negotiators opened their bid on 12 August. On the 14th, the Russians raised the crucial question about access for the Red Army through Poland and Romania, in order to support these countries against German aggression. Although France was prepared to accept this without Poland's permission by 22 August, the British refused to agree to the Soviet request without the consent of Warsaw. In fact, on the day on which the Allied military negotiations with Russia had begun, the Soviet government had instructed chargé Astachov to convey their readiness to discuss details of an agreement with Germany. On the 14th Ribbentrop expressed himself willing to go to Moscow in person. Two days later the Germans made it clear that they were prepared to offer a non-aggression pact of twenty-five years' duration and a joint German–Russian guarantee of the Baltic states.[84]

[81] Cf. H.-A Jacobsen, in Geyer, op. cit., p. 277.

[82] Cf. E.M. Robertson, *Hitler's Prewar Policy and Military Plans, 1933–9* (London, 1963), pp. 166, 172–3.

[83] *DGFP*, Series D, Vol. VI, No. 729

[84] *DGFP*, Series D, Vol. VII, No. 50.

This offer Stalin could hardly refuse, and on 22 August 1939 Ribbentrop left for Moscow to finalise the agreement. On the same day Hitler addressed his senior commanders and their chiefs of staff. According to his remarks on this occasion it had been his original intention to reach agreement with Poland, the better to fight the West in due course before moving against Russia at a later date – a scenario which we saw in Chapter 3 had emerged in outline during the Czech crisis in 1938. Hitler then confirmed that Poland's obstinacy had compelled him to deal with that state first. During his talk he passed on the dramatic news of Ribbentrop's departure to sign a non-aggression pact with the Soviet Union that would enable Germany to dispose of Poland without, hopefully, any effective resistance from Britain and France. At the same time, Hitler made reference to Germany's economic difficulties. These were more acute in the early part of 1939 and in his statement on the 22 August Hitler observed: 'It is easy for us to make decisions. We have nothing to lose; we have everything to gain. Because of our restrictions our economic situation is such that we can only hold out for a few more years. Göring can confirm this. We have no other choice; we must act'.[85]

What doubts Hitler's audience may have had about the chances of localising a war against Poland were lessened by the news of the coming agreement with Russia – a belated fulfilment of the dreams of key German military leaders in the 1920s and in vastly changed circumstances. Were Soviet suspicions of the West's intention to turn Hitler against the Soviet state paramount? We can be reasonably sure now that Chamberlain and his colleagues had no desire for Hitler to be unleashed against the Soviet Union, but: 'Once this diagnosis of western policy had been accepted in Moscow, only one conclusion could be drawn: if the Western alliance could not be achieved, then let Hitler at all costs strike west and let Russia purchase immunity by "non-intervention". This was the conception embodied in the pact of 23 August 1939.'[86] Stalin was able to achieve his breathing space of immunity from German attack, was able to devote more attention to the threat from Japan in the Far East. By means of the secret clauses in the Nazi–Soviet pact which divided Poland and the Baltic into zones of influence, Stalin secured Germany's agreement to the establishment of an advanced defensive bastion beyond the Soviet frontiers. 'It was significant that this bastion was, and could only be, a line of

[85] Cited by Carr, op. cit., pp. 118–19.

[86] G. Niedhart, *Grossbritannien und die Sowjetunion 1934–9. Studien zur britischen Politik der Friedenssicherung zwischen den beiden Weltkriegen* (Munich, 1972) seems to dispose of this familiar belief.

defence against potential German attack, the eventual prospect of which was never absent from Soviet reckonings.'[87]

There is little reason to doubt this, even though historians have recently emphasised the diversity of views within the Soviet government on foreign policy.[88] Equally there remains litle doubt that Hitler's intention to settle the score with Russia in due course remained. Not that German plans for the Soviet Union were any more thoroughly worked out before the Second World War than they were for Russia before the First World War. Nonetheless, the Eastern Department of Rosenberg's *Aussenpolitische Amt*, (p. 60) under Georg Leibrandt's energetic guidance, had managed during the 1930s to involve numerous Russian Germans in their efforts to prepare schemes for the future dismemberment of Russia. These had little doubt about Hitler's views on Russia and Bolshevism.[89] It was to be the day on which the attack on the Soviet Union was ordered, 18 December 1940, before Leibrandt was given the task of drafting a possible scheme for the administration of Russia. That was still a distant prospect in August 1939. On 24 August 1939, with the Soviet–German Non-Aggression Pact in the bag, the immediate concerns of Hitler centred around Poland, and that will be considered in Chapter 5.

[87] Carr, *German–Soviet Relations*, p. 136.

[88] See D.C. Watt, *How War Came. The Immediate Origins of the Second World War, 1938–1939* (London, 1989), pp. 216ff.; J. Haslam, *The Soviet Union and the Struggle for Collective Security* (New York, 1984).

[89] Jacobsen, *Nationalsozialistische Aussenpolitik*, pp. 86–9, 448, 449, 463.

CHAPTER FIVE

Germany and East Europe

Two historians of 'East Europe' once wrote: 'We admit that the concept of an Eastern Europe which excludes Russia and includes many territories far more "central" than "eastern" is, in many ways, an artificial one; we can only plead that the wit of man has not yet devised for this area any term which is not objectionable on grounds either of accuracy or of euphony.'[1] This search cannot be pursued here, where Germany's policies are the principal concern. To an important extent German policy towards East Europe capitalised on the regional diversities, but in political terms the Versailles peace settlement provided one obvious constant of interest to Berlin; the newly independent successor states of Russia and Austria–Hungary were to make up a cordon sanitaire or 'barrier', a concept which was formulated by the Western Powers at the close of 1919 (p. 27).

Conceived by many as stretching from the Baltic to the Aegean, the 'barrier' rested on two blocs, centring respectively on Poland and Czechoslovakia. The central importance of these two powerful states in the French 'system' of eastern alliances was underlined by the Franco-Polish treaty of March 1921 and the Franco-Czech treaty of 1924. The former, complete with a secret military convention, was to operate in the event of unprovoked attack on either party from a third power; the latter was a political agreement providing for the

[1] C.A.Macartney and A.W. Palmer, *Independent Eastern Europe. A History* (London/Melbourne/Toronto, 1966), p. v. A good discussion of East Europe and the peace, with appropriate bibliographical references, is in V. Aschenbrenner, *et al.* (ed.), *Die Deutschen und ihre östlichen Nachbarn. Ein Handbuch.* (Frankfurt am Main/Berlin/Bonn/Munich, 1967). In addition, see R. Olzey, *Eastern Europe 1740–1945* (2nd edn) (London, 1986); I.T. Berend, *The Crisis Zone of Europe. An Interpretation of East–Central European History in the First Half of the Twentieth Century* (Cambridge, 1986); A. Teichova, *Kleinstaaten im Spannungsfeld der Grossmächte* (Munich, 1988).

common defence of the status quo. Both reflected France's determination to keep Germany in check in line with its traditional policy, now that its former Russian ally had gone, as well as to keep the two 'outcasts' of Versailles apart.[2]

The barrier was to be extended to the north and south of the two states through the efforts of the East European countries themselves, supported by France. To the north, Poland sought to bring about a 'Baltic bloc' with the Baltic states – Estonia, Latvia and Lithuania – as well as with Finland, along the lines thrown up by the Conference of Balduri in 1920. It was agreed here that economic, military and political treaties were to be negotiated to make the whole greater than the sum of its parts.[3] The high points in this area were the Warsaw Accord of 17 March 1922, which pledged Poland, Estonia, Latvia and Finland to concert in the event of attack by a third power, and the Treaty of Arbitration signed between these states in January 1925 at Helsinki. To the south of Poland was the 'Little *Entente*', made up of Czechoslovakia, Yugoslavia and Romania and arrived at by means of a Czech–Yugoslav defensive alliance on 14 August 1920, a Czech–Romanian 'defensive convention' of 23 April 1921 and a Yugoslav–Romanian alliance of 5 June 1921. The Little *Entente* was, however, directed chiefly against Hungarian revisionism as well as against the idea of *Anschluss* between Austria and Germany.[4]

There were inherent weaknesses in these political groupings of interwar East Europe which stemmed from the peace settlement. At the same time a bare recital of these treaties alone expresses graphically the political energies expended in the area and gives an idea of the difficulties likely to be faced by Germany's own policies. The overriding concern of Weimar *Ostpolitik* was the revision of the German–Polish borders. All parties wanted Poland's borders changed but, as elsewhere, the events of 1921 reinforced the opinion of moderate parties and political leaders in the Weimar Republic that revision depended in the last resort on the co-operation of the Allied

[2] A detailed study of the genesis of the French alliances with Poland and Czechoslovakia is P.S. Wandycz, *France and her Eastern Allies, 1919–1925. French–Czechoslovak–Polish relations from the Paris Peace Conference to Locarno* (Minneapolis, 1962); K. Hovi, *Cordon Sanitaire or Barrière de l'Est: the Emergence of the New French East European Alliance Policy, 1917/19* (Turku, 1975); K. Hovi, *Interessensphären im Baltikum. Finland im Rahmen der Ostpolitik Polens 1919–22* (Helsinki, 1984).

[3] A. Tarnowski, *Two Polish Attempts to Bring About a Central East European Organization* (London, 1943); M.K. Dziewanowski, *Joseph Pilsudski: A European Federalist 1918–1922* (Stanford, 1969); *Minutes of the Baltic Conference Held at Balduri in Latvia in 1920*, Latvian Legation (Washington DC, 1960).

[4] Cf. Macartney and Palmer, op. cit., pp. 254ff.

Powers. This was underlined by the policy of fulfilment, which also required the Republic to take some action at least against the illegal frontier defence units which had been skirmishing with Poland immediately after the First World War. It required, too, the acceptance by Germany of the partition of Upper Silesia in October 1921 (p. 26). Germany could not conceive of attacking Poland alone. Against a Poland allied with France such an attack was an even more remote contingency. For such reasons historians of the Weimar Republic were wont to argue that German policies in East Europe were 'inactive' before the signature of the Rapallo Treaty between Germany and Russia in April 1922 (p. 69).

THE ECONOMIC DIMENSION OF WEIMAR *OSTPOLITIK*

Such a view underestimated the importance of Germany's economic policies and was a result of concentrating too much on the more obvious diplomatic overtures. An important trade treaty was signed between Germany and Czechoslovakia in 1920, as was a provisional agreement with Latvia. By 1921 German governments began to respond still more to the pressure of their economic experts and business interests in Germany for a more concerted attempt to penetrate East European markets, particularly the northern bloc of states. In 1921, Germany was in the process of trying to negotiate trade agreements with Latvia, Estonia and Lithuania. This reflected the relative political consolidation of the area as Russia made peace with Poland and the Baltic states in 1920–21. Germany's eastern trade policies have to be seen as part of the broader European 'race for Russia'. It was widely believed that economic penetration of the border states was an essential prelude to this; they were to be 'stepping stones' to the still unknown and chaotic Russian interior. German governments sought to negotiate most-favoured-nation agreements with the border states in order to provide at least an adequate framework for the activity of private German business.[5]

Germany's progress was visible from its recovery during 1921/22 of a greater share of East Europe's economic life from its chief

[5] J.W. Hiden, 'The significance of Latvia: A forgotten aspect of Weimar *Ostpolitik*', *The Slavonic and East European Review*, **53**, No. 132 (July 1975): 392; J.W. Hiden, *The Baltic States and Weimar Ostpolitik* (Cambridge, 1987), pp. 93ff.

commercial rival in the area, Great Britain. The German advance had its roots in the grave economic difficulties under which the eastern states laboured in the postwar world. They suffered alike from their severance from larger economic units which independence brought with it. All felt compelled to consolidate that independence by fostering industrialisation and foreign trade to offset their predominantly agrarian economies. All, however – with the possible exception of Czechoslovakia, and even this state was backward in some branches of industry – were in a poor position to achieve this without foreign capital and expertise.[6] In this situation, the very economic ills and weaknesses which so disadvantaged Germany after Versailles in its competition with Europe's big industrial powers were potential advantages in the depressed markets of East Europe. Germany's cheaper goods, its historic network of trading contacts with Eastern Europe and its pressing need for raw materials as well as for markets for its industrial products combined to give it a stronger position in the third year of peace.

The Weimar Republic's pursuit of trade treaties with the Eastern European states in the earliest years of peace demonstrates the close connection between economics and politics in modern times. From the outset, Weimar governments regarded the improvement of its economic position in East Europe as the best, if not the only way of improving the highly unfavourable political situation for Germany. The power of economic realities had to be exploited to offset anti-German fears in East Europe. For this reason, the negotiation of trade treaties was accompanied by efforts to 'draw a line' under past disputes and to settle outstanding differences between Germany and the states arising from the war. These agreements invariably covered wartime reparations claims, disputes about the liquidation of German property and the position of German minorities. The dilemma for Germany was to strike a balance between a satisfactory resolution to such problems and the need to placate its eastern neighbours by contributing constructively towards their economic development.

In this context it is not easy to regard the Treaty of Rapallo, which Germany and Russia signed during the World Economic Conference at Genoa in April 1922, simply as a 'threat' to the border states (p. 69). The Rapallo Treaty did indeed shatter the assumption of East European leaders that they could automatically profit from compe-

[6] A. Polonsky, *The Little Dictators: The History of East Europe Since 1918* (London, 1975), pp. 9–10; I.T. Berend and G. Ranki, *Economic Development in East Central Europe in the 19th and 20th centuries* (New York/London, 1974).

tition among the great powers for economic penetration of Russia. Such expectations helped to explain what one German economic expert called the 'hither and thither' of East European policies; an unwillingness to contract possibly dangerous and binding ties.[7] However, as the text of the Rapallo Treaty reveals, there was a similarity in type if not in scale of problems outstanding between Germany and Russia on the one hand and Germany and the East European states on the other. Thus the Rapallo Treaty was exploited by Germany as a model for the settlement of still outstanding disputes in its negotiations for trade agreements with the border states. Such a pursuit of settled relations contrasted sharply with the simmering feud between Berlin and Warsaw and therefore helped to increase the reservations of Poland's neighbours about involvement in any bloc directed against Germany and the Soviet Union. At the same time, the pursuit of settled relations with the Eastern European states could improve the Republic's own economic position. It could also help German minorities as will be seen, and could put Germany in a more favourable position to penetrate Russia.[8]

The Rapallo Treaty marked a turning point in that afterwards Germany discussed East European problems more fully with the Soviet government. This is demonstrated by the dramatic increase after 1922 in the number of German Foreign Office files under the rubric *Randstaatenpolitik* (border states policy). Paradoxically, more frank exchanges helped to bring out underlying differences both of principle and emphasis between the respective regimes in Berlin and Moscow. This is not so obvious in the case of Poland, the focal point of interest in most studies on Germany and East Europe in the interwar years. Rapallo provided the context for sporadic German–Russian exchanges about 'pushing Poland back to its ethnic frontiers', but the use of force remained out of the question for Germany. *Reichswehr* leader Seeckt's gleeful welcome of the uneasiness in the West about suspected secret military arrangements in the Rapallo Treaty against Poland, had much to do with the fact that the effect was achieved without the existence of such a dangerous alliance.[9] The benefits to Germany of Russian pressure on Poland

[7] Hiden, *Baltic States and Weimar*, pp. 119–123. On the inflated expectations of the East European states before Genoa and the bitter disappointment after Rapallo, Edgar Anderson, 'The USSR trades with Latvia: The treaty of 1927', *Slavonic Review*, **21** (1962): 299.

[8] Cf. O. Lehnich, *Währung und Wirtschaft in Polen, Litauen und Estland* (Berlin, 1923), p. 253.

[9] Cf. G. Post, *The Civil–Military Fabric of Weimar Foreign Policy* (Princeton, 1973), pp. 42ff.

were evident in 1923, when it was feared that Warsaw would act in conjunction with France over the Ruhr invasion (p. 70). Throughout the 1920s, however, Germany's military and naval leaders were obsessed not with the problem of attacking Poland but of defending Germany from possible Franco-Polish attacks.[10]

The Weimar Republic's interest in co-operating with Russia to keep Warsaw in a state of apprehension was naturally extended to counter the Franco-Polish activity in the regional alliance systems which were summarily mentioned at the outset of this chapter. Poland's position in the Baltic alliance projects was of obvious concern to Berlin, anxious to prevent any strengthening of the status quo for Poland's Baltic position. The Baltic states were of obvious concern, too, for Germany's strategists, given that they assumed Polish hostility in any conflict.[11] In addition, Germany regarded Lithuania as a natural counterweight to Poland because of the impasse in Polish–Lithuanian relations after Poland's seizure of Vilna in 1920 (p. 29). Germany's growing economic importance for these small states was indisputable. The political implications of this were seen, for example, in the consistent attempt by Berlin's economic negotiators to have Poland excluded from the list of 'neighbour states' which Estonia, Latvia and Lithuania wanted to exempt from the general most-favoured-nation provisions which they were willing to grant Germany.[12] Fortunately for Germany, the economies of the states in the projected Baltic bloc were too similar to afford more than limited regional co-operation.[13] In 1926 Germany was at last able to sign a full-scale economic treaty with Latvia and ended its outstanding disputes. The treaty with Estonia had to wait until 1929, but the provisional German–Estonian agreement of 1923 underpinned German trade, as did that with Lithuania in the same year.

Although Germany's Foreign Office shared to some extent the views of Seeckt that Russia's Baltic interests were not to be threatened – a policy rooted in Bismarck's Germany – it did not share Russia's phobia about the small countries. There were even discussions after

[10] Ibid., pp. 101ff., 107–8; R. Grathwol, 'Gustav Stresemann. Reflections on his foreign policy', *Journal of Modern History*, **45**, No. 1 (March 1973): 66.

[11] Cf. Seeckt's views and utterances on this subject in October 1923, F.L. Carsten, *Reichswehr und Politik* (Cologne/Berlin, 1964), p. 155. See also J. Hiden, P. Salmon, *The Baltic nations and Europe. Estonia, Latvia and Lithuania in the Twentieth Century* (London/New York, 1991), pp. 59ff.

[12] Hiden, 'The Significance of Latvia', op. cit., p. 406.

[13] Cf. Reinhold Brenneisen, *Lettland. Das Werden und Wesen einer neuen Volkswirtschaft* (Berlin, 1936), pp. 118, 123. Cf. G. von Rauch, *The Baltic States. The Years of Independence, Estonia, Latvia, Lithuania 1917–1940* (London, 1974), pp. 123–8.

the Estonian–Latvian defence alliance of 1923 about possible German–Russian guarantees of Estonia and Latvia. These came to nothing, apart from Russia's reservations, because it was ultimately impossible for Berlin to see how to guarantee Estonia and Latvia, with whom it had no territorial disputes, without guaranteeing Lithuania. This was an impossibility if Germany was to preserve a claim to Memel. For similar reasons, in 1925/26, German experts abandoned the idea of a mooted customs union with Lithuania.[14]

Without doubt, economic realities undermined the Baltic bloc in the end, but as well as this there was constant diplomatic effort from Berlin and Moscow to disrupt the alliance projects. Both the German and Soviet governments capitalised on Lithuania's absence from the projects, one of the most important reasons for their failure given the reluctance of Estonia and Latvia to join a bloc with Poland without their Baltic cousin. In 1926 the Soviet Union signed a non-aggression pact with Lithuania. Confidential German–Russian exchanges prior to this ensured that the text did not damage Germany's ultimate claim to Memel.[15] At the same time, Germany was compelled to work hard to curtail the fear of the Soviet threat in the Baltic states, particularly after the failed communist coup in Estonia in 1924. To some extent it was German policy to convince the Baltic leaders that it could exploit its standing with Moscow after Rapallo to persuade the Russians to be more understanding of Baltic problems.[16] Finally, Germany's good relations with Finland, stemming from German military aid against the Bolsheviks in 1918, played their part in turning that country from the Baltic alliance projects and towards Scandinavian pastures. The final meeting of Baltic foreign ministers to discuss such schemes took place in 1925.

The Weimar Republic's economic *Ostpolitik* was also effective in the states to the south of Poland in the 'barrier'. German governments and business regarded South-East Europe as a natural market for Germany. The weak, or in the case of Czechoslovakia and Austria, partially developed industries, needed German aid. Furthermore, the spending power of the states could be raised by more intensive agricultural development and by the greater use of largely unexploited

[14] Cf. *ADAP*, Series B, Vol. II, I, pp. 1–5; C. Höltje, *Die Weimarer Republik und das Ostlocarno Problem 1919–1934* (Würzburg, 1958), p. 2. See also, Hiden, *Baltic States and Weimar*, pp. 165–7.

[15] *ADAP*, Series B, Vol. II, I, pp. 459–60, 461–2, 471–2.

[16] Hiden, 'The Significance of Latvia', op. cit., p. 412. An impressive study is H.I. Rodgers, *Search for Security. A Study in Baltic Diplomacy 1920–1934* (Hamden, Connecticut, 1975).

natural resources. 'We aim to create suitable conditions for Germany's commercial dealings with and in these countries by means of agreements on economic relations (business transactions, laws pertaining to aliens, legal aid, etc.).[17]

The success of this strategy rested on not making the question of *Anschluss* 'actual'. That would have further narrowed Germany's freedom of movement by hardening French resistance as well as that of Italy. The latter was France's chief rival for influence after Mussolini's seizure of power brought the inevitable 'forward' Italian policy in South-East Europe (p. 171).[18] The international financial guarantees to Austria in 1922 were conditional on Vienna renouncing *Anschluss*. As Stresemann said in 1927: 'It is best to let this matter rest for the time being, for at the moment the *Anschluss* is only a nightmare for the other powers.'[19] Similarly, the Weimar Republic was reluctant to get too involved with Hungary, in spite of good relations from their wartime alliance: 'because this would load us up with the ballast of Hungarian desires to win back territories lost to Czechoslovakia, Roumania, Austria and Yugoslavia'.[20] Germany could not be too obviously 'active' in South-East Europe any more than it could in North-East Europe in the 1920s.

Yet the political effects of economic penetration remained important. It was agreed by the German Foreign Office that Germany's interest in Austria could be served by that state remaining independent, as long as its political and economic ties with other powers were not closer than they were to Germany, and as long as Austria kept clear of any regional federation which excluded Germany.[21] Germany's economic weight in Austria reinforced the political arguments against that sort of development. To take another example, although Romania was seen as offering no political advantage to Germany and Berlin was anxious to avoid conflict with Russia over Romania's possession of Bessarabia, Yugoslavia was regarded as potentially the most valuable ally in South-East Europe. Notwithstanding Rapallo, the German Foreign Office wanted to curtail Soviet influence in Yugoslavia. Moreover: 'it would be important for us if

[17] *ADAP*, Series B, Vol. III. Doc. 175.

[18] See Chapter 6.

[19] *ADAP*, Series B, Vol. VII, p. 250. Cf. Schubert–Stresemann talk of 16 July 1927 where both agreed on the need to bind Germany and Austria closer together, but felt that it was preferable for Austria to remain independent. *ADAP*, Series B, Vol. VI, p. 84.

[20] Source, note 17. Cf. *ADAP*, Series B, Vol. IV, Doc. 71, Schubert conversation with Hungarian Ambassador to Berlin on 27 Jan. 1927).

[21] *ADAP*, Series B. Vol. III. Doc. 175.

the development of our relations with Yugoslavia produced a weakening of the Little Entente, with the result especially that Czechoslovakia could not count in the future on any, even moral, support from Yugoslavia against Germany'.[22] Finally, postponing *Anschluss* was essential to the cause of German-Czech *rapprochement* after 1919. This in itself was valuable in helping to prevent the Polish–Czech agreement, which the French wanted to strengthen the ties between Poland and the Little *Entente.* As a detailed examination of France's alliances with Poland and Czechoslovakia 1920–25 concluded: 'The bulk of foreign trade of both Czechoslovakia and Poland went to Germany, giving rise to the view that East Central Europe was a natural area of German economic influence.'[23]

THE PROSPECTS FOR PEACEFUL REVISION

By the mid-1920s then, the discrepancies between the political commitments of the East European states to the Allied Powers and their economic links with Germany were becoming painfully obvious. Precisely this consideration reinforced the strategy of Weimar governments of working with the West to achieve more movement in the East rather than relying exclusively on exploiting the Russian connection. As Beneš of Czechoslovakia remarked in December 1924: 'Thus we must not look unfavourably on Germany, must on the contrary work with every means to contribute towards a *rapprochement* between Germany and France, in order to reconcile our political and economic interests.'[24] This was valuable in Germany's Locarno initiatives. The Czech acceptance of the need for an arbitration agreement with Germany made it easier for Berlin to represent Poland's hesitancy as truculence.[25]

In the last resort, Germany managed in 1925 to exploit its relations with the Western Powers at Locarno to secure the effective differentiation between its western and eastern borders and to frustrate any prospects of an *Ostlocarno*. Reluctantly, the French were compelled to accept the fact that the German–Polish and German–Czech arbitration

[22] Cf. AA to Belgrade, 2.1.26, *ADAP*, Series B. Vol. III, Doc. 18, pp. 43–5.

[23] Wandycz, op. cit., p. 372.

[24] Cited by M. Alexander, *Der Deutsch–Tschechoslowakische Schiedsvertrag im Rahmen der Locarno Verträge* (Munich/Vienna, 1970), p. 27.

[25] Ibid., pp. 33ff. F. Gregory Campbell, *Confrontation in Central Europe. Weimar Germany and Czechoslovakia* (Chicago/London, 1975), pp. 43ff.

agreements of 1925 were not an integral part of the Rhineland Pacts (p. 74). Moreover, France was compelled to renegotiate its alliance of 1921 with Poland in order to relate it to the broader requirements of action within the League of Nations. The automatic guarantee of aid of the Franco-Polish pact of 1921 was no longer there. From then on such aid was contingent on a battery of qualifications.[26]

The political ties remained between France and East Europe, but Locarno marked another stage in French disillusionment as well as in that of its East European allies. It emphasised the fact the France's primary concern was the defence of its own territory, and in this respect indirectly furthered the Weimar Republic's revisionist cause. At the same time although the use of force was not positively excluded by the arbitration agreements, in fact their very existence testified to the need of Germany to achieve revision with rather than against the Western Powers.[27] The arbitration agreements were of the type favoured by Germany, since they left open the prospect of territorial revision. Less well known is the fact that they were also useful in Germany's overall drive to achieve settled relations with its East European neighbours and to eliminate sources of friction.[28] The leverage obtained for German policy in East Europe in the mid-1920s came not from its relationship with Russia alone but from the progress made by Germany in striking a balance between its commitments and interests in East and West as a whole, which is exactly what the East European states were trying to achieve.

This whole process was slow and painful, but it is apparent in retrospect that 1925/26 witnessed the more effective merging of the economic and political strands in Germany's East European policies. Stresemann's tenure at the Foreign Office was marked at first by his tendency to assume, like the head of his Eastern Department, von Dirksen, that Poland's continuing domestic and economic crisis could be exploited. Theirs was the strategy of making economic aid to Poland dependent on territorial revision. The year 1925 was not only that of Locarno but of the German–Polish customs war.[29] Seen in the light of the foregoing analysis, this can be regarded as a more explicit

[26] Cf. Wandycz, op. cit., pp. 363–4. J. Korbel, *Poland Between East and West. Soviet and German Diplomacy Towards Poland 1919–33* (Princeton, 1963), pp. 179–80. Cf. Z.J. Gasiorowski, 'Stresemann and Poland before Locarno', *Journal of Central European Affairs*, **18** (April 1958): 43.

[27] K.D. Erdmann, 'Das Problem der Ost-oder Westorientierung in der Locarno Politik Stresemanns', *Geschichte in Wissenschaft und Unterricht*, **6**, (1955): 147.

[28] Cf. Alexander, op. cit., Chapter X.

[29] See Harald von Riekhoff, *German–Polish Relations 1918–1933* (Baltimore/London, 1971), pp. 164ff.

form of economic warfare than that already *implicit* in Germany's trade treaty policies in Eastern Europe after 1919. Reference to that strategy, however, is at once a reminder of Germany's own economic needs. Commercial warfare in East Europe was potentially risky, a double-edged weapon. In addition there were political dangers to Germany's cause if it were seen to be too openly thwarting Poland's recovery. Ulrich Rauscher, Germany's Ambassador to Warsaw, argued for example that the customs war was damaging Germany's own economic prospects without political benefit. State Secretary Schubert saw little hope of bringing Poland to heel by financial pressures. Many German industrialists shared Rauscher's viewpoint and were not slow in saying so.[30]

Not surprisingly, these considerations counted for more as the policy of Stresemann was clarified. Open financial warfare accorded ill with the Locarno strategy. Because of this there were pressures for Germany to define its aims against Poland, the better to attain concrete agreement. On 16 November 1925 Dirksen penned the memorandum on which this tactic was based. Germany's specific demands against Poland were to include the Corridor, Danzig, East Upper Silesia and some parts of Lower Silesia. Some modification of the Posen border was desired but the German Foreign Office was prepared to consider abandoning Posen. This underlined the fact that strategic rather than ethnic considerations were paramount. To increase the viability of this scheme, Poland was to have a free port in Danzig as well as internationally guaranteed rights of rail and river traffic. This was to be exempt from tariffs and there would be adequate transit privileges across German territory to the Baltic. 'In short, rights analogous to those accorded Germany in the corridor.'[31]

The seizure of power in Poland by Marshal Pilsudski in 1926 opened an era of relative stability for Poland. Without doubt this played its part in reinforcing the changing German tactics. After 1926, revision was pushed more firmly into the future and it was in Berlin's best interests, having distinguished between economic policy and political objectives, to improve relations with Poland while giving more patient attention to Germany's overall international position. In keeping with Locarno and Germany's accession to the League of Nations in 1926, Stresemann embarked on the long-term policy of persuading the Western Powers, France in particular, to accept the

[30] Post, op. cit., pp. 21–2, 35.

[31] C.M. Kimmich, 'The Weimar Republic and the German–Polish borders', T.V. Gromada (ed.), *Essays on Poland's Foreign Policy 1918–39* (New York, 1970), p. 39.

necessity of change in Germany's Eastern borders. At the same time, work began on the day-to-day task of normalising relations between Germany and Poland; of settling respective claims from the war, the question of each country's minorities and the trade treaty. In short, as Stresemann put it, Weimar's Polish policy grew from its Western policy.[32]

None of this, however, was particularly welcome for Poland and the 'economic imperialism' of Weimar *Ostpolitik* can be more clearly seen by the second half of the 1920s.[33] Although the *Anschluss* issue was not pressed by German governments during the 1920s and their priorities lay with revising the German–Polish border, Germany's economic policies threw up the wartime shadow of *Mitteleuropa* in the most uncomfortable way for the East European states (p. 11). During a visit by Beneš to Berlin in May 1928, Schubert could refer to the prospect of 'a large-scale economic co-operation between Germany, Czechoslovakia and Austria'. Such a union was 'completely logical'. For Beneš, and indeed for the other leaders of East Europe, the problem remained one of improving regional integration and strength without being too hopelessly involved in great-power politics. Beneš' understatement was masterly: 'The political arguments against such an association were very strong all the same.'[34] How correct was his assessment of some, though by no means all, German leaders can be inferred from a private letter from State Secretary Bülow to the German Ambassador in Prague, Koch, in 1931.

> The inclusion of Czechoslovakia in our economic system is entirely in line with the long-term policy of the Reich as I visualise it. Once the German–Austrian customs union had become a reality, I calculate that the pressures of economic necessity will compel Czechoslovakia within a few years to adhere to it one way or another. I would see this as the beginning of a development which would be likely to lead to the satisfaction of vital German interests, difficult to satisfy in other ways. I am thinking of German–Polish frontier problems. If we should succeed in incorporating Czechoslovakia in our economic bloc, and if meanwhile we should also have established closer economic relations with the Baltic states, then

[32] Cf. Post, op. cit., pp. 37–8; Riekhoff, op. cit., p. 131.

[33] Significantly, the Polish Press in the Weimar era saw no virtues in Stresemann's foreign policy. Cf. F. Golczewski, *Das Deutschlandbild der Polen 1918–1939. Eine Untersuchung der Historiographie und der Publizistik* (Düsseldorf, 1974), pp. 245–6. For more general perspectives see M. Broszat, *Zweihundert Jahre deutsche Polenpolitik* (Munich, 1963).

[34] For this quote, J.W. Bruegel, *Czechoslovakia Before Munich. The German Minority Problem and British Appeasement Policy* (Cambridge, 1973), p. 96. On Beneš' foreign policy a convenient essay is, P.S. Wandycz, 'Foreign Policy of Eduard Beneš 1918–1938', In V.S. Mamatey and R. Luza (eds), *A History of the Czechoslovak Republic 1918–1948* (Princeton, 1973), pp. 216–38.

> Poland with her unstable economic structure would be surrounded and exposed to all kinds of dangers: we should have her in a vice which would perhaps in the short or long run make her willing to consider the idea of exchanging political concessions for tangible economic advantages.[35]

Surveying the situation at the onset of economic crisis in Europe it remains difficult, however, to see how Germany's strategy could ever have forced Poland to agree to revision since that was quite impossible on domestic grounds for Polish governments after 1918. It could also be suggested that decades of peaceful co-existence would be needed to achieve even a real and lasting understanding between the two states. At the same time, credit must be given for the fact that Stresemann's policies at least sought to accustom German opinion to the sort of long-term perspectives where a *modus vivendi* would no longer be automatically ruled out. In the last resort, it would depend on political pressures and on the distribution of domestic forces in both states. In view of these, it is all the more remarkable that, notwithstanding the constant stress at 'high policy' level of Germany's determination to revise its borders with Poland, some progress was made on a day-to-day basis to improve relations. Even while the customs war was under way economic relations continued to reflect some mutual interest. Above all, there is much evidence that Stresemann made a sustained effort to convince hostile critics in Germany of the wisdom of this approach, as for example when he counselled moderation even during private meetings with anti-Polish circles in East Prussia during 1927.[36] Nor was nationalist pressure able to deflect German policy from its strategy before the onset of crisis in 1929.

This was also confirmed by the relative success of Weimar governments in preventing disputes over German minorities in East Europe from disrupting the overall strategy of peaceful revision which reached its climax under Gustav Stresemann. There were undoubtedly very powerful pressures in Germany, especially on the right of the political spectrum, for a policy of active support for the cause of the *Auslandsdeutsche* (Germans abroad), particularly those Germans left in

[35] Bruegel, op. cit., p. 100.

[36] *ADAP*, Series B, Vol. VII, pp. 520–6, Stresemann lecture of 16 Dec. 1927. For an argument seeking to expose the contradictions between the 'high-level' insistence on revised borders and the day-to-day efforts to reach limited agreement, for example over minorities, see H. Lippelt, '"Politische Sanierung". Zur deutschen Politik gegenuber Polen, 1925/6', *Vierteljahrshefte für Zeitgeschichte*, **19**, No. 4 (1971): 329. This minimises the inherent promise in many of Germany's minorities policies, which were not just a device. Grathwol, op. cit., pp. 53–4 cites the views exchanged between Briand and Chamberlain on the possibility of peaceful change in the German–Polish border.

Poland. The vast majority of the numerous organisations which sprang up in the Weimar Republic for the care of Germans abroad were of a conservative–rightist complexion and some of their appeal was to aggressive nationalism. In East Europe above all, the support of German settlements was seen by many as an essential aid in preserving a claim to later revision. Recent investigations have shown only too clearly that side of the minority movement. The government-sponsored 'private' organisation, the *Deutsche Stiftung*, had at its disposal sums of money which it used to strengthen German groups in East Europe and in Poland in particular. Elaborate measures of secrecy were used to conceal such sums at a time when Germany was representing to the outside world its financial difficulties in order to get rid of reparations debts.[37] However, care must be taken not to assume that the Republican governments automatically endorsed the more extreme political sentiments of some *Auslandsdeutsche* leaders. It was a maxim of German Foreign Office strategy not to create the impression that Germany was supporting its minorities simply in the interests of irredentist claims.[38]

Forceful attempts to exploit the German minorities in the cause of German foreign policy were seen as likely to increase the pressures of the host countries against the *Auslandsdeutsche*. Secondly, the financial sums available from official and private sources were far too small to do anything other than help the minorities towards 'self-help'. They would have to survive on their own resources and, in the last resort, that entailed some effort to come to terms with the host country and to play a responsible role in its economic, political and social life. The progress of this vision depended on many variables, but some success was achieved by the mid-1920s, notably by the Baltic Germans or by the Germans in Czechoslovakia. As such, this was part of a broader international effort for the various minorities to work together to improve their legal position and to build on the cultural and welfare activities which were permissible under international law.

The problem of German minorities was obviously far greater in extent than any other European minority issue, but when Germany

[37] Cf. N. Krekeler's, *Revisionsanpruch und geheime Ostpolitik. Die Subventionierung der deutschen Minderheit in Polen, 1919–33* (Stuttgart, 1973). This is a rather exaggerated study in many respects notwithstanding its valuable findings. Cf. E. Ritter, *Das Deutsche Ausland-Institut in Stuttgart 1917–1945. Ein Beispiel deutscher Volkstumsarbeit zwischen den Weltkriegen* (Wiesbaden, 1976), p. 25. For a balanced discussion, see B. Schot, *Nation oder Staat? Deutschland und der Minderheitenschutz* (Marburg an der Lahn, 1988).

[38] J.W. Hiden, 'The Weimar Republic and the problem of the *Auslandsdeutsche*', *Journal of Contemporary History*, 12 (April 1977): 281.

joined the League in 1926 its strategy was to try to develop the process of minority protection in conjunction with the efforts of the various international minority organisations.[39] It does not therefore seem adequate to view the *Auslandsdeutsche* movement after 1919 simply as an extension of German revisionist policy, though many German nationalists would have welcomed that. At the very least, the *Auslandsdeutsche* problem, which was so pressing in East Europe, must also be seen in the light of the struggle within German politics for a more realistic and co-operative foreign policy strategy. The degree of co-operation reached between minorities and their host countries was viewed by the Foreign Office and many economic experts as directly related to the prospects of German trade with the country concerned. Settled German groups were to play their part in directing German trade towards their host countries.[40]

No doubt, this was part of the overall effort to increase German influence in East Europe and as such was hardly all that welcome to France or even Britain, but pursued in some conjunction with them it offered the prospect of a balance which the West could come to accept. Indeed, this was confirmed by the Soviet Union's own growing uneasiness over Germany's foreign policy strategy under Stresemann (p.119). Germany's economic standing in East Europe before the onset of economic crisis was, by dint of great effort, strong. It had generally active trade balances, taking payment in cash from the eastern states and using this to pay its reparations debts. Its political standing still left much to be desired, but it was vastly improved since 1919 and stood in marked contrast to Russia's own economic and political performance in East Europe. The Soviet Union was still not recognised formally by Czechoslovakia, Yugoslavia, Romania and Hungary by the end of the decade. Of the East European states only Lithuania 'was willing to maintain anything more cordial than the stiffest of formal relations with Russia, if so much'.[41]

Such factors must raise further doubts about general charges of German–Soviet co-operation against East Europe, which we suggested earlier was a by-product of much of the writing on the 'Rapallo legend'. There were indeed echoes of Brest-Litovsk here in Weimar Germany's *Ostpolitik* (p. 11), but the changed context of international collaboration must be taken into account when drawing such parallels.

[39] *ADAP*, Series B, Vol. I, I, pp. 202–7.

[40] Cf. Hiden, 'Problem of the *Auslandsdeutsche*', pp. 280–1. Cf. Schot, *Nation oder Staat*, pp. 49–50.

[41] Macartney and Palmer, op. cit., p. 246.

Germany was likely to profit from Russia improving its own economic performance in East Europe and from generally improving trade relations, but Berlin's continuous effort to settle differences with its small neighbours suggests that the physical presence of these states was not entirely unwelcome. As Russia turned to settle its own internal problems at the close of the decade and resumed the policy of non-aggression pacts with East Europe, it was apparent that a string of independent states could serve to protect Russia, too, for the time being.[42]

Since the radicalisation of German politics after 1929 brought a resurgence of ultra-nationalism it could hardly fail to disrupt the cautious and skilful policy pursued by Weimar governments in East Europe since 1919. The most obvious proof of this was the pursuit of a more active Austrian policy by Stresemann's successor at the Foreign Office, Julius Curtius. Planning for a customs union between Germany and Austria had become an *idée fixe* of his foreign policy and he broached the matter with the Austrians in late February 1930.[43] By this time, State Secretary Schubert, who had advised against the union, had already been replaced by Bülow (p. 80). Since the proposed union was an obvious step towards *Anschluss* its announcement on 21 March 1931 was politically incendiary, given France's known opposition. The enforced abandonment of the customs project brought about the resignation of Curtius. It was a sharp reminder for Germany of the interlocking nature of its security in east and west. Taken in conjunction with the impatient declarations of intent by Brüning and his successors against Poland, and the growing hard line inside Brüning's own Centre Party towards the Polish problem, the abortive customs union marked a significant step beyond Stresemann's *Ostpolitik* even if, arguably, inherent in that policy (cf. p. 45).

By contrast with the enforced passivity in the Weimar Republic's policies towards East Europe after the Austrian fiasco, the Soviet Union's growing preoccupation with internal consolidation and its fears about the Japanese threat in the Far East (p. 129) provided impetus for the settlement of relations with its small western neighbours. The Litvinov protocol of 1929 did not quite fulfil the Soviet intentions of securing the allegiance of the Baltic states under Russia's aegis to the Kellogg–Briand Pact to outlaw war (p. 77), since Poland

[42] Cf. H.-A. Jacobsen, in D. Geyer (ed.), *Osteuropa Handbuch. Sowjetunion, Aussenpolitik* (Cologne/Vienna, 1972), pp. 223ff.

[43] S. Suval, *The Anschluss Question in the Weimar Era. A Study of Nationalism in Germany and Austria, 1918–32* (Baltimore/London, 1974), pp. 148–9. For a valuable overview, F.H. Carsten, *The First Austrian Republic 1918–1938* (London, 1986).

joined it too.[44] By 1932 the Soviet desire for peace in the west had advanced to the stage where Moscow gave up its earlier insistence on not signing pacts with blocs of states. It concluded non-aggression treaties with Finland, Latvia and Estonia. In the summer Russia signed a similar pact with Poland, and after overcoming Romania's objections, cleared the way for the Franco-Soviet Non-Aggression Pact of 29 November 1932.[45] One of the props of German–Soviet political relations had gone, notwithstanding Russia's reassurances and the outwardly correct German–Soviet diplomatic relations: the Soviet government had bound itself not to assist any aggressor against Poland, directly or indirectly, for the duration of the conflict. There was nothing left of the spirit of 1920 (p. 28).

On paper therefore, the 'barrier' against Germany in East Europe looked even more formidable by 1933 than in 1919. Not only France but Russia as well were party to it, and the combined military might of France and its two major eastern allies, Poland and Czechoslovakia, far outweighed Germany's. The Little *Entente*, too, suddenly seemed more solid. Germany's economic position in East Europe was affected by the crisis, as will be seen. Since France suffered much later from the world economic crisis than Germany and East Europe, its own weight appeared disproportionately greater in East European politics. French influence on the Danube reached a high point with the Lausanne agreement in July 1932.[46] In fact, within a short time the resurgence of Germany confirmed that this situation was temporary; the cracks in the structure of the East European 'barrier' were still there. As elsewhere, however, notwithstanding some continuities, Germany's priorities in East Europe had shifted after 1933. As before, this is best appreciated by tracing Hitler's mental picture of East Europe.

EASTERN EUROPE IN HITLER'S STRATEGY

The attachment of Hitler to the idea of securing Germany's continental base by dismembering and colonising Russian territory provided

[44] For a suitably hostile treatment of Russia's aims see A.N. Tarulis, *Soviet Policy Towards the Baltic States, Estonia, Latvia and Lithuania, 1918–1940* (Indiana, 1959), pp. 78–83. Cf. R. Ahmann, *Nichtangriffspakte: Entwicklung und operative Nutzung in Europa, 1922–1939* (Baden-Baden, 1988), pp. 76ff.

[45] In general see W.W. Scott, *Alliance Against Hitler. The Origins of the Franco–Soviet Pact* (Durham, North Carolina, 1962).

[46] Macartney and Palmer, op. cit., p. 299.

one key to his general reflections. Such an aim enforced consideration of the 'lands between'. Hitler's fixation with his ultimate solution to the Russian problem diminished in the first instance the long-term importance of Poland. Clearly, Hitler recognised the significance of coping with Poland's hostility towards Germany, the more essential since Poland would hardly fail to be concerned about the conflict with France which Hitler envisaged in the 1920s. Compromise with Poland was one of the most obvious ways to relieve the danger of a two-front conflict. But, in the event of a German victory, the German–Polish border dispute of the Weimar era would be utterly irrelevant. Thus, tactical agreements with Poland were far more readily acceptable to Hitler than they were to most other German politicians in the 1920s.[47] Hitler was consequently less worried than his predecessors about the effects of such a policy on German–Baltic relations. The Baltic countries were marked out by Hitler as an ideal area for German colonisation, along with the Ukraine. The extended effort made by Weimar Germany to keep the Baltic states separate from Poland was hardly worthwhile from this vantage point.[48]

Hitler also showed less concern for another *leitmotif* of Weimar *Ostpolitik*, namely the concern to exploit Germany's relations with the states south of Poland to put additional pressure on Warsaw. On the contrary, an agreement with Poland would release energies to be concentrated on securing South-East Europe as a vital strategic base for the later penetration of the Soviet Union and the quest for *Lebensraum*. This consideration was possibly far more important than any 'Austrian' outlook of Hitler's.[49] Of course, again in contradiction to Weimar official policy, Hitler was obsessed with the need for *Anschluss* and did not hesitate to say so publicly and often in the 1920s. *Anschluss* would extend the racial basis of the future Germany in the most obvious and desirable way. Moreover, Austria's strategic importance for dealing with Czechoslovakia was indisputable. Hitler commented often on the power of this state, his 'spearhead in the side of Germany'. Contrary to Weimar policy, whose restraint over the matter of *Anschluss* had facilitated comparatively reasonable relations between Berlin and Prague, Hitler assumed Czechoslovakia's hostility in the last resort. Accordingly he accepted that the Germans there

[47] Cf. the discussion by G.L. Weinberg, *The Foreign Policy of Hitler's Germany. Diplomatic Revolution in Europe, 1933–6* (Chicago/London, 1970), pp. 14, 57–74. A valuable study for background is M. Burleigh, *Germany Turns Eastwards. A Study of Ostforschung in the Third Reich* (London, 1988).

[48] H. Rauschning, *Hitler Speaks* (London, 1939), p. 46.

[49] Weinberg, *Foreign Policy*, p. 18.

would eventually be useful to him in putting pressure on the Czech leadership. He maintained contact with 'sympathetic' German elements in Czechoslovakia in the 1920s.[50]

The perennial problem of Italy was certain to arise in pursuing active policies in the south-east, as the AA had been aware. By and large the Republican governments had avoided antagonising Italy as far as possible in its East European policies, notably over the *Anschluss* and over Hungary, since by the mid-1920s Italy was playing a leading role in the Balkans. There was little desire for active co-operation with Italy over South-East Europe because of the possible ramifications on Germany's domestic situation of allying with the fascists. Stresemann made this quite clear in private.[51] Admittedly, both Italy and Germany had a general interest in offsetting France's influence over the Little *Entente*. But Italy was still hostile to any increase in Germany's power in East Europe in 1933. However, an alliance with Italy was one of Hitler's earliest firm conclusions from his reflections on international relations (p. 174), and this was bound to affect his views on East Europe. The desire for an agreement with Italy made it easier for Hitler to conceive of Hungary as an ingredient in his alliance system than it had been for Weimar Germany. After the assumption of power of Gömbös in 1932, Hungary was increasingly the client of Italy. Not that Hitler conceived of Hungary as playing a very prominent role, although contact between the authoritarian elements in Hungary and the Nazis dated from 1923.[52] Interestingly, although economic considerations played their part in modifying this after 1933, Hitler regarded Yugoslavia – the Weimar Republic's favourite target for friendly relations in South-East Europe, and the only other East European state mentioned in any detail by Hitler before 1933 – as Italy's enemy and a friend of France.[53]

Whereas Weimar *Ostpolitik* sought to isolate Poland and in general to increase Germany's weight in East Europe in its own power-political interests and those of its minorities, Hitler regarded it primarily in terms of creating a basis for a policy of future conquest. For the new regime after 1933 the question of German minorities was transformed into one about their potential contribution to the expansion of Germany's racial basis. The ideology of the Nazis appeared to

[50] Ibid., p. 20; R.M. Smelser, *The Sudeten Problem 1933–8. Volkstumpolitik and the Formulation of Nazi Foreign Policy* (Clinton, Mass., 1975), pp. 50–1.

[51] Cf. *ADAP*, Series B, Vol. VII, p. 247.

[52] G. Schubert, *Anfänge nationalsozialistischer Aussenpolitik* (Cologne, 1963), pp. 168–80.

[53] Weinberg, *Foreign Policy*, p. 20.

have much in common with beliefs prevalent in the *Auslandsdeutsche* movement under the Weimar Republic. However, while the organisation of the movement was taken over by the Nazis, there was a deliberate attempt to disavow the policies of the Weimar Republic towards German minorities and to instil a new sense of purpose. Although playing a lesser role at first, the AO and APA (p. 60) expressed the intention of the government to exploit minority issues in a way markedly different from the official policy of the Republic.[54] Those who stress the continuities in the *Auslandsdeutsche* movement, would do well to note this as well as the dogged survival among Germans abroad of efforts to keep on good terms with their host states, in spite of the inevitable resurgence of interest in Nazism in the world of *Auslandsdeutsche*.[55]

The ground for the agreement with Warsaw was prepared throughout 1933 by the regime deliberately keeping down friction between Poland and Danzig after the Nazi electoral victories there in the spring. Only by completely ignoring the logic of Nazi racial policy could one suppose that this was anything more than a tactical move, true to Hitler's general belief in the need to relieve his position by temporary agreements. But this desire was matched by Poland's, whose disillusionment with France was deepened after Hitler's early successes in exposing the tactical disunity and weaknesses of the Western Powers (p. 90). The Poles were upset by the projected four-power pact, which Mussolini saw as channelling German revision towards Poland and diverting it from South-East Europe.[56] As Stresemann had exploited good relations with France to increase pressure on Poland, Hitler cultivated Poland to isolate France. The ending of the eight-year-old German–Polish trade war by an economic treaty was followed shortly afterwards by the German–Polish Non-Aggression Pact of 26 January 1934. This, taken in conjunction with the 1932 agreement between Poland and the Soviet Union, was expected to help Poland preserve its balance between East and West.

[54] Cf. the official pamphlet of Emil Ehrich, *Die Auslandsorganization der NSDAP* (Berlin, 1937), pp. 7–8; MacAlister Brown, 'The Third Reich's mobilization of the German Fifth Column in East Europe', *Journal of Central European Affairs*, **19** (1959): 128–48.

[55] H.-A. Jacobsen, *Nationalsozialistische Aussenpolitik, 1933–8* (Frankfurt am Main, 1968), p. 602 argues that by 1937 at most 6 per cent of Reich Germans outside the Reich were Nazi Party members.

[56] Cf. R. Debicki, *Foreign Policy of Poland, 1919–1939* (New York, 1962), pp. 63ff. More generally, R. Breyer, *Das Deutsche Reich und Polen, 1932–7* (Würzburg, 1955); M. Broszat, op. cit., pp. 239ff.

The illusion was sustained for the moment by the cooling of German–Soviet relations after 1933.[57]

Hitler's success in breaking so decisively with Weimar foreign policy and concluding a bilateral pact in the midst of a plethora of Western efforts to achieve four-power co-operation was considerable (p. 88). Although German–Polish relations continued to be troubled 'their alignment with each other dramatically altered the situation in East Europe'.[58] Above all, the agreement made it easier for Germany to concentrate on South-East Europe. The need for this was underlined by the premature attempt of the Austrian Nazis to impose *Anschluss* on Austria in the abortive coup of 1934. Hitler had to accept that action would have to be taken against Austria at a later date. Meanwhile relations with the Nazi elements there could be strengthened.[59] Similarly, closer relations were developed with the pro-Nazi elements in Czechoslovakia, and after 1935 more systematic support was given to Henlein's Sudeten German Party. Controversy still exists as to how much these 'agents of Nazism' could be or were manipulated before 1938, but at the very least they were disruptive elements whose exploitable value to Hitler was always potentially high.[60] They were there and that was enough for the moment in so far as dramatic foreign policy initiatives in East Europe were not yet possible, even with the German–Polish agreement to build on. Such initiatives were dependent on the general pace of Germany's recovery and rearmament, as well as on a more favourable international setting.

In 1934, the French attempted to organise a regional structure including Poland, Russia, Germany, Finland and the Baltic states, the so-called Barthou project. The failure of this *Ostlocarno* underlined the desperation of French diplomacy. It could hardly overcome British hesitation in the face of German and Polish refusals to enter such a multilateral arrangement, quite apart from the distrust between Britain and the Soviet Union so evident during these exchanges. The

[57] G. Wollstein, *Vom Weimarer Revisionismus zu Hitler. Das deutsche Reich und die europäische Grossmächte in der Anfangsphase der nationalsozialistischen Herrschaft* (Bonn, 1973), pp. 302–3; Korbel, op. cit., pp. 275–86. For the idea that Pilsudski considered a preventive war against Germany, see the literature cited by Weinberg, *Foreign Policy*, p. 57. On Danzig at this time, H.S. Levine, *Hitler's Free City: A History of the Nazi Party in Danzig, 1925–1939* (Chicago, 1973).

[58] Weinberg, *Foreign Policy*, p. 74.

[59] Ibid., p. 106. A useful survey is J. Gehl, *Austria, Germany and the Anschluss, 1931–8* (London, 1963). See also, R. Luza, *Austro–German Relations in the Anschluss Era* (Princeton, 1976); D. Ross, *Dollfuss und Hitler. Die deutsche Österreich–Politik 1933–4* (Hamburg, 1966); G. Shepherd, *Engelbert Dolfuss* (Vienna/Cologne, 1961). Note also Carsten, *Austrian Republic*.

[60] Cf. Smelser's measured conclusions, op. cit., pp. 243–4.

one offshoot of this project was the Baltic *Entente* of 1934 between Estonia, Latvia and Lithuania, but this was rather an attempt to opt out of international conflicts.[61] There appeared, even then, little prospect of stopping Germany with Russian aid. The Franco-Soviet and Soviet–Czech pacts of 1935 could not disguise the patchy state of Allied diplomacy in East Europe. The Soviet agreement to help out Czechoslovakia was dependent on prior French action, and the real measure of France's intent was its continuing refusal to give military teeth to its agreement with the Soviet Union.[62] Nor could the resistance of the East European states to including Russia be ignored. The prospects for a Danube pact were equally poor. In 1936, the year of Germany's intensified rearmament programme, Poland's inclination to maintain a friendship with Germany was strengthened by the remilitarisation of the Rhineland. This made even less likely speedy and effective French aid in the event of war, particularly since France and Britain were increasingly troubled by conflicts in the Mediterranean (p. 93). In the same year, the German–Austrian agreement gave the possibility of further leverage to Hitler should he so choose to exploit it. This was, of course, still dependent in part on the progress of German–Italian relations (p. 178).

THE ECONOMIC LEVERS OF NATIONAL SOCIALIST POLICY

Meanwhile, a less dramatic but nonetheless effective process was going on: namely the Nazi effort to remould economic realities in East Europe. The general effects of the world economic crisis in East Europe cleared the ground for a new German economic *Ostpolitik*. The worsening financial conditions of the East European states after 1929 made impossible the continued payment for German commodities by cash. The alternative for the predominantly agrarian states was to persuade Germany to take an increased share of their agricultural produce. That was made difficult by the protective duties which the Brüning regime placed on such imports, which in turn reflected the social realities of his domestic base and the influence of the agrarian interest groups in his government (p. 48). Germany's preferential

[61] Cf. Scott, op. cit., pp. 166–77. On the Baltic *Entente*, Rodgers, op. cit., pp. 106–7. Hiden and Salmon, *Baltic Nations*, pp. 95–6.

[62] Scott, op. cit., pp. 262–7.

customs agreements with Hungary, Bulgaria and Romania were signed in 1931, but were not put into force. Although Germany was compelled to take commodities from East Europe in order to maintain their own imports there, its trade balance with most of the eastern states became passive. In general terms Germany retreated from the fairly strong economic position which it had built up in the 1920s.[63]

This situation was even more unacceptable to the new regime than it was to the old one. The increasingly autarchic trend in Germany's economic development from Brüning onwards, brought with it both a passive trade balance and a great shortage of foreign currency with which to buy the raw materials so necessary to the new regime, thereby creating greater pressures for Germany to pay for such imports with finished goods. The need soon arose for special agreements with the East European countries. The latter had a similar problem of non-convertible currency and a need to offload their surplus agricultural produce as well as a demand for finished goods. Indeed, their plight was all the more desperate as a result of the depression. The compulsion of the East European states to increase their foreign trade was far greater than the desire for foreign currency which France, for example, had pumped into East Europe in the 1920s. Germany's temporary agreement with Yugoslavia in July 1933 (to replace the lapsed treaty of 1927) clearly revealed the trend.[64]

However, the framework for the new German policy was not properly in place until 1934, when Schacht's 'New Plan', with its import controls, export subsidies and currency arrangements was introduced. An agreement with Hungary on 23 February 1934 and one with Yugoslavia on 1 May 1934 confirmed the basic pattern. Ostensibly most-favoured-nation treaties, the agreements were accompanied by a series of secret clauses securing preferential openings in German markets for agricultural produce. Unlike Brüning, Hitler was able to overcome the resistance of the agricultural lobby in Germany. The Third Reich did not even demand special concessions for its industrial products to these countries. In effect, a currency-free exchange of goods was instituted.[65]

[63] Macartney and Palmer, op. cit., pp. 289–90. A helpful overview is J. Bellers, 'Deutsche Aussenwirtschafts Politik seit 1918', *Neue Politische Literatur* (1988, No. 3), pp. 373–92.

[64] Weinberg, op. cit., p. 116. The position of British and French capital investment in South-East Europe remained strong in comparison with Germany, notwithstanding the changing patterns of trade. Alice Teichova, 'Die deutsch–britischen Wirtschafstinteressen in Mittelost-und Südosteuropa am Vorabend des Zweiten Weltkrieges', in F. Forstmeier and H.-E. Volkmann (eds), *Wirtschaft und Rüstung am Vorabend des Zweiten Weltkrieges* (Düsseldorf, 1975), p. 285.

[65] Cf. H.J. Schröder, 'Südosteuropa als "Informal Empire" Deutschlands, 1933–9. Das Beispiel Jugoslawien', *Jahrbücher für Geschichte Osteuropas* 23 (1975): 72–3.

It has rightly been emphasised that, 'The bilateral foreign trade system manifested in the "New Plan" constituted the decisive instrument for the economic and political penetration of the South-East European states, which were regarded by the Nazi regime from the beginning as an important area of influence for German policy.'[66] A German Foreign Office view on the treaties with Hungary and in Yugoslavia commented on 'their political significance above their commercial content, since they were designed to create in Hungary and in Yugoslavia two points of support for German policy in the Danube region, above all to counteract French and Italian policy directed against German interests.[67] The political influence created by economic policies helped to explain why Poland and Czechoslovakia avoided such agreements with Germany. The economic treaty with Poland of 1934 did not therefore lead to a dramatic growth in German–Polish trade (see Tables 4 and 5).[68] By contrast, the case of Yugoslavia shows that, whereas in 1933 England, Italy and France took some 30 per cent of Yugoslav imports and exports compared with Germany's share of 13 per cent, by 1936 Germany had 27 per cent, the other three powers 13 per cent. The growth of German influence posed potentially difficult questions for relations between the Third Reich and fascist Italy. It had the advantage to Hitler, however, of disrupting France's efforts to integrate the economic development of the Little *Entente* in the 1930s.[69]

The extent to which the Nazi regime continued to reinforce the complementary role of South-East Europe to the economy of the Third Reich offered pressures never available to the Weimar regime. The expansionism inherent in National Socialist economic penetration of South-East Europe became more blatant after 1936. With the introduction of the Reich's Four-Year Plan German armaments exports began arriving in Yugoslavia. Significantly, the 'second phase' of German economic penetration from 1936 was notable for a greater degree of co-operation between Germany, Italy and Austria. After

[66] *DGFP*, Series C. Vol. II. pp. 592–6; cf. J. Freymond, *Le IIIe Reich et la Réorganisation économique de l' Europe 1940–2. Origines et Projets* (Leiden, 1974), pp. 83–8.

[67] *DGFP*, Series C, Vol. II, pp. 592–6; Schröder, 'Sudosteuropa', p. 77.

[68] Cf. B. Puchert, 'Die deutsch–polnische Nichtangriffserklärung von 1934 und die Aussenwirtschaftspolitik des deutschen Imperialismus gegenüber Polen bis 1939', *Jahrbuch für Geschichte der UdSSR und der Volksdemokratischen Länder Europas*, **12** (1969): 339–54.

[69] Schröder, 'Südosteuropa', p. 84. For more figures see Table 6. W.S. Grenzebach Jr, *Germany: Informal Empire in East–Central Europe. German Economic Policy towards Yugoslavia and Romania 1933–1939* (Stuttgart, 1988).

the *Anschluss*, a big offensive of German capital took place in Yugoslavia, and by 1938 the Third Reich's commanding position was shown by the fact that it took some 40–50 per cent of Yugoslavia's import and export figures, whereas Yugoslavia's share of Germany's total was about 3 per cent (see Table 6).[70]

If attention is now redirected to 1937/38, when Hitler was beginning to take the sort of risks which were inconceivable in 1933, we can concern ourselves with the details of Germany's East European policies in the last years of peace. Clearly, the dominant German economic role in East Europe played its part in limiting the range of responses to political problems by the East European states themselves and by the Western Powers. The attempt by the latter to counter German economic penetration of South-East Europe was too belated. In any case the benefits to the area of Nazi economic policy were far from negligible.[71] In general, the vision of the East European policy which Hitler outlined to Hermann Rauschning was becoming clearer: an Eastern alliance: Poland, the Baltic States, Hungary, the Balkan States, the Ukraine, the Volga Basin, Georgia. An alliance but not of equal partners, it was to be an alliance of vassal states, with no army, no separate foreign policy, no separate economy.[72] Here, rather than in the machinations of the Weimar Republic's East European policies, was the authentic echo of Brest-Litovsk (p. 11). As in 1918, the chief victim of this forecast was Russia; as in 1918, however, the ultimate implications for the Western Powers could hardly be ignored.

Over the *Anschluss*, Hitler reaped the benefit of the doubt. Its relative ease of accomplishment disguised the real risks and was the

[70] Schröder, 'Südosteuropa', p. 89. Cf. R. Schönfeld, 'Deutsche Rohstoff-sicherungspolitik in Jugoslavia, 1934–44', *Vierteljahrshefte für Zeitgeschichte*, **24** (1976): 215–58. Freymond, op. cit., pp. 77–9, shows that the *Anschluss* increased the impulses in South-East Europe for closer economic ties with Germany. On the extent to which the area became a 'closed system' under German influences, particularly after 1936, cf. H. Raupach, 'Strukturelle und institutionelle Auswirkungen der weltwirtschaftskrises in Ost-Mitteleuropa', *Vierteljahrshefte für Zeitgeschichte*, **24** (Jan. 1976): 38–56.

[71] Macartney and Palmer, op. cit., p. 314. Studies taking the issues further are: M. Adam, *Allianz Hitler–Horthy–Mussolini. Dokumente zur Ungarische Aussenpolitik 1933–4* (Budapest, 1966), M. Broszat, 'Deutschland und Ungarn-Rumänien. Entwicklung und Grundfaktoren national-socialistischer Hegemoniale- und Bündnispolitik 1938–41', *Historische Zeitschrift*, **206**, (1968): 45–96, A. Hillgruber, *Hitler, König Carol und Marshall Antonescu. Die deutsche–rumänische Beziehungen 1938–44* (2nd edn, Wiesbaden, 1965), G. Reichert, *Das Scheitern der Kleinen Entente. Internationale Beziehungen im Donauraum von 1933 bis 1938* (Munich, 1971), W. Treue, 'Das Dritte Reich Deutschlands, Grossbritannien und Frankreichs, 1933–9, *Vierteljahrshefte für Zeitgeschichte*, **1** (1953): 45–64.

[72] Rauschning, op. cit., p. 41. On the Baltic see H.G. Schröter, *Aussenpolitik und Wirtschaftsinteresse Skandinavien im aussenwirtschaftlichen Kalkül Deutschlands und Gross Britanniens 1918–1939* (Frankfurt, 1983).

result of an increasingly fatalistic acceptance by Western leaders that the *Anschluss* was indeed a 'family affair', as Göring subsequently put it. Moreover, Austria had been undermined by the persistent internal agitation of the Nazis within it. Admittedly, the timing of the *Anschluss* was not Hitler's. The Austrian Chancellor, Schuschnigg, after having been browbeaten by Hitler in a meeting in Berchtesgaden on 12 February 1938 into giving far-reaching concessions, including the participation of Hitler's follower, Seyss-Inquart, in the Austrian Cabinet as Austrian Minister of Security and of the Interior, belatedly rebelled. When he announced a referendum on Austria's future on 9 March in order to put Hitler in the wrong before world opinion, he virtually compelled Hitler to take action. The directive for invasion was issued on 10 March. Hitler's ensuing nervousness and the fact that Göring's 'ice-cold' will helped strengthen the Führer's resolve to force the issue,[73] must not be allowed to obscure the inevitability of this step in the long run. The fact that Hitler abandoned his initial idea of a satellite government under Seyss-Inquart in favour of immediate *Anschluss* only after his tumultuous reception in Linz on the day of military action, 12 March, provides further evidence of the Führer's appetite growing with success. In any event, the support of Italy was announced in a telephone call from Rome by Philip of Hesse on the evening of 11 March. Hitler's calculations about British unwillingness to resist the *Anschluss*, proved to have been correct. The Austrians had already decided not to resist the invasion with Schuschnigg's broadcast on the evening of 11 March.

MUNICH AND AFTER

Only in a highly academic sense can there continue to be discussion in 1938 of Hitler's 'opportunism' and his 'response to external stimuli' in taking action next over Czechoslovakia.[74] The timing of the crisis over Czechoslovakia which developed through 1938 was again not

[73] J. Fest, *Hitler* (London, 1974), p. 547. On *Anschluss*, see H. Amberger *et al.* (eds), '*Anschluss' 1938. Eine Dokumentation* (Vienna, 1988).

[74] Cf. D.C. Watt, 'Hitler's visit to Rome and the May weekend crisis: A study in Hitler's response to external stimuli', *Journal of Contemporary History*, **9**, No. 1 (Jan. 1974): 23–32. G.L. Weinberg suggests that Hitler never intended to reach agreement with the Czech government, 'Secret Hitler–Benes negotiations in 1936–7', *Journal of Central European Affairs*, **19** (1959/60), p. 74. Cf. A. Speer's description of Hitler studying a map of Central Europe after the *Anschluss* to show how Czechoslovakia was caught in a pincer, *Inside the Third Reich* (London, 1971), p. 167.

entirely of Hitler's making, but to press this point too far is to ignore the logic of National Socialist foreign policy. The additional economic advantages derived by the Third Reich from the *Anschluss*, including valuable ores, additional steel capacity and some forty-four million RM foreign exchange reserves, helped to sustain the tempo of rearmament in Germany.[75] The immense strategic advantages to be derived from the *Anschluss* added their weight to the pressures for taking action against Czechoslovakia (p. 57). Shortly after the *Anschluss* the Czechs partially mobilised over the weekend 20/21 May 1938, in response to false rumours of German troop movements. Much has been made of the fact that a few days later, on 28 May, the final directive for *Plan Green* (p. 98) had the words about Hitler's 'unalterable decision to smash Czechoslovakia by military action in the near future', substituted for the phrase that it was not Hitler's intention 'to smash Czechoslovakia without provocation in the near future through military action'. The second phrase had appeared in the original draft of *Plan Green* submitted by Keitel to the Führer on 20 May.[76] The significant fact must remain that military action against Czechoslovakia had been mooted earlier. What was more apparent after the weekend crisis was the need for relatively speedy action to capitalise on Germany's increasingly precarious advantages in rearmament. Accordingly, Hitler set the deadline of 1 October 1938 for the operation against the Czechs.[77]

The gradual realisation of Hitler of the need to settle with the West before dealing with the Soviet Union (p. 97) gave the Führer even greater interest in localising any conflict with Czechoslovakia. Not surprisingly, therefore, Hitler insisted that the growing dispute between the Sudeten Germans and the Czech government was an internal matter for Czechoslovakia, while maintaining undercover support of the Sudeten German Party and co-ordinating tactics with Henlein. Their agreed approach was, in effect, to seek confrontation since they were to demand more than the Czechs could reasonably be expected to give in the way of self-determination for the three and a half million Germans in Czechoslovakia. As the crisis developed, fuelled by the mixture of genuine grievances of the Sudeten Germans, who had been hit badly by the economic hardships of the Great

[75] W. Carr, *Arms Autarky and Aggression. A Study in German Foreign Policy, 1933–9* (London, 1972), p. 86; A. Bullock, *Hitler. A Study in Tyranny* (London, 1960 printing), p. 399.

[76] The drafts are in *DGFP*, Series D, Vol. II, pp. 300–2, 358.

[77] W. Bernhardt, *Die deutsche Aufrüstung, 1934–1939* (Frankfurt am Main, 1969), pp. 92ff. analyses the Czech crisis in terms of Germany's military/strategic situation.

Depression, and by the rapid growth of sympathy with the Third Reich in the Sudeten German ranks after the *Anschluss*,[78] the fiction that Germany was standing by simply awaiting the outcome became increasingly difficult to sustain. Indeed, it was the express policy of the Czechs to show that the minority dispute was simply a pretext for German aggression. Fortunately for Hitler, and in this sense A.J.P. Taylor's emphasis is warranted, the Allies were prepared to do much of his spadework for him.[79] Not only did they adhere to the notion that agreement between the Prague regime and the Sudeten Germans was possible, but played into Hitler's hands by trying to find out what solution was acceptable to Berlin.

Hitler, and above all his generals, could hardly have foreseen the extent to which Chamberlain would involve himself, but in any case Hitler was increasingly prepared to risk the opposition of Britain and France (p. 101). The military arrangements for action against Czechoslovakia continued to progress. On 3 and 9 September, Hitler discussed further the details of *Plan Green* with Keitel and Brauchitsch. The 'concealed' build-up of forces and supplies was by then an open secret as the British despatches reveal.[80] When Hitler's speech at the Nuremberg party rally on 12 September, was followed on the 13th by a rising in the Sudetenland, it was hardly doubted in Europe that Hitler would use force. The sudden decision of Chamberlain on 13 September, to have direct talks with Hitler, and the subsequent meetings with the British Premier at Berchtesgaden and Godesberg, on 15 and 22 September, respectively, confirmed to Hitler that he was correct in assuming he could probably have his way with Czechoslovakia. The claims of the Poles and Hungarians against Czechoslovakia, which Hitler had been encouraging, were now advanced by the Führer as one of the reasons why it was too late for anything short of the Sudetenland being handed over to the Third Reich between 26 and 28 September. This suggestion, put forward in the Godesberg memorandum, was indeed as the Czechs said, an

[78] Cf. the struggles within the ranks of the Germans in Czechoslovakia after the *Anschluss*, Bruegel, op. cit., pp. 170–2.

[79] A.J.P. Taylor, *The Origins of the Second World War* (London, 1964), pp. 209ff. On Munich, apart from material cited in the chapter on Germany and the Western Powers, see K. Robbins, *Munich 1938* (London, 1968), B. Celovsky, *Das Münchener Abkommen von 1938* (Stuttgart, 1958); A. Crozier, 'Prelude to Munich. British foreign policy and Germany', *European Studies Review*, **6**, 1976: 357–81; R. Douglas, *In the Year of Munich* (London, 1977).

[80] And the Germans knew this. Cf. *DGFP*, Series D, Vol. II, Doc. 409, memorandum by Weizsäcker on the fact that: 'There is no question therefore of an element of surprise.'

'ultimatum'.[81] Hitler's 'concession' of extending the time limit for evacuation of the Sudetenland to 1 October was well in line with his existing military plans.

The Munich settlement gave Hitler the chance to occupy the Sudetenland in stages between 1 and 10 October. Plebiscites were to be held in disputed areas and an international guarantee of the remainder of the Czech state was made conditional on prior satisfaction of Polish and Hungarian claims. In effect, Hitler interpreted the settlement as a green light for subsequently dismantling the rest of the Czech state. On 21 October the Army was ordered to be ready to dispose of Czechoslovakia by a surprise attack, and even by 17 December to assume that there would be no resistance from the other powers.[82] By 5 November 1938, as if to celebrate the anniversary of the Hossbach memorandum, the extent of Germany's hold in South-East Europe was underlined by the so-called Vienna Award. Italy and Germany arbitrated on Hungary's belated attempt to carve its share from the Czech cake. Significantly, the Vienna settlement reflected Germany's strategic interests by preventing the junction of Poland and Hungary across Slovakia.[83] The exploiting of the disgruntled Slovak separatist movement by the Germans was barely necessary in view of the growing isolation of the rump Czech state from its erstwhile defenders. This was more than confirmed by the farce of the international commission which was supposedly settling the disputed claims left over from the Munich Conference.[84] Slovakia declared its independence under German pressure on 14 March 1939. The luckless President Hâcha was bullied into giving the necessary 'request' for German troops to protect the Czech people. The Rape of Prague on 15 March finally brought the military solution of which Hitler had been deprived by the Munich Conference.

The events of March 1939 strengthened Germany's growing economic and political penetration of East Europe since 1933 and played a vital role in the progress of rearmament in the Third Reich. The question of Poland was also raised in more pressing form. That Poland was still conceived as a sort of junior partner in any expansion eastwards was apparent from exchanges between Ribbentrop and the

[81] *DBFP*, 3rd Series, Vol. II. pp. 518–19.

[82] *DGFP*, Series D, Vol. IV, Doc. 81.

[83] Ibid., Doc. nos. 39, 99. Cf. T.L. Sakmyster, 'Hungary and the Munich crisis. The revisionist dilemma', *Slavic Review*, **32**, No. 4 (1973): 730.

[84] L.B. Namier, *Diplomatic Prelude* (London, 1948), p. 55 still has the most satisfactorily scathing judgement on the commission. On Slovak separatism and German policy see J.K. Hoensch, *Die Slowakei und Hitlers Ostpolitik* (Cologne, 1965).

Polish Ambassador to Berlin, Josef Lipski. These began on 21 October 1938. The German seizure of Memel from Lithuania in March 1939 was a reminder of how things had changed since the Weimar Republic 'fell over backwards' to retain Lithuania's friendship against Poland.[85] At the same time, the seizure of Prague and Memel were a clear indication of what Germany's friendship could mean. What the Germans demanded from Poland, at the least, was satisfaction over its claims to Danzig and the corridor. This was precisely what the Poles could not accept. In short, it was clear by March 1939 that the Poles could not balance for ever between Germany and Russia. Nor could they by then continue to have Germany's friendship without paying dearly for it. The Soviet Union's help they would not have at any cost. The Anglo-French guarantees of Poland and Romania after the Rape of Prague settled Hitler's immediate priorities. On 3 April orders were given to prepare for a new contingency, military action against Poland if it continued to be awkward, *Case White*. By 28 April, Hitler had denounced the German–Polish Non-Aggression Treaty of 1934. The smouldering Danzig issue provided ample opportunity for screwing up tensions during the summer of 1939.[86] So Poland's immediate fate came to rest on the outcome of Hitler's policy towards the USSR during the last year of peace.

Just as the requirements of military planning, which stemmed from Hitler's determination to attack Poland, impelled the Nazi regime to reach agreement with Moscow, so the German–Soviet agreement in turn had to be put to the acid test of the reactions of the Western Powers. Hitler had drawn what appeared to be an obvious conclusion from Chamberlain's continuing reluctance in 1939 to grant Poland the financial aid it demanded. Namely, that effective and speedy direct aid to Poland was unlikely.[87] Whether or not Britain would still go to war over Poland was, as Hitler's talks to his military leaders on 23 May and 22 August 1939 could not disguise, an open question. Doors soon began to close rapidly when on 24 August Chamberlain reaffirmed the British guarantees to Poland, and on the next day the treaty which formally founded the Anglo-Polish alliance was signed between London and Warsaw.

It was hardly Hitler the 'opportunist' who gave the order to attack

[85] E.-A. Plieg, *Das Memelland, 1920–1939* (Würzburg, 1962).

[86] Levine, op. cit., On the Danzig issue, A. Prazmowska, 'The role of Danzig in Polish–German relations on the eve of the Second World War', in J. Hiden, T. Lane (eds), *The Baltic and the Outbreak of the Second World War* (Cambridge, 1992), pp. 74–94.

[87] *DGFP*, Series D, Vol. VI, Doc. 480.

Poland on 25 August 1939, at 3 p.m., or who, after cancelling it a few hours later, gave the same order on 31 August at lunch-time. The diplomatic machinations filling in the time between the two commands to attack have been set out at length in all too many books. Of course Hitler might have lost his nerve on the 25th, faced with the double dose of bad news about the Anglo-Polish alliance and the refusal of Italy to rush to war. Yet these were hardly *entirely* unexpected events, and in any case they did not prevent Hitler from making war on Poland as he had intended since April 1939.

CHAPTER SIX

Germany and Italy

Perhaps this chapter should have been entitled 'Germany and the Mediterranean', but Italy was indisputably the most important Mediterranean power for Germany. Moreover, this book has so far given attention both to the 1920s and 1930s, and in the 1920s, when the German Army was barely adequate, let alone its Navy, the role of the Mediterranean in German foreign policy was not the most hotly debated issue. The published documents from the German Foreign Office for the 1920s hardly mention the Mediterranean when dealing with Italy. Spain and Portugal figure on only a handful of occasions.

There were reasons for the *Auswärtiges Amt's* (AA) reticence towards Italy in the 1920s. The acid test for German policy-makers was to what extent could relations with other powers help Germany's revision of the Versailles peace. When applied to Italy in the immediate postwar years, the answers to this question were not impressive. In a sense this was utterly predictable. Italy was one of the peacemakers; one of the beneficiaries of the Versailles peace settlement. Not only was it given additional territory, notably Trieste and a more favourable border with Yugoslavia, it was a recipient of German reparations payments and Rome provided important legal backing to the French occupation of the Ruhr in 1923.[1] In addition, Italy acquired the South Tyrol to create a strategically viable frontier at the Brenner Pass. This was a source of contention and the 1920s were littered with German–Italian exchanges about the Italianisation of the Germans in the Alto Adige. Finally, Italy's determination to prevent the *Anschluss*

[1] E.E. Rosen, 'Mussolini und Deutschland, 1922–3', *Vierteljahrshefte für Zeitgeschichte*, **5** (1957): 17 ff.

between Germany and Austria, forbidden by Versailles, remained another sore point between the two powers.

On the other hand, there was considerable disappointment in Italy at its treatment by the Allied Powers at the Peace Conference. Italian nationalists considered themselves cheated both in the Adriatic and in Africa; felt themselves robbed of gains promised by their wartime agreements with Britain and France, Fascism, afterall, 'swept to power on a wave of popular if misconceived Italian disappointment at the Versailles peace settlement'.[2] Why did German governments not exploit the circumstances created by Mussolini's arrival in power in Rome in October 1922? One obvious answer was that Weimar governments had little taste for risking the bedfellowship of Italian fascism even on domestic grounds, as Stresemann made clear in private.[3] The distaste for fascism in moderate Weimar political circles was thoroughly matched by the Duce's own contempt for Weimar democracy.

Ideological incompatibility was not the only or even the most important obstacle to the emergence of a German–Italian revisionist bloc in the 1920s, as many German nationalists desired. As we have already seen, the policy of fulfilment testified to the realities of power in Europe after 1919 (p. 65), and Germany could not risk coming into conflict with Britain and France over Italy. This was made particularly apparent under Stresemann. In his term as Chancellor in 1923 he left Mussolini in no doubt – when asked by the Italians to immobilise part of the French Army on the Rhine in the event of an Italian–Yugoslav conflict – that, 'Germany, being compelled to devote itself to its economic re-establishment and to the solution of the reparations problem, could not see its way to taking sides in such a conflict.'[4] In the event, Italy remained on paper one of the victor powers, and Mussolini did not formally endorse the call for a revision of the European peace settlement until the summer of 1928. Nevertheless, the outlines of a future Franco-Italian conflict continued to be drawn after 1923.

This was bound to concern Germany and this is best appreciated by considering first the perspective given to fascist diplomacy in the interwar years by more recent researches. The study of Italy's foreign policy has been liberated from the once dominant belief that Mussolini

[2] A. Cassels, 'Mussolini and German nationalism, 1922–5', *Journal of Modern History*, **35**, No. 2 (June 1963): 137.
[3] See Note 51 of Chapter 5.
[4] Cassels, op. cit., pp. 139–40.

was merely an 'opportunist'.[5] The twists and turns of Italy in the 1920s contributed to this impression, but they stemmed largely from Italy's inability to revise the European order on its own. Even so, it was obvious to many contemporaries that 1922–32 was far from being the 'decade of good behaviour' in fascist foreign policy.[6] Quite apart from the use of force by the Italians against Fiume and Corfu in the immediate postwar years, Neurath, German Ambassador to Rome and later Hitler's foreign minister, viewed Mussolini as deliberately trying to escape the tutelage of his Versailles allies. While ambivalent in his attitude even towards Britain (for the traditional diplomatic circles in Rome, Italy's best friend), it was against France that Mussolini's hostility was directed.[7] In a report of 2 December 1924 Neurath expressly related Mussolini's changed attitude towards Germany to his long-term interest in overthrowing Versailles.

Mussolini's efforts, Neurath urged, were directed at 'making the Mediterranean into an Italian sea. There France stood as an obstacle and he began to prepare for the struggle with this opponent. Thus . . . the reversal of his attitude to Germany.' Mussolini believed that the order created by Versailles in Europe could not last.

> In the new war which would break out between France and Germany, Italy, led by Mussolini, would place itself at Germany's side in order jointly to defeat France. If this were to happen, Mussolini would claim as the reward of victory the whole of the present French North African coast in order to found a great Latin Empire in the Mediterranean.[8]

Jens Petersen's impressive study of the origins of the Axis takes up Neurath's vision, and analysing, too, the internal forces at work in Italy after the fascist seizure of power, observes:

> Fascist Italy, after an initial phase of internal consolidation, began an expansionist foreign policy from 1925/26 which, impelled powerfully by domestic expectations, demanded political, economic, colonial and territorial expansion and in the long term strove to create an Italian Mediterranean Empire, which was to be reinforced on African soil by the extension of existing colonial possessions.[9]

[5] See above all Jens Petersen, 'Die Aussenpolitik des faschistischen Italien als historiographisches Problem', *Vierteljahrshefte für Zeitgeschichte*, **22**, No. 4 (1974): 417–57.

[6] H. Stuart Hughes, 'The early diplomacy of Italian Fascism', in G.A. Craig and F. Gilbert (eds), *The Diplomats 1919–1939* (Princeton, 1953), pp. 216ff., rather exaggerates the extent to which the Italian Foreign Office was able to restrain fascism in the 1920s.

[7] *ADAP*, Series B, Vol. IV, report of Neurath of 27 Jan. 1927, pp. 166–70.

[8] Report cited in Petersen, op. cit., p. 249.

[9] Jens Petersen, *Hitler, Mussolini. Die Entstehung der Achse Berlin–Rom, 1933–6* (Tübingen, 1973), p. 495.

The fact that the turning point in Italian foreign policy coincided with Germany's entry to the League and with the pacts of Locarno to which Italy was also a partner, made it even more important for Berlin that relations with Rome were kept 'normal, even friendly' but nothing more.[10] Disputes over the South Tyrol and over Austria were there to provide a convenient excuse for Stresemann politely to decline some warm Italian invitations for him to visit Mussolini.[11] Beneath the surface normality, relations continued to be distinctly cool. In a talk at the German Foreign Office on 18 May 1927, which included *Reichswehr* officers, the AA justified its present refusal to send air attachés to Rome after the ending of the Inter-Allied Military Control Commission (p. 77) because, 'we hold as undesirable, any measure which implies a stand for Italy against France'.[12] In short, just as Italy's overtures to Germany reflected according to Neurath the state of Franco-Italian hostility, so Germany's official policy towards Italy remained very much a function of its western policies. Yet Germany could not be indifferent to Italy, not least because of its concern with Austria and South-East Europe.

BALKAN ISSUES

In a sense, Italy's policies in the Balkans stemmed from the need to reorientate Italian foreign policy after the collapse of the Hapsburg Empire, but the expansionist nature of Italy's activity in South-East Europe was self-evident. In particular, Italy's growing domination over Albania was confirmed by a bank and loan agreement in March 1925. On 27 November 1926, and 22 November 1927, the first and second Treaties of Tirana tied the two countries more firmly together. The first pledged mutual support of the two partners in maintaining Albania's territorial, judicial and political status quo and the second widened these commitments into a defensive alliance.[13] Italy viewed its very considerable investment in Albania not as a normal economic one but as basically political and strategic. Above all, its efforts were directed against Yugoslavia. This was a reversal of the Italo–Yugoslav

[10] *ADAP*, Series B, Vol. VII, Köpke, AA, to Rome, 23 Dec. 1927, pp. 565–6.

[11] *ADAP*, Series B, Vol. VI, pp. 427–30, talk between Stresemann and Grandi at Geneva, 11 and 12 Sept. 1927.

[12] *ADAP*, Series B, Vol. V, pp. 368–9.

[13] J. Rothschild, *East Central Europe Between the Two World Wars* (Seattle/London, 1974), p. 364.

rapprochement in the first part of the 1920s (Rapallo Treaty of 1920, Italo–Yugoslav Friendship Treaty of 1924; economic agreements of 1924/25.) More importantly, Italy's opposition to Yugoslavia in its Adriatic policy was regarded by the French as part of the wider Italian challenge to their own position; Yugoslavia was after all a member of the French-sponsored Little *Entente* (p. 138). French fears were apparently justified by the friendship agreements concluded on 5 April 1927 between Italy and Hungary, chief enemy of the Little *Entente*. The reaction of Paris to the more overtly active Italian policy in the Balkans after 1925 was to conclude a further agreement with Yugoslavia in December 1927. The treaty made it apparent to all 'that the Italian–Yugoslav conflict had broadened out to a confrontation in the Balkans between Rome and Paris'.[14]

As noted in Chapter 5, Berlin regarded economic influence in the Balkans as a useful aid to checking France and the Little *Entente*. While the German Foreign Office tended to favour good relations with Yugoslavia in this connection, it was also well appreciated that, in the words of Graf Prittwitz of the German Embassy staff in Rome in September 1928:

> 'Without doubt we need the Italians for anything coming under the term Danube policy, and I think that we also have apparently far-reaching possibilities of coming to agreement with them [Italians] there. The initiatives in all such matters must, however, be left to the Italians . . . otherwise the price of compensation will be too high. . .'[15]

Indeed, the Italians had intimated more than once that their attitude towards the question of *Anschluss* was not final, although such references had been invariably coupled with remarks on the need for German–Italian agreement over the South Tyrol.[16] In 1927, the Italo-Yugoslav conflict over Albania posed the sort of problem for Germany which Stresemann was anxious to avoid. It increased the pressures on Berlin to take an either/or stand on the Italian–French conflict underlying Balkan struggles. It therefore provided an interesting test case for Germany's official relations with Italy in the 1920s.

Ideally Berlin wished to remain neutral, an obvious way out. For this reason any conflict in the Balkans was to be avoided as far as possible. The State Secretary of the AA, Carl Schubert, agreed as much with the Italian Ambassador to Berlin, Count Aldrovandi, on 19 March, 1927.[17] In late March 1927, however, the suggestion was

[14] Petersen, *Hitler, Mussolini*, p. 5; cf. Rothschild, op. cit., p. 228.
[15] *ADAP*, Series B, Vol. VI, pp. 486–8. Prittwitz to AA, 21 Sept. 1927.
[16] Cf. Ibid., Prittwitz to Schubert, 25 Aug. 1927, pp. 305–6.
[17] *ADAP*, Series B, Vol. V, pp. 10–13, Schubert memorandum of 19 March 1927.

made by the British Foreign Minister, Austen Chamberlain, that British, French and German officers in Belgrade should investigate Mussolini's charges against Yugoslavia. These were that the Yugoslavs were intending to make an attack on the Yugoslav–Albanian border and that Belgrade's rearmament confirmed this.[18] Faced with the prospect of having to offend either the Western Powers, Italy or Yugoslavia, there was only one possible choice for Stresemann. It was Schubert who conveniently listed in a memorandum dated 25 March 1927, ten reasons why Germany could not refuse to take part in the projected action with Britain and France. In particular, point three of the memorandum stressed that since it was the first big political question involving Germany but not directly touching it, 'We must give a clear answer, because we must keep to the lines of our policy.' This was made clear by point eight: 'It has been our firm policy to work for co-operation with the big European powers. We have said this all over the place for years.' On the first occasion when Germany's attitude was put to the test, there could be therefore no question of shirking the issue.[19] Germany's participation in the exercise was accompanied by earnest assurances both to Italy and Yugoslavia about Germany's goodwill.[20]

This sort of development in Weimar–Italian relations was only possible in the 1920s for quite specific reasons. Firstly, the priorities of German foreign policy under Stresemann and the German Foreign Office were firmly established. Secondly, Italy was still not extensively challenging the European status quo, as was demonstrated by Italy's continued membership of the League of Nations and its participation in the Locarno pacts. Both factors ensured that the troublesome issues between Berlin and Rome, notably over Austria and the Balkans, were latent rather than actual, but they must be kept in mind. They provided additional evidence of the larger and more important realities underlying the Locarno era. Not surprisingly, the Italian leader worried about the Franco–German *rapprochement*, the policy of Thoiry and the much-publicised goodwill between Stresemann, Briand and Chamberlain (p. 75). Such developments stood in diametrical opposition to the situation he desired: that is the freedom to exploit European unrest for Italy's benefit. Yet one has only to raise the question about a change in the relationship between Germany and France to grasp the importance to Italy of disrupting Stresemann's

[18] Ibid., Schubert memorandum of his talk with the English Ambassador on 24 March 1927, pp. 54–8.

[19] Ibid., pp. 63–4.

[20] Ibid., Docs. 53, 67.

diplomacy. The force of these remarks can be seen by taking account of Mussolini's contacts with German rightist–nationalist circles after 1919. These form a counter-theme to German–Italian diplomatic relations and run like 'a red thread' through the 1920s.[21]

MUSSOLINI AND NATIONAL SOCIALISM IN THE 1920s

Mussolini was alerted to the strength of German nationalism from a visit he made to Germany six months before gaining power. From this he concluded: 'Despite the Republic and perhaps in consequence of the Republic, the whole of Germany is moving uniformly and progressively to the right.'[22] Late in September 1923, Karl Helfferich, of the German National People's Party, spoke bitterly to the Italian Ambassador, Bosdari, of his contempt for the policy of fulfilment and of the need for a foreign policy based on a break with France. He hoped that 'in view of possible radical changes in international politics Germany and Italy will not delay in coming to an understanding'. Although Mussolini felt on hearing such views that it was not then opportune to take action, he wanted Bosdari to maintain cautious contacts.[23] In October–November 1923 no less than *Reichswehr* Chief Seeckt and General Paul Hasse spoke of a war of revenge against France to the Italian Naval Attaché in Berlin. Reference was made to possible Italian diplomatic aid in evading the Allied Military Control Commission and Italian assistance was asked for in Germany's rearmament.[24] Such unofficial channels continued to be used, often bypassing Italian diplomatic circles. They helped to fuel the rightist criticism of Berlin's official policy of restrained correctness towards Italy.

Inevitably, considerable mutual interest developed early on between the Bavarian nationalist/separatist groups and Italian fascism. Geographical proximity alone made this inevitable, although none of the groups in South Germany were ready to accept Italian possession

[21] Petersen, *Hitler, Mussolini*, p. 10. For further arguments against the idea of Weimar–Italian collaboration against Versailles, V. Torunsky, *Entente der Revisionisten? Mussolini und Stresemann, 1922–1929* (Cologne/Vienna, 1988).

[22] Cassels, 'Mussolini and German nationalism', pp. 138–9.

[23] Ibid., p. 140. See also the discussion by A. Cassels, 'A.J.P. Taylor and Italy', in G. Martel (ed.), *Origins of the Second World War Reconsidered. The A.J.P. Taylor Debate after Twenty-Five Years* (London, 1986), pp. 73–96.

[24] Ibid., pp. 143–4. Petersen, *Hitler, Mussolini*, pp. 11–13 is more cautious in his judgement here.

of the Alto Adige.[25] It was in this connection that Hitler's views on Italy came to be of considerable interest to Mussolini. Ideological considerations were not prominent in Hitler's earliest reflections on Italy, if his *Table Talk* is to be credited.[26] It was rather that the logic of Hitler's desire to overthrow Versailles led him to argue the need for an alliance with Italy as well as with Britain (p. 84). On 1 August 1920 Hitler had said: 'The basic demand is: away with the Peace Treaty! To this end above all we must take all steps to exploit the conflicts between France and Italy, so that we get Italy on our side.' This idea remained firmly fixed in Hitler's mental world. France was the fatal enemy of Italy as well as Germany and both would have to fight France for their existence, as Hitler was later to argue in his *Second Book*.[27]

By September 1922 Hitler had already become part of the network of unofficial contacts fostered by Mussolini's henchmen in Germany. The introduction originated in a visit to Rome of Hitler's foreign policy advisor, Kurt Lüdecke, who used Ludendorff's name to get an audience with Mussolini.[28] From these exchanges Hitler heard of Mussolini's concern for the Alto Adige. Notwithstanding the call in the Nazi Party programme for the uniting of all Germans, Hitler was urging at the close of 1922/23 that:

> 'Germany must go with Italy, which has experienced its national rebirth and has a great future. To this end a clear, binding renunciation of the Germans in South Tyrol must be given by Germany. The babble about South Tyrol, the futile protests against the fascists, only damage us because they alienate us from Italy. In politics there is no sentiment.'[29]

Although aware of Nazi complaisance on this point, and advised that the Nazis were the most promising of the German rightists for Italy's purposes, Mussolini was not apparently that helpful during Hitler's attempted *putsch* in November 1923.[30] This event cooled the immediate concern of Mussolini for the Bavarian rightists, although prominent Nazis, notably Göring, went into exile in Italy. Yet contacts remained between the Italians, the *Stahlhem* and the DNVP as well as the NSDAP, and after Hitler left prison at the latest, Mussolini was

[25] Petersen, *Hitler, Mussolini*, pp. 146–7; cf. W.W. Pese, 'Hitler und Italien 1920–6', *Viertaljahrshefte für Zeitgeschichte*, **3** (1955): 113–26.

[26] Cf. E. Jäckel, *Hitlers Weltanschauung* (Tübingen, 1969), p. 34.

[27] Quote from Pese, op. cit., p. 113; *Zweites Buch*, p. 187.

[28] Cassels, 'Mussolini and German nationalism', pp. 147–8; Petersen, *Hitler, Mussolini*, pp. 14–15.

[29] G. Schubert, *Anfänge nationalsozialistischer Aussenpolitik* (Cologne, 1963), p. 77.

[30] Cassels, 'Mussolini and German nationalism', says Mussolini was not that helpful; Petersen, *Hitler, Mussolini*, p. 15 implies that he might have helped.

giving financial aid to the National Socialist movement. Some time between 1925 and 1928 Italian arms were also supplied for the South German rightists.[31]

As for Hitler, his most significant variation on his Italian theme was to be found in his *Second Book*. Here he reasoned that of the two would-be allies, Britain and Italy, only the latter was a certain partner for a 'new' Germany. It had achieved its revolution and under fascism put its national interests to the fore. Britain, by contrast, was tainted by suspect Jewish elements in the governmental establishment.[32] Of course, this writing was unknown to Mussolini and to others, but it is interesting that on 5 June 1928 Mussolini made a speech to the Italian Senate publicly referring for the first time to the need for revision of the Paris treaties the better to ensure lasting peace. Irrespective of their views, events began to move in the direction of Mussolini and Hitler with the onset of crisis in 1929. The more open conflicts in Germany over foreign policy ensured that rightist circles were ever more attracted by the prospect of defying the Allied Powers, and that with Rome's help. The evidence for this was the fact that by 1928/29 the idea of abandoning the Tyrol was finding more acceptance in the bourgeois-rightist political circles and was no longer confined to sections of the NSDAP.[33] Important as was the Alto Adige issue in cementing ties between fascism and German rightists it would be to take a too narrow view to argue that the key to Mussolini's German policy 'lay in the Alto Adige'.[34] There remained the bedrock of Italy's hostility towards France and the fact that Germany's worsening relationship with its Locarno partner – particularly after Stresemann's death in 1929 – encouraged Mussolini to renew his efforts to win over Berlin.

These became more marked under Brüning's government. The open espousal of revision by Italy opened up a greater range of possible areas for co-operation. Both powers rejected the Briand plan for a united Europe and Italy supported the German line on the disarmament issue, against the French efforts to get security before disarmament, (p. 87). There was little doubt, however, that Mussolini hoped for more than such limited co-operation. Notwithstanding the friendly reception of Brüning on his visit to Italy in 1934, it remained a maxim in the German Foreign Office to maintain, as Curtius put it, 'friendly reserve' towards the Italian ogling. More tangible proof of

[31] Ibid., pp. 14–18, 24ff.
[32] Ibid., pp. 29 ff.
[33] Ibid., pp. 28, 497.
[34] Cassels, 'Mussolini and German nationalism', p. 156.

Italy's goodwill was required in the Wilhelmstrasse before any commitments were made against France.[35] In fact, Brüning was the victim of Italy's double-edged policy. While flirting with the German government of the moment the Italians were taking a still closer interest in the future leaders of Germany. Rome provided a not insignificant contribution to the erection of the Nazi-nationalist Harzburg front through the efforts of Guiseppe Renzetti, chief go-between of the fascists and the German Right. Göring, now a Reichstag deputy, was making daily visits to the Italian Embassy and when Hitler finally became Chancellor in 1933 at the head of a rightist coalition it was regarded by the Italians as their victory too, the breakthrough to the 'fascist era'.[36]

THE AUSTRIAN FACTOR

The real interest arises from the fact that, at the same time, Hitler's arrival in power gave urgency to the basic dilemma of German–Italian relations. Namely, to what extent was German revisionism – useful as it was to Italy's own cause – to be reconciled with Mussolini's ambitions? The question had already been dramatically posed in 1931, when Italy was thoroughly alarmed at the abortive German–Austrian Customs Union. It was also clear, from various exchanges between Rome and Berlin in 1931/32, that it would be difficult to reconcile German–Italian economic interests in South-East Europe. The area was marked out for German trade and business and began to figure more prominently in Germany's attention with the onset of the world economic crisis after 1929 (pp. 158–9). Mussolini said in June 1932 to the Austrian *Heimwehr* leader, Starhemberg, Austria must not be incorporated into a Greater Germany, which would mean that Italy had fought in vain over the Adriatic during the war. 'Trieste would cease to be Italian. That Italy can never allow. . . . If Austria ceases to exist, there will be no more order in Central Europe – great dangers will then menace Italy. An independent Austria must remain a priority for Italian foreign policy.'[37] Or as he saw the situation after

[35] Petersen, *Hitler, Mussolini*, pp. 37–8.

[36] Ibid., pp. 497–8; Elizabeth Wiskemann, *Fascism in Italy: Its Development and Influence* (London, 1969), pp. 56–7.

[37] E.R. von Starhemberg, *Between Hitler and Mussolini* (London, 1942), p. 94.

the German–Austrian Customs project of 1931: 'We can march with Germany on the Rhine but not on the Danube.'[38]

As it happened, it was to prove impossible for Mussolini to march with Germany on the Rhine and not on the Danube – the one went with the other like a horse and carriage. The quotations are, however, a convenient reminder of the conflict of interests between Germany and Italy, which did not conveniently disappear for all the ideological affinities between Nazism and fascism.[39] The Concordat negotiated with the Vatican in July 1933 helped Hitler to ease relations with the Roman Catholic Church in Germany, but it did not signal any great advance in German–Italian relations. Hitler's accession to power, with the question-mark hanging over Germany's policy for Britain and France, gave an anxious Mussolini greater immediate freedom of movement than he had had before. There seemed little reason for premature ties with Berlin. Significantly, Mussolini's version of the four-power pact (p. 88) attempted to divert Germany from the South-East towards East Europe, and its chief effect was to weaken France's standing in East Europe. Similarly, after Germany had left the League and the Disarmament Conference, Italy was to be found signing a joint declaration with Britain and France on 17 February 1934 on the need for Austria's independence. On 17 March 1934 Mussolini continued his efforts to provide a bulwark against German expansion towards South-East Europe by concluding the 'Rome protocols' with Dollfuss of Austria and Gömbös of Hungary. The three states pledged themselves to political consultation and further economic co-ordination.

Against this background there was little prospect of immediate agreement between Mussolini and Hitler when, in accordance with Hitler's wishes, the two dictators met in June 1934 – Hitler's first visit abroad since assuming power. It has been suggested that the meeting was not as disharmonious as it has sometimes been portrayed. Yet Hitler did not find much more than a quiet listener to his views.[40] Mussolini may have received the impression that Hitler was not willing to force the pace of events in Austria, although the Führer was unable to say so openly in view of his domestic audience.[41] At any rate, the *putsch* by the Austrian Nazis shortly afterwards and the murder on 25 July 1934 of the Austrian Chancellor, Dollfuss, brought a low point in German–Italian relations. By 21 August Mussolini and

[38] Petersen, *Hitler, Mussolini*, p. 50.
[39] Cf. A. Cassels, *Fascist Italy* (London, 1969), pp. 82–3.
[40] Jäckel, op. cit., p. 54.
[41] H. Graml, *Europa zwischen den Kriegen* (Munich, 1969), pp. 297–8.

the new Austrian Chancellor, Kurt von Schuschnigg, specifically reaffirmed the Rome protocols, and on 6 September 1934 Mussolini made a public speech expressing the ill-feeling between Rome and Berlin: 'Thirty centuries of history enable us to look with majestic pity at certain doctrines taught on the other side of the Alps by the descendants of people who were wholly illiterate in the days when Rome boasted a Caesar, a Virgil and an Augustus.'[42] Sour resentment was not the monopoly of the Duce. The Führer, too, was bitterly disappointed by the Italian reaction to events in Austria and it was not to be until January 1936 that Hitler drew a line under past German–Italian differences.[43]

In the intervening two years it must be said that the logic of the position of Germany and Italy reasserted itself. The period opened inauspiciously for Hitler with the continuation of Italy's *rapprochement* with the Western Powers, and in particular with the advances made in Franco-Italian relations, first under Foreign Minister Barthou and then his successor, Laval. However, the *rapprochement* with Italy was, like that between France and Russia, essentially the product of French fears over Germany; it was, like the agreement between France and Russia, as limited by long-standing realities. Admittedly, the Mussolini–Laval agreement in Rome on 7 January 1935 promised Franco-Italian co-operation in the event of any threat to Austria's independence or any attempt by Germany to remilitarise the Rhine. A gesture was made towards settling Italian–French differences in Africa when Mussolini abandoned territorial claims in Tunisia in return for France's economic disinterest in Ethiopia (except for the rail line Addis Ababa–Djibuti).[44] After the reintroduction of conscription by Germany in March 1935, Italy protested bitterly and the Stresa Front appeared a few weeks later (p. 90).

Italy did not, however, share the attachment of France to the European status quo, as had been evident enough from Mussolini's original suggestion for a four-power pact in 1933. That was proof in itself of Mussolini's readiness to entertain a far-reaching revision in Europe, provided it was in Italy's interests. In the summer of 1935, the German representative in Rome, Hassell, was speculating on the various possibilities of preventing Italy from throwing in its lot with France. There was no obvious note of urgency.[45] Indeed, the Franco-

[42] Ibid., p. 298.

[43] M. Funke, *Sanktionen und Kanonen. Hitler, Mussolini und der internationale Abessinienkonflikt, 1934–6* (Düsseldorf, 1970), p. 176.

[44] Ibid., p. 32.

[45] *DGFP*, Series C, Vol. IV, pp. 3–5. Report of 1 Aug. 1935.

Italian agreement could not conceal the fact that both powers were following opposed policies in the Balkans. Nor could it conceal the fact that Mussolini interpreted the French–Italian exchanges on Africa as a green light, as he did Britain's failure during the Stresa meeting to warn him against an adventure in Abyssinia. It is by no means clear that Laval expressed his willingness to give Mussolini a free hand in Ethiopia during their exchanges in Rome in January 1935.[46] But the Italian–Ethiopian crisis had been in progress since December 1934 and on 18 April 1935 the first Italian troops landed at Massawa, Eritrea. Throughout the summer this expeditionary force was increased to 200,000 troops. On 3 October 1935 the Italian invasion of Abyssinia began.[47]

The Italian involvement with Abyssinia is invariably regarded as the turning point in German–Italian relations, although in recent scholarly studies on the Axis and on the Abyssinian conflict there is some difference of emphasis and interpretation. Petersen's study of the Axis concluded that the alliance between the two dictators north and south of the Alps was inevitable. By contrast others stressed the continuing reserve on both sides and argued that the war simply created an 'alliance-worthy situation', which in no way had to lead to the 'Axis'.[48] Neither explanation is unduly concerned by questions about the actual timing of Mussolini's Abyssinian adventure. Both stress instead the long-term revisionism and imperialism of Italian fascism, although Petersen relates the opening of the conflict to the precise state of Germany's rearmament. The Germans were strong enough to worry Britain and France, but not yet prepared to tackle Italy's position in Central and South-East Europe.[49] From our vantage point, it is enough to note that Berlin regarded the growing embroilment of Italy with Ethiopia with some satisfaction. As early as May 1935, the Germans were aware of Italy's friendly overtures, notwithstanding the policy of the Stresa Front nor the fact that Mussolini was annoyed by the Anglo-German Naval Agreement (p. 92). The German Foreign Office interpreted Italy's approaches as evidence of Mussolini's difficulties in Africa, and Neurath stressed 'We have no

[46] E.M. Robertson, *Hitler's Prewar Policy and Military Plans* (London, 1963), p. 49; cf. the sources cited by Funke, op. cit., p. 32. note 99.

[47] For basic information on this, Angelo Del Boca, *The Ethiopian War 1935–41* (Chicago/London, 1969).

[48] Petersen, *Hitler, Mussolini*, p. 502. Unlike E. Wiskemann's earlier study, *The Rome–Berlin Axis, a History of the Relations Between Hitler and Mussolini* (London, 1949), Petersen is not prone to see Mussolini as completely dominated by Hitler's will; Funke, op. cit., p. 177.

[49] Petersen, 'Die Aussenpolitik des faschistischen Italien', p. 457.

occasion to free the Italians from this dilemma prematurely. Perhaps a situation will arise from this in which we can negotiate and solve the Austrian question with Italy.'[50]

Hitler, too, viewed the question of Italy in conjunction with that of Austria, and continued to be uneasy about the Third Reich's estrangement from Mussolini. The development was somewhat at odds with the Führer's long-standing views on German–Italian relations. Evidence of this was his insistence in late June 1935, that the Italian Ambassador to Berlin, Vittorio Cerutti, be replaced by someone more suitable – a move clearly intended to capitalise on the friendlier overtures coming from Rome. Typically, Hitler used Mussolini's unofficial go-between, Guiseppe Renzetti, to pass on his views. Mussolini's agreement to the change of personnel was prompt and Bernardo Attolico subsequently took up the Berlin post. Evidently a change of atmosphere was designed to create the conditions for a change of policies. Hitler did not of course express German lack of interest in Austria, but he made placatory noises to Renzetti on 21 June 1935, and again disclaimed personal responsibility for the abortive Nazi *putsch* in Austria in 1934. These developments did not mean that Hitler was prepared to support Mussolini unreservedly in Italy's conflict with Abyssinia. While tacitly encouraging Mussolini's Abyssinian undertaking Germany remained neutral during the conflict.[51]

THE EMERGENCE OF THE 'AXIS'

This was a perfectly logical policy for the Nazi regime. Nazi Germany's own economic predicament in 1935/36 and Hitler's continued efforts to keep on good terms with Britain argued against extensive German material aid for Italy's struggle in Africa after the imposition of economic sanctions by the League in October 1935. Nonetheless, the interest of the great powers in the Abyssinian conflict seemed to offer a welcome chance for Germany to intensify its own rearmament policies. At the back of Hitler's mind was the conviction that only a rearmed Germany could tempt Italy finally from the Western Powers.

[50] Funke, op. cit., p. 40. Cf. Hassell (Rome) to AA, 30 May 1935, *DGFP*, Series C, Vol. IV, pp. 230–4 on the change of mood in Rome about Germany.

[51] Cf. G.L. Weinberg, *The Foreign Policy of Hitler's Germany. Diplomatic Revolution in Europe 1933–6* (Chicago/London, 1970), pp. 234–5.

> A genuine understanding between the Führer and the Duce was therefore unlikely until a well-armed Germany emerged as an attractive partner for an Italy which had come under pressure. Consequently, Hitler was bound to be strongly interested in a sharpening of the Abyssinian conflict, indeed this offered a virtually ideal opportunity, to divert outside attention from Germany's rearmament, and in this way to prolong the 'truce' between Germany and the Western Powers, which Hitler urgently needed to create the preconditions for the active foreign policy he wanted.[52]

It followed also, from his friendlier overtures in the summer of 1935 and from his long-term views, that Hitler did not want to see Mussolini defeated, a rather unwelcome precedent for resistance to aggression.[53] Germany's neutrality was benevolent, although its economic relations with Italy were not intensified to the extent that Mussolini had reason to be exactly overjoyed.[54]

The aptness of Nazi Germany's Italian policy was shown by Mussolini's deteriorating relations with Britain and France during the Abyssinian crisis. If proof were needed that Mussolini's foreign policy was determined by the long-standing realities of Italy's position as a 'late power',[55] it could be given from a study of these relations. Even though Britain and France made every conceivable effort to reach agreement with Mussolini, which culminated in the abortive Hoare–Laval pact of December 1935, the Italians refused to abandon the struggle. On 28 December 1935, the Italians denounced their pact with France. It was logical, when the Italian undertaking in Abyssinia took longer than Mussolini had expected and when Italy's international position looked bleak, that overtures were again made to Berlin. On 6 January 1936, Mussolini finally told von Hassell that Italy had nothing against Austria becoming a satellite of the Reich and even went so far as to assure him that the Stresa front was finished as far as Italy was concerned, an assurance which Hitler used to draw a line under the events of 1934.[56] On 11 July 1936 a German–Austrian agreement was concluded along the lines suggested by Mussolini to Hassell in January. Germany pledged itself to respect the internal and external independence of Austria and Vienna promised to follow a 'German' foreign policy and to bring the Nazi opposition into more responsible positions.

Some historians have insisted that with the upturn in Italy's venture

[52] Funke, op. cit., p. 42.
[53] Weinberg, *Foreign Policy*, p. 236.
[54] Funke, op. cit., p. 81.
[55] Petersen, *Hitler, Mussolini*, pp. 495–6.
[56] Funke, op. cit., pp. 102–3.

in Abyssinia in February 1936, Mussolini's readiness to make concessions waned.[57] Others have implied that Italy was still half hoping for Anglo-French acceptance of her Abyssinian undertaking. However, Rome became disillusioned when in April and May Britain refused to abandon the League policy towards the Abyssinian crisis – although its actions during the conflict had not prevented an Italian victory![58] On the other hand, fears that Mussolini would not be so amenable once Italy had secured a victory in Africa, probably played a part in Hitler's decision to advance his plans to remilitarise the Rhineland. On 14 February 1936, Hitler had instructed von Hassell to speak to Mussolini and by 22 February had received general assurances that the Duce would take no action against Germany, should Hitler use the pending ratification of the Franco–Soviet pact to renounce Locarno.[59] Germany did not exactly co-ordinate the Rhineland remilitarisation with Italy. Nor did Hitler's hollow promise to the Western Powers at the time of the Rhineland crisis, that Germany was ready to rejoin the League, exactly please the Duce. Mussolini had himself considered threatening to leave the League, to pressure Britain and France into giving Italy greater freedom of movement in Africa.[60] Yet, with the successful remilitarisation of the Rhineland, indispensable prerequisite to Germany's long-term strategic planning, the scales tipped decisively in Hitler's favour. What the West could have offered Italy to offset the pull of the Third Reich thereafter appeared doubtful to say the least.

In 1936 the passivity of the Western Powers seemed more evident than ever, and strengthened the inclinations of both Hitler and Mussolini to take greater risks. Ultimately, therefore, their shared interest in flouting the principle of collective security found them following roughly parallel paths.[61] The Spanish Civil War, 'so often said at the time to be inspired by Axis collusiveness', was not so inspired.[62] Nonetheless, the conflict in Spain after General Franco's *putsch* against the legal Madrid government on 17 July 1936, greatly intensified the forces impelling Germany and Italy towards each other. Italy's prompt support of Franco was predictable. Working on the assumption that Franco had little chance of success without Italian

[57] Ibid., p. 176.
[58] Weinberg, *Foreign Policy*, p. 269.
[59] *DGFP*, Series C. Vol. IV, Doc. 579.
[60] Graml, op. cit., p. 334.
[61] Funke, op. cit., p. 177. Cf. G. Carocci, *Italian Fascism* (London, 1975), p. 122.
[62] D.C. Watt, 'The Rome–Berlin Axis. Myth and reality', *Review of Politics*, **22** (1960): 120. For studies of the civil war, S. Ellwood, *The Spanish Civil War* (London, 1991); P. Preston (ed.), *Revolution and War in Spain, 1931–1939* (London, 1984).

aid, Mussolini clearly expected to profit from an improvement in Italy's position in the Western Mediterranean. That in turn increased pressure on the French by cutting them off from North Africa in the event of future war. Inevitably, what little goodwill remained between France and Italy soon vanished. In reality, of course, Franco refused to become over-dependent on any country. In the last resort, therefore, the more Mussolini manœuvred himself into a position where he was committed for intervention, the more an alliance with Germany became a necessity; it was no longer a fall-back, as it were, to strengthen his own position in the international arena.[63]

It may well be that such considerations did not figure prominently in Hitler's original decision to intervene on Franco's behalf, although they can hardly have been entirely absent in view of his reflections on Italy and France in the 1920s. As a matter of fact, Hitler had also briefly envisaged Spain as a possible member of Germany's alliances during the 1920s,[64] but Spanish–German relations were little more than correct before 1933, and were barely changed by the Nazi seizure of power. Spain's friendship was with Britain and France above all, and until the Spanish Civil War Hitler had little opportunity to prise this relationship apart. On the night of 25–26 July, during his stay in Bayreuth for the Wagner festival, Hitler took the decision to intervene in Spain. He did so against the wishes of the German Foreign Office, which was in favour of a policy of neutrality. Instead he took the advice of the two officials of the AO in Spain who had brought Franco's request for war materials and aircraft from Morocco. These men were Adolf Langenheim, the highest Nazi dignitary in Morocco and the economic expert of the local Nazis, Johannes Bernhardt.[65] Hitler himself made a reference to the importance of Spanish raw materials, and economic interests clearly influenced in part the decision to intervene.[66]

This was not, however, the primary motive. Nor was the desire to test planes and war materials – although both economic gains and opportunities for such testing resulted from German intervention. It was Hitler's prime aim to prevent the emergence of a Spain dominated by Bolshevik influences – a not surprising fact in the year in which his anti-Bolshevik stance on the world stage became more pro-

[63] Graml, op. cit., p. 340.

[64] H.-H. Abendroth, *Hitler in der spanischen Arena. Die deutsch-spanischen Beziehungen im Spannungsfeld der europäischen Interessenpolitik vom Ausbruch des Bürgerkrieges bis zum Ausbruch des Weltkrieges* (Paderborn, 1973), p. 17.

[65] Weinberg, *Foreign Policy*, p. 288.

[66] Ibid., p. 289.

nounced. In addition, Hitler was trying to prevent the emergence of a Franco-Spanish bloc – 1936 was after all the year of the Popular Front. Hitler's motives were further clarified by his remark in November 1936 to the German chargé in Spain, Faupel:

> 'His exclusive aim was that, once the war had ended, Spain's foreign policy would be influenced neither by Paris, London or Moscow and therefore in the final conflict for the reorganisation of Europe, which was certainly to be expected, Spain would not be in the camp of Germany's enemies but most likely the friend of Germany.'[67]

This was more than enough to account for the despatch of the earliest German supplies and planes to Franco to transport the General and his followers to the Spanish mainland. If Hitler did not have any specific idea of prolonging the conflict in Spain when he reached his decision to intervene on the night of 25/26 July,[68] the general considerations outlined above ensured that he quickly realised the advantages of a protracted struggle in Spain.

Hitler was to affirm in the Hossbach memorandum of 5 November 1937 (p. 97), that the upheaval in Spain carried with it the possibility of war between Italy and the Western Powers and offered the chance for freer movement for Germany in East Europe. The risks to Hitler in supporting Franco were minimal owing to the farce of 'non-intervention' perpetrated by the other powers. An international committee to supervise this policy was set up in London in September 1936, but its chief distinction was that it made it easier for Hitler and Mussolini to intervene in Spain. Hitler received an additional bonus. The reluctance of the Western Powers materially to aid the legal government of Spain made inevitable the increase in Soviet support. In turn, this increased the aversion of France and Britain to supporting the legal Spanish government. Here was fertile ground for Hitler's efforts to be regarded as the defender against Bolshevism.[69] At a far lesser cost than Italy suffered, Germany's intervention achieved far from negligible economic gains – particularly in the shape of much-needed raw materials, including iron ore. In the winter of 1936–37 alone, Germany imported 335,513 tons of Spanish iron ore, and by the end of 1937 Britain had been replaced by Germany as the chief recipient of Spanish ores. In 1937 alone, Hisma, the organisation controlled by Bernhardt, shipped a total of 1,620,000 tons of iron ore, 956,000 tons of pyrites, 7,000 tons of tungsten, copper and

[67] Abendroth, op. cit., p. 36.
[68] Weinberg, *Foreign Policy*, p. 290.
[69] M. Muggeridge (ed.), *Ciano's Diplomatic Papers* (London, 1948), p. 87.

bronze.[70] But the main prize for Hitler remained the 'capture' of Mussolini.[71]

Dramatic evidence of this was provided by Mussolini's pointed reference for the first time on 1 November 1936, to the Rome–Berlin Axis 'round which all those European states which are animated by a desire for collaboration and peace may work together'. Mussolini's reference to the Axis followed a visit to Berlin of his son-in-law, Count Ciano, Italian Foreign Minister since July 1936. The Ciano visit had been prefaced by the exploratory mission to Mussolini of Hitler's Minister of Justice, Hans Frank, on 23 September. Apart from receiving further German reassurances about Austria, Mussolini found that Hitler 'regards the Mediterranean as a purely Italian sea. The interests of the Germans are turned towards the Baltic, which is their Mediterranean.'[72] This was more or less what Mussolini liked to hear. It was not that surprising that after Ciano had conversed with Hitler in Berlin on 24 October 1936, he was able to sign a nine-point protocol with Neurath. This covered in more detail various aspects of German–Italian co-operation.[73]

It is, of course, important to bear in mind the distinction between the 'myth and reality' of the Axis; give due weight to the mutual antagonisms and suspicions that remained between Berlin and Rome and Hitler and Mussolini.[74] However, the mutual distrust in Axis circles could hardly outweigh the shared frustration of Hitler and Mussolini at the obstacles posed by Britain and France to the respective plans for expansion of two dictators. The Axis expressed the awareness of the Italians that their own resources were simply not sufficient to allow them to dominate both South-Eastern Europe and the Mediterranean. The Axis promised in effect a delineation of spheres of interest, although these were hardly elaborated in detail. The implication was that Italy could have the Mediterranean, Germany, East Europe. It was equivalent, as one German historian has argued, to a joint declaration of war on the status quo.[75]

The meaning of the Axis was apparent from the connections drawn by Hitler between Italy's foreign policy and his own attitude towards

[70] G.T. Harper, *German Economic Policy in Spain during the Spanish Civil War, 1936/9* (The Hague, 1967), p. 88.

[71] Graml, op. cit., p. 341.

[72] Muggeridge, op. cit., pp. 43–8. But on the Mediterranean see G. Schreiber, *Marineführung und deutsch–italienische Beziehungen 1919–1944* (Stuttgart, 1978).

[73] A. Bullock, *Hitler. A Study in Tyranny* (London, 1952), pp. 321–2.

[74] D.C. Watt, 'The Rome–Berlin Axis', p. 522.

[75] Graml, op. cit., p. 341.

Britain. Hitler's uncertainty over Britain was revealed when he told Ciano in October that

> 'German and Italian rearmament is proceeding much more rapidly than rearmament in Great Britain, where it is not only a case of producing ships, guns and aeroplanes, but also of undertaking psychological rearmament, which is much longer and more difficult. In three years Germany will be ready, in four years more than ready; if five years are given, better still'.

There is no need in this chapter, even if it were possible, to attempt to trace in detail the relationship between Hitler's gradual disillusionment with Britain and the development of Italian–German relations 1936–39, any more than there is a need to revisit the series of crises in Austria and East Europe 1938–39, which were covered in Chapter 5 and which the German–Italian relationship certainly made easier for Hitler to deal with. It will be enough finally to trace the path towards the 'Pact of Steel'.

THE 'PACT OF STEEL'

Before this was concluded in May 1939, Italy joined the Anti-Comintern Pact on 6 November 1937 – a pact concluded between Germany and Japan on 25 November 1936. This agreement, formed under the guise of fighting Bolshevism, contained a secret part which committed Germany and Japan to benevolent neutrality in the event of either power being involved in a conflict with the Soviet Union. Considered by its initiators as a particularly daring step, it implicitly designated another area of expansion for the third 'fascist' power, Japan.[76] The Anti-Comintern Pact was related not only to Hitler's desire to make the Soviet Union weaker, but also to his effort to pressure Britain into an agreement with Germany (see Chapters 3 and 4). It illustrated the global nature of Hitler's viewpoint. Indeed, the most striking development thereafter was Japan's further activity against mainland China, from July 1937, which increased the risks of confrontation with the great sea powers, Britain and America. This was certainly in keeping with the policies of Ribbentrop, one of the chief supporters of the German–Japanese pact, and the man now anxious to erect the 'worldwide triangle' based on Berlin, Rome and Tokyo. Mussolini's adherence to the pact hardly boded well for a

[76] Th. Sommer, *Deutschland und Japan* (Tübingen, 1962), p. 19.

future *rapprochement* between Italy and Britain. On 11 December 1937, Italy left the League.

From such a perspective it is not easy today to view German–Italian relations after 1936 in terms of an 'empty collection of formulas' inspired by Ribbentrop, or to overemphasise the inevitable and continuing differences between Germany and Italy during the ensuing period of 'pact-making'.[77]

That Ribbentrop was anxious to include Italy in a broader pact followed from his antipathy towards Britain. Ribbentrop's entry to the German Foreign Office roughly coincided with the *Anschluss*, and while this may not have endeared him to the Italians, Austria's fate underlined the progress of Germany in relation to Italy. The *Anschluss* was among other things a logical if cynical exploitation of the situation created by the Axis. During Hitler's visit to Italy on 5–7 May 1938, Ribbentrop proposed the next step with an agreement providing for regular three-monthly meetings of foreign ministers or their deputies. In addition, Italy and Germany were to consult in the event of any threat to their common interests. There was to be a secret protocol promising military support if either signatory were involved in a war and permanent staff contacts were foreseen. Mussolini refused. A year later, however, the so-called 'Pact of Steel' concluded between Germany and Italy on 22 May 1939, committed Italy to the sort of arrangement which Mussolini had declined in 1938.[78] Article III stressed: 'If, contrary to the wishes and hopes of the High Contracting Parties, it should happen that one of them became involved in warlike complications with another Power or Powers, the other High Contracting Party would immediately come to its assistance as an ally and support it with all its military forces on land, at sea and in the air.'

There are, of course, various ways of interpreting this last phase of German–Italian relations. By far the most common approach is to show how the Germans manœuvred the Italians into accepting such a far-reaching pact. This, it is argued, was concluded under false pretences because Hitler did not reveal to the Italians until too late his intention to take not only Danzig but the whole of Poland, with the risk of general war.[79] Such an interpretation derives support from the rather low opinion held of Italy's military help by the leaders of Germany's armed forces. In a document of 26 November 1938,

[77] Watt, 'The Rome–Berlin Axis', p. 533.
[78] Ibid., p. 534.
[79] M. Toscano, *The Origins of the Pact of Steel* (Baltimore, 1967), p. 42.

Hitler's new strategic directives for staff talks with Italy foresaw the latter power playing a diversionary role in the Mediterranean, while Britain, France and Germany fought a war on France's frontiers. When the Italian–German staff talks did eventually take place on 4 April 1939, Hitler had second thoughts and ordered the deferment 'for the moment, of the military–political bases and the strategic and operational questions arising therefrom'. The Italians were convinced by the German insistence that the staff talks be on technical matters, that war was not envisaged for two or three years.[80] Only when Ciano came to Salzburg on 11 August 1939, did he find out the real nature of Germany's plans. His diary paints a graphic picture of his horror and rage at Germany's duplicity and at the German assumption that, in the coming conflict with Poland, Britain and France would stand aloof.[81] There followed the well-known Italian device of presenting the Germans with so many conditions for Italy's entry into any war that it was hoped to deter Hitler from his plans.[82]

There are, however, alternative explanations. It is, for example, misleading to seek for detailed evidence of German–Italian collaboration at every point of the way after 1936. This does less than justice to the international context in which the Axis powers operated *before* the advent of war, which imposed on Italy especially, as the weaker power, a continuing semblance of co-operation with Britain and France. Nor does it fully acknowledge the way in which the Nazi leaders tended to *assume* spheres of influence.[83] Petersen's study of the Axis and his general reflections on Italy's foreign policy in the twentieth century lend enormous weight to the belief that there was a long-term identity of interest between German and Italian nationalist/rightist forces; that Mussolini was not, as was argued earlier in this chapter merely an opportunist, but had far-reaching plans which the fascists themselves recognised and interpreted at the time. Thus G. Bortolotto in his *Storia del Fascismo*, published in Milan in 1938, wrote:

> In the very year of the conclusion of the Locarno treaties, the Duce took the first direct steps to get compensation for the unjust treatment of Italy at the Versailles peace negotiations. After confidential negotiations with Britain, Mussolini signed a protocol which dealt with the Ethiopian legacy. From that time the Duce worked ceaselessly to prepare a new

[80] Watt, 'Rome–Berlin Axis', pp. 536–7.

[81] For the talks between Ciano and the Germans, 12–13 August 1939, *DGFP*, Series D, Vol. VII, Docs. 43, 47.

[82] *DGFP*, Series D, Vol. VII, Doc. 301.

[83] Cf. Toscano, op. cit., p. 330.

> undertaking. To realise the fascist state in the full sense of the word means to create an empire.[84]

From such a vantage point, the fluctuations in German–Italian relations in the 1930s appear in a different light: 1936 was indeed the turning point, bringing as it were the institutionalisation of the German–Italian community of interest. The Abyssinian crisis had in any case already wrecked the Anglo–Italian *Entente*.[85] Although flirtations between Rome and the Western Powers form a counter-point, they were not the main theme of the years 1936–39. Italy's 'mediation' at Munich, its participation thereafter in the share-out of South-East Europe, its attack on Albania in 1939 in the wake of Hitler's Prague coup, all combine, as did the conclusion of the 'Pact of Steel' itself, to convince the observer that Mussolini's Italy *was* indeed tied to Hitler's Germany. Had Mussolini wanted to exploit any freedom of movement created by the growing conflict between Germany and the Western Powers in 1938/39, he had only to take his eyes off British and French interests in Africa and the Mediterranean. This we know he did not do, probably could not do. In view of this, the fact that the Germans did not tell all to the Italians in the last years of peace shows only that the Nazi regime was as selfishly pursuing its own interests as was the fascist government beyond the Alps. It did not mean that Hitler had no need for Italy's support in a war, although he began the conflict without it. No doubt Mussolini and his entourage were struck by Hitler's mistaken assumption during 1939, but characteristically – that is not simply following Hitler but following Italian lines too – Italy soon threw itself into the fray after the fall of its long-term enemy, France. Neurath was right, after all.

[84] Petersen, 'Die Aussenpolitik des faschistischen Italien', pp. 455–6.
[85] A. Cassels, *Fascist Italy*, p. 90.

PART THREE
Conclusion

CHAPTER SEVEN

Hitler's Place in German Foreign Policy?

The question of Hitler's place in German foreign policy was already being asked in the 1930s, but it was dramatically revived by Fritz Fischer's book on the First World War, published in 1961.[1] The 'Fischer debate' broadened into one concerning continuities in German history. One important result of this debate has been the greater in-depth examination of the domestic/political structures of the German state as it existed between 1871 and 1945. The central theme of such studies is easy to identify. On the one hand, it is the determined survival of an archaic social structure based on privilege and wealth. The extent to which the powerful conservative classes of Germany, landed and industrial, were able to retain power determined in the last resort the limits of reform. Their hold was not broken in 1918/19 and they played a crucial role in bringing Hitler to power in 1933. Hitler 'seemed to them to be the right servant to carry out their aspirations'.[2]

On the other hand, Hitler's success was also the outcome of growing support from Germany's petit bourgeoisie in the face of economic misery. Their demands, together with those of the conservative sectors of German society accentuated the pressures on Weimar governments to adopt dramatic foreign policy postures. Foreign successes were the 'drug' to divert attention from domestic ills, the hoped-for means to 'integrate' German society. In principle, it has been argued, 'Hitler's programme integrated all the political demands, economic requirements and socio-political expectations in German society since the days of Bismarck.'[3]

[1] Translated as *Germany's Aims in the First World War* (London, 1967).
[2] K. Hildebrand, *The Foreign Policy of the Third Reich* (London, 1973), p. 144.
[3] Ibid., p. 146.

Fruitful as it was in raising questions about the interaction of domestic and foreign policy in the German state, the model of explanation so crudely outlined above tended to obscure other important aspects of Germany's foreign policy. It became a powerful machine in its own right, making it increasingly difficult to give due attention to other 'continuities' in Germany's history. These were admittedly referred to, but still often received only token consideration in writing on Germany's foreign policy. Although such an explanatory framework brought out the significance of comparisons between 'Germany's role' in the First and Second World Wars, it threatened to distort the study of the Weimar Republic's foreign policy; it correctly argued that Hitler was *not* simply an 'interlude' in Germany's history and foreign policy, but implied, wrongly, that Stresemann was.[4]

This was more difficult to sustain once historians began to suggest, partly in reaction to Fischer and his followers, that similarities existed between the foreign policy of the Weimar Republic and the then West German state. It followed that the foreign policy of the Federal Republic, with its markedly realistic attempt to coexist between East and West, while much more part of the Western bloc than it ever was after 1919, was as rooted in Germany's past as was Hitler's policy.[5]

In other words, it is all too easy to exaggerate the similarities between German policy before 1914 and before 1939 and this also applies to comparisons between German policies 1914–18 and 1939–45, when the conditions of war and geography drew attention to obvious strategic continuities in the Reich's history.[6] Here we wish to emphasise, however, the racist and revolutionary ideology which underpinned Hitlerian expansion, and which distinguished it from earlier episodes in German history. Ironically, some of those very German historians who have stressed the continuities in German foreign policy 1871–1945 were most incensed by A.J.P. Taylor's suggestion that Hitler was just another German statesman. What Taylor did above all in his book, *Origins of the Second World War*, was to redirect attention to the comparative international context in which Hitler functioned. It is precisely this comparative context, however, which brings out more obviously the important differences between the Weimar Republic's foreign policies and those of Hitlerian Germany.

[4] Ibid., p. 142.

[5] G.B. Benecke, *Society and Politics in Germany, 1500–1750* (London, 1974).

[6] Cf. K. Megerle, *Deutsche Aussenpolitik 1925. Ansatz zu aktiven Revisionismus* (Frankfurt am Main, 1974), p. 131.

This is because such a context reveals most effectively how Hitler deliberately exploited other 'continuities', namely those in British, French, Russian, Italian and East European history, in order to launch his own foreign policy 'programme'. Doubts about how far Germany's leaders in the First World War can be said to have had anything comparable in the way of a 'programme' also need to be expressed more forcefully when comparisons are made between Germany in the First and Second World Wars. Although Hitler's foreign policy 'integrated', or sought to integrate, the component parts of German society, and although it overlapped in places with the traditional aspirations of the conservative establishment, of the nationalists and so forth, it could not be deduced in its entirety from such premises. It was more, far more than the sum of any of these parts, otherwise there would not have been the strains there were in Germany after 1933; there would have been no opposition, even if admittedly hamstrung by its own equivocal stance on expansionism, no discomfort, no desperate leaps forward, no risky foreign policy gambles to paper over yawning cracks in the domestic structure of the Third Reich. These there were in plenty.

Hitler's views on the Western Powers in the 1920s can certainly be represented in some respects as part of the mainstream of revisionism in Germany after the Treaty of Versailles. His desire for a war of revenge against France found plenty of support from other nationalists and Army leaders, and in many ways it would have been surprising if this had not been the case after four years of war followed smartly by a painful defeat. Surprising, that is, within the framework of European nationalism in the early twentieth century. Nor was Hitler's decision to seek accommodation with Britain exactly a novel one. As we saw, many in the Weimar Republic hoped that Britain's goodwill could be used to Germany's advantage. Both Wirth and Stresemann played this card, but they were also aware that it had a limited application. Both realised that fairly well-defined boundaries were set by France's readiness for compromise. It was for such reasons that Stresemann attached so much weight to reaching an understanding with France. To regard Britain as an ally in a war against France would have been inconceivable to any of the Weimar governments. Stresemann and Hitler drew diametrically opposed conclusions from the Ruhr crisis of 1923.

By the end of the 1920s the gap between Stresemann's diplomacy and that favoured by Hitler was still considerable. Although the rising tide of nationalism in Germany rapidly undermined the vision of most of the Locarno protagonists, there was still enough room for international co-operation to revise the reparation plan and to launch hopeful initiatives for closer economic and political integration in Europe. This only ten years after the most painful confrontations between victor and vanquished. Large bodies of political opinion in Germany, France and Great Britain endorsed this process of *rapprochement*. True, Brüning's policies towards the West soon reflected the political radicalisation inside Germany and more than confirmed the depth of anti-Versailles sentiment in the Republic. True, Hitler has rightly been shown to have consciously built on this and to have exploited the 'continuities' of Germany's situation to pose as a traditional German statesman. The fact that he felt obliged to adopt this procedure is, paradoxically, also evidence of the continuing strength of the ideal of international co-operation which Stresemann and others had generated.

There remains the inescapable fact that within a very short space of time Hitler had shattered the illusions of the mid-1920s. The long-standing quest for great-power status in the German state was freed from the restraints which Weimar governments had managed to impose in the interests of realism; freed from the attempt to negotiate in common with the Western Powers for a larger German slice of the international spoils. What attempts were made at 'co-operation' by Hitler served only to free Germany from *any* restraints. The startling differences between this process and what had been attempted by Germany between 1919 and 1929, even 1933, were confirmed by the *continuing* efforts of Britain and France to resurrect the corpse of Locarno. Only when such continuities are put alongside the Third Reich's policies can we fully understand the break in Germany's policies.

This is of course far from exempting from blame German policy-makers in the Weimar Republic. It simply emphasises the degree to which National Socialist foreign policy was able to transform many of Germany's traditional demands. This point becomes more striking when we take note of the relationship seen by Hitler between Germany's western policies and those towards the Soviet Union. Of course, Hitler's '*Ostimperium*' had its roots in Germany's eastern policies during the First World War – Brest-Litovsk lived again, as it were, in Hitler's world of ideas. Like the German war leaders of 1914–18, Hitler embraced the logic of German geography and reasoned that only a Germany made stronger by the acquisition of land and resources in the east could withstand a lengthy conflict with the 'world powers'. The nature of Hitler's vision, however, was very different from that of his Wilhelmine predecessors. Hitler's anti-

Bolshevism and the dependence of the Third Reich on gains in the east to maintain the Nazi revolution make it impossible to take the comparison too far. The First World War leaders followed an expansionist policy in the east primarily to help them preserve a conservative reactionary status quo, not a racially driven revolution of German then European and, ultimately, world society! Still less apt are some of the comparisons made between the Weimar Republic's Russian policies and those of the Third Reich.

The most significant feature of the Weimar Republic's Russian policies in the long term might well be the progress that was achieved in attempting to integrate Germany's policies towards the West and East. Indeed, the balance of domestic forces in Germany made this attempt imperative. With the moderate groups behind the 'Weimar coalition' heavily committed to co-operation with the West and German rightists and nationalists equally determined not to give up the Russian connections, Rapallo and Locarno were two rather inescapable landmarks and, from the present vantage point, appropriate, too, to international realities. Those historians who have drawn a line linking Rapallo with the Nazi–Soviet Non-Aggression Pact of 1939 have played down the not unimportant point that the latter agreement was, in fact, a prelude to attacking the Soviet Union! As Hitler said: 'Everything I do is directed against Russia; if the West is too stupid and blind to grasp this, I shall be forced to reach agreement with the Russians, to attack the West and then, after its defeat, turn against the Soviet Union with my combined forces.' After all, that is precisely what he did.

In this respect the argument that both the Rapallo agreement of April 1922 and the Nazi–Soviet pact of 1939 were made at the expense of the states between Germany and Russia needs to be qualified. Was the 1939 agreement, with its accompanying secret arrangements for delimiting German and Soviet spheres of interest in East Europe really to be seen as the formulation of a new order already implicit in the Rapallo 'partnership'? The fate of Poland as a result of the Nazi–Soviet Non-Aggression Pact provides at first glance persuasive evidence for such an interpretation. However, to accept this without reservations is to ignore the complexity of the realities created in East Europe after 1919. Like it or not, the economic and political forces in the European system made inevitable a resurgence of Germany's traditional influence in East and Central Europe, and this is bound to happen again now that Germany is reunited. As we argued, Weimar governments were hardly unaware of the political advantages to be derived from economic penetration. At the same time, neither the policies of the East European states themselves nor the policies of the Western Powers were able or likely to provide a feasible alternative to Germany's long-term revival. From an East European perspective, Germany remained a great power even in 1919.

This did not have to be entirely harmful. Proof of this was provided by the tacit acceptance by the Western Powers of Germany's dominating economic role in the 'lands between'. The Locarno arrangements also revealed the effort behind the Weimar Republic's moderate revisionist strategy to extend co-operation with the Western Powers to embrace East Europe. This was indeed very much on Germany's own terms but the progress, in relative terms, of German–East European relations 1919–29 threw into relief the sort of perspectives that were well and truly absent after 1933, but which reappeared painfully after the Second World War. In the 1920s the East European states also faced the same problem as Germany in the realm of East–West relations. They all had to reach agreements and to develop ties with the West, while preserving a tolerable relationship with the Soviet Union. In the 1930s British and French governments tried to preserve something of this arrangement. They preferred the inevitable and growing German presence in East Europe not to upset the interests of the continent as a whole.

Hitler's conceptions made this quite impossible. The states in the east were there to provide launching-pads for grander adventures and reservoirs of material to fuel Germany's continuing development. The sort of economic penetration practised by the Third Reich in 'East Europe' had recognisable antecedents in the Weimar Republic's policies, but became, as we saw, something more, and served different ends. National Socialist policies went further even than the grandiose nineteenth-century dreams of *Mitteleurope* because they were made to serve a dangerous revolutionary order. As we also suggested, this transformed the problem of the German minorities in the lands between, although once again some of the roots of Hitler's policies towards the *Auslandsdeutsche* may be found in the Weimar era.

Hitler himself assumed, correctly as it turned out, that the nature of Italian fascism made Italy a natural ally for a Nazi Germany. The long-term antipathy between Italy and France gave the two 'fascist' states a more certain foundation for friendship and co-operation. By contrast, Franco-Italian hostility in the 1920s brought the Weimar governments to the conclusion that Italy was not to be encouraged in case it threatened to endanger the process of Germany's *rapprochement* with the Western Powers. Although the Republic's foreign policy-makers accepted the importance of Italy for future developments in

South-East Europe, it remains difficult to see how German–Italian differences in the Balkans could have been reconciled without the dramatic change effected in German–Italian relations after 1933. This followed from Hitler's determination to pursue an expansionist policy which encouraged Mussolini's own tendency to 'forward' policies, but in time presented the Duce with an ever-diminishing range of alternatives from which to choose. Nevertheless, Mussolini's Italy put itself in Germany's path in the first place and the respective personalities of Mussolini and Hitler played a crucial role in the formation of the 'Axis'.

Their own prominent roles in the formation of their states' respective foreign policies underlined the real novelty of the 1930s in the international arena: that is the pursuit of ends by states for whom ideology and power politics were inextricably tied together. In the 1930s Hitler set out to change realities in the light of a global view which had no room for such accommodation. In the 1920s there was at least a more or less continuous adjustment to changing international realities and German foreign policy pursued a course which seemed likely for a time to strike an acceptable balance between 'German' and 'European' interests. The probability of that balance being struck again today by a reunited Germany is very high. For this reason it is possible to view without alarm the leading German role in the European-wide task of reconstruction which has arisen from the collapse of the former Soviet Union.

Quoting Himmler's view in January 1944 that a Greater Germany would emerge from the war as Europe's world power and would then have the task of reorganising the other peoples of Europe, Hans-Adolf Jacobsen's fine study of Nazi foreign policy observed:

> These and similar utterances, as well as the practice of national socialist policy of conquest and destruction in Europe, prove once again, how inextricably tied together were the foundations (until 1933), the tactics (until 1939) and the aims of National Socialist foreign policy (until 1943) – logical consequences of the Nazi 'Weltanschauung'. Looked at historically, it may therefore be more sensible to describe the *foreign policy of Germany after 1933* as *National Socialist foreign policy,* in that this fateful year and the further development of German history until the war's end, should be seen *less in the light of continuity* but rather *in terms of a revolutionary break.*

Importantly, Jacobsen recognised some of the similarities between parts of the Nazi policy and more general aims of nineteenth- and twentieth-century Germany, but this did not lessen the force of his final judgement. Hopefully, this present short study will leave the reader with enough interest to pursue in more detail exactly how and why Nazi foreign policy differed from that of the Weimar Republic. All we have done is to put the 1920s and the 1930s together and would like to urge in conclusion that this is the best way to understand both.

Bibliographical Essay

The footnotes to this book contain detailed references to foreign language literature and source materials on German foreign policy in this century. The present essay therefore confines itself to a brief discussion of relatively recent and useful books in English.

GENERAL

Studies providing background information on German foreign policy abound. An informative general history of the Weimar Republic, giving bibliographic guidance and an indication of major historical controversies, is E. Kolb's, *The Weimar Republic* (London, 1988). For the final stages of the Republic, see J. von Krüdener (ed.), *Economic Crisis and Political Collapse. The Weimar Republic 1924–1933* (Oxford, 1988) and the important study by H. James, *The German Slump. Politics and Economics, 1924–1936*, (Oxford, 1984). Information on political parties and foreign policy is in E.L. Evans, *The German Centre Party 1870–1933* (Illinois, 1981); B.B. Frye, *Liberal Democrats in the Weimar Republic. The History of the German Democratic Party and the German State Party* (Carbondale, 1985); R.P. Grathwol, *Stresemann and the DNVP. Reconciliation or Revenge in German Foreign Policy 1924–1928* (Kansas, 1980); L.E. Jones, *German Liberalism and the Dissolution of the Weimar Party System* (London, 1988); R. Breitman, *German Socialism and Weimar Democracy* (Chapel Hill, 1981).

The domestic context of German policy has even fuller coverage for the 1930s. K.D. Bracher's *The German Dictatorship. The Origins,*

Structure and Consequences of National Socialism (London, 1971) is still worth consulting, but perhaps more challenging ideas are in M. Broszat, *The Hitler State. The Foundation and Development of the Internal Structure of the Third Reich* (London, 1981). H.W. Koch (ed.) *Aspects of the Third Reich* (London, 1985), also has essays on foreign policy. A number of historiographical surveys of the literature provide further guidance. These include: I. Kershaw, *The Nazi Dictatorship. Problems and Perspectives of Interpretation* (London, 1985); J. Hiden, J. Farquharson, *Explaining Hitler's Germany. Historians and the Third Reich* (2nd edn, London, 1989); K. Hildebrand, *The Third Reich* (London, 1984). R.J. Evans, *In Hitler's Shadow. West German Historians and the Attempt to Escape from the Nazi Past* (London, 1989), has been overtaken, as it were, by the reunification of Germany, but his book provokes thought.

General surveys of the foreign policy of Germany for the interwar period include, for the 1920s, M. Lee and W. Michalka, *German Foreign Policy 1917–1933. Continuity or Break* (Leamington Spa, 1987). This is heavy going but touches on most of the key issues. K. Hildebrand's well-written *German Foreign Policy from Bismarck to Adenauer. The Limits of Statecraft* (London, 1989), covers more ground and is preferable to his *The Foreign Policy of the Third Reich* (London, 1973). The late W. Carr's fine book, *Arms, Autarky and Aggression. A Study in German Foreign Policy 1933–1939* (London, 1973), still serves well as an introduction. Note also G. Weinberg, *The Foreign Policy of Hitler's Germany, 1937–1939* (Chicago, 1980). Richard Overy's elegant work spans foreign policy and economic issues and his *Goering, The 'Iron' Man* (London, 1984) is essential reading. His concise *The Nazi Economic Recovery 1932–1938* (London, 1982) is a good starting point for economic issues, and can be supplemented by other detailed studies, including J.R. Gillingham, *Ruhr Coal, Hitler and Europe. Industry and Politics in the Third Reich* (London, 1985) and P. Hayes, *Industry and Ideology. I.G. Farben in the Nazi Era*, (Cambridge, 1987).

Since the first edition of the present book a number of new surveys of the origins of the Second World War have appeared, most of which introduce key debates of recent years. P.M.H. Bell's *The Origins of the Second World War in Europe* (London, 1986), is highly readable as well as reliable. So too is W. Carr's *Poland to Pearl Harbor. The making of the Second World War* (London, 1985). The two volumes complement each other well. The uproar which A.J.P. Taylor's book on war origins caused is recalled in G. Martel (ed.), *The Origins of the Second World War Reconsidered. The A.J.P. Taylor Debate after Twenty-Five*

Years (London, 1986). An enviably well-argued account of the final months of peace is provided by D. C. Watt, *How War Came. The Immediate Origins of the Second World War, 1938–1939* (paper edn, London, 1991).

D.C. Watt's extended essay, *Too Serious a Business. European Armed Forces and the Approach to the Second World War* (London, 1975), highlights, among other things, strategic issues underlying German foreign policy between the wars. For these see also V.R. Berghahn, *Militarism. The History of an International Debate 1861–1979* (Leamington Spa, 1981), and the stimulating and clear study by W. Murray, *The Change in the European Balance of Power 1938–1939. The path to Ruin* (New Jersey, 1984).

On Hitler and his ideas there is much to choose from. Ian Kershaw's short but reflective book, *Hitler* (London, 1990), is to be recommended, although it shows little interest in foreign policy as such. In that respect E. Jäckel's earlier, *Hitler's Weltanschauung. A Blueprint for Power* (Connecticut, 1972) is still essential reading, as is Jäckel's *Hitler in History* (Hannover, New Hampshire, 1984). N. Rich stresses the importance of ideology in National Socialist foreign policy, *Hitler's War Aims. Ideology, the Nazi State and the Course of Expansion* (2 vols, London, 1973–74). G. Stoakes has written a rather stolid but undeniably full discussion of the origin of Hitler's ideas, *Hitler and the Quest for World Dominion. Nazi Ideology and Foreign Policy in the 1920s* (Leamington Spa, 1986).

THE PEACE SETTLEMENT

G. Schultze's *Revolutions and Peace Treaties* (London, 1972), remains one of the most useful general introductions to the postwar settlement, and does not seem to have dated as much as A.J. Mayer's massive *Politics and Diplomacy of Peacemaking. Containment and Counterrevolution at Versailles, 1918–1919* (London, 1968). A.P. Adamthwaite is excellent on *The Lost Peace 1918–1939. International Relations in Europe* (London, 1980), and is more appealing than R. Henig, *Versailles and After. Europe 1919–1933* (London, 1984). A key issue of the peace is considered by L.S. Jaffe, *The Decision to Disarm Germany. British Policy Towards Postwar German Disarmament 1914–1919* (London, 1985). But the best writing on the subject is to be found in the work of German historians, notably that of P. Krüger (see Introduction). For an interesting link between Versailles and the

1930s, A. Lentin, *Guilt at Versailles. Lloyd George and the Pre-history of Appeasement* (London, 1985).

GERMANY, BRITAIN AND FRANCE

There remains a need for a major study of German–Allied relations for the interwar years which takes full account of newer documentation and, above all, offers a more balanced assessment of the differences which existed between Paris and London on the subject of Germany after 1918.

F.L. Carsten, *Britain and the Weimar Republic* (London, 1984), is a study based on extensive extracts from the British Public Record Office. A major problem of German–Allied relations during the 1920s, reparations, is outlined by B. Kent, *The Spoils of War. The Politics, Economics and Diplomacy of Reparations 1918–1932* (Oxford, 1989), but indispensable is S. Schuker, *The End of French Predominance in Europe. The Financial Crisis of 1924 and the Adoption of the Dawes Plan* (North Carolina, 1976).

There are a number of major studies of British foreign policy which at the same time illuminate German foreign relations. M. Howard's brilliant, *The Continental Commitment. The Dilemma of British Defence Policy in the Era of Two World Wars* (paper edn, London, 1974), has stood the test of time. A. Orde, *British Policy and European Reconstruction after the First World War* (Cambridge, 1991); G.C. Peden, *Keynes, the Treasury and British Economic Policy* (London, 1988) and G. Schmidt, *The Politics and Economics of Appeasement. British Foreign Policy in the 1930s* (Oxford, 1986), provide insights into Britain's difficulties in responding to the challenge of Germany. A pro-French, anti-British account of the interwar years is C. Bloch, *Le IIIe Reich et le Monde* (Paris, 1986), while A. Adamthwaite, *France and the Coming of the Second World War, 1936–9* (London, 1977), is less provocative but more reliable.

Relevant strategic issues are examined by B.R. Posen, *The Sources of Military Doctrine. France, Britain and Germany between the World Wars* (London/New York, 1984); U. Bialer, *The Shadow of the Bomber. The Fear of Air Attacks and British Politics 1932–1939* (London, 1980); B. Bond, *British Military Policy between the Two World Wars* (Oxford, 1980) and J. Gooch, *The Prospect of War. Studies in British Defence Policy 1847–1942* (London, 1981). The title of P. Kennedy's general overview, *The Realities behind Diplomacy. Background Influences on British External Policy 1865–1980* (London, 1981), speaks for itself.

GERMANY AND RUSSIA

There is an enormous literature on the subject of German–Russian relations, particularly for the years immediately following the First World War. Much of this literature, however, now seems quaint, overdramatising as it did the earliest contacts between the Versailles 'outcast', Germany and the ostracised Soviet regime. The collapse of the USSR and the re-emergence of a united Germany offer major opportunities to re-examine the 1920s, when German policy in East Europe was perfectly capable of launching constructive and helpful initiatives beneath the public rhetoric of revisionism.

Most of the studies of the 1920s which have lately attempted a balanced discussion of Weimar–Soviet relations are in German. Hardly any recent attempts in English to tackle the subject have been satisfactory, as witness the hastily compiled and unsubtle analysis offered by the collective of R.H. Haigh, D.S. Morris and A.R. Peters, *German–Soviet Relations in the Weimar Era. Friendship from Necessity* (London, 1985) and *The Years of Triumph. German Diplomatic and Military Policy 1933–1941* (London, 1986). An American study of *The Genoa Conference. European Diplomacy 1921–1922* (North Carolina, 1984) by C. Fink must count as another lost opportunity to reassess a major episode in Weimar–Soviet relations, although it is very detailed. The English reader could turn to H. Pogge von Strandmann, 'Rapallo – strategy in preventive diplomacy: new sources and new interpretations', in V.R. Berghahn, M. Kitchen (eds), *Germany in the Age of Total War* (London, 1981), pp. 123–46, which at least gets behind some of the myths of Weimar–Soviet relations.

An older and sensible study is that by W. Lacqueur, *Germany and Russia. A Century of Conflict* (London, 1965). A memoir–history which can be consulted with profit and which spans the interwar period is G. Hilger, A.J. Meyer, *The Incompatible Allies* (New York, 1971). Juri Hochman, *The Soviet Union and the Failure of Collective Security, 1934–1938* (New York, 1984), is detailed but suffers from a determination to put most of the blame on the Soviet Union for the failure of collective security. The most balanced account, and one which emphasises the diversity of opinion inside the Soviet policy-making élite, is that by J. Haslam, *The Soviet Union and the*

Struggle for Collective Security in Europe, 1933–1939 (New York, 1984).

GERMANY AND EAST EUROPE

An older study, that by C.A. Macartney and A.W. Palmer, *Independent Eastern Europe* (London, 1962), is valuable as a general point of reference, although like many general books on 'East Europe' it has little to say on the Baltic states. This is true, too, of A. Polonsky's otherwise excellent short account, *The Little Dictators. The History of East Europe since 1918* (London, 1975). R. Okey, *Eastern Europe 1740–1985. Feudalism to Communism* (2nd edn, London, 1986,) is readable, but still more so is R. Pearson, *National Minorities in Eastern Europe 1848–1944* (London, 1983). I.T. Berend, *The Crisis Zone of Europe. An Interpretation of East Central European History in the First Half of the Twentieth Century* (Cambridge, 1986), has, like the other general books, a great deal of information about German policies.

As with Soviet–German relations in the interwar period, many of the books on Germany and East Europe – infected as they often were by the tensions of the Cold War – now look badly dated. An unusually fair discussion of *German–Polish Relations 1918–1933* (Baltimore and London, 1971), is offered by H. von Riekoff. Fairness also characterises F.G. Campbell's, *Confrontation in Central Europe. Weimar Germany and Czechoslovakia* (Chicago and London, 1975). See also S. Suval, *The* Anschluss *Question in the Weimar Era. A Study of Nationalism in Germany and Austria* (Baltimore/London, 1974) and F.L. Carsten, *The first Austrian Republic 1918–1938* (London, 1986). For the Baltic region in the 1920s, H.I. Rodgers, *Search for Security. A Study in Baltic Diplomacy 1920–1934* (Hamden, Connecticut, 1975) and J. Hiden, *The Baltic States and Weimar Ostpolitik* (Cambridge, 1987). The Danzig issue is covered by C. Kimmich, *The Free City. Danzig and German Foreign Policy 1919–1934* (New Haven, London, 1968).

For the 1930s, M. Burleigh, *Germany turns Eastwards. A study of Ostforschung in the Third Reich* (Cambridge, London, 1988) offers an interesting approach. A valuable general study is L. Radice, *Prelude to Appeasement. East Central European Diplomacy in the Early 1930s* (Boulder, Colorado, 1981). N. Levine's, *Hitler's Free City. A History of the Nazi Party in Danzig, 1925–1939* (Chicago, 1973) is augmented by the provocative work of A. Prazmowska, *Britain, Poland and the*

Eastern Front, 1939 (Cambridge, 1988). On Czechoslovakia, J.F.N. Bradley, *A Short History of Czechoslovakia* (Edinburgh, 1978); R.M. Smelser, *The Sudeten Problem 1933–1938.* Volkstumspolitik *and the Formation of Nazi Foreign Policy* (Folkestone, 1975), and J.W. Bruegel, *Czechoslovakia before Munich* (Cambridge, 1973). For South-East Europe, W.S. Grenzebach, Jr, *Germany's Informal Empire in East Central Europe. German Economic Policy towards Yugoslavia and Rumania, 1933–1939* (Stuttgart, 1988). For the Baltic region at this time, consult J. Hiden, P. Salmon, *The Baltic Nations and Europe. Estonia, Latvia and Lithuania in the Twentieth Century* (London, 1991), as well as J. Hiden, T. Lane (eds), *The Baltic and the Outbreak of the Second World War* (Cambridge, 1992).

GERMANY AND ITALY

A. Cassels' early account, *Fascist Italy* (London, 1969) must still be mentioned precisely because it is interesting on foreign policy. A number of newer studies are also helpful, including P. Brooker, *The Faces of Fraternalism. Nazi Germany, Fascist Italy and Imperial Japan* (Oxford, 1991); M. Clark, *Modern Italy 1871–1982* (London, 1984). Books concentrating on foreign issues include M. Toscano, *The Origins of the Pact of Steel* (Baltimore, 1967); M. Knox, *Mussolini Unleashed. Politics and Strategy in Fascist Italy's Last War 1939–1941* (Cambridge, 1984). An overview is provided by C.J. Lowe, F. Marzar, *Italian Foreign Policy, 1870–1940* (London, 1975).

On Spain and its civil war, M. Blinkhorn, *The Spanish Civil War* (London, 1987), is a short but authoritative account. A recent study is by S. Ellwood, *The Spanish Civil War* (London, 1991), and much of interest is to be found in P. Preston (ed.), *Revolution and War in Spain, 1931–1939* (London, 1984.

Tables and Map

Table 1 Gross national product and military expenditure in Germany, the United States and England, 1929–45

Year	*Germany (billions RM)*			*United States (billions $)*			*Great Britain (billions £)*		
	GNP	*Million expended*	*per cent*	*GNP*	*Million expended*	*per cent*	*National income*	*Million expended*	*per cent*
1929	89	0.8	1	104	0.7	1	4.2	0.1	2
1932	58	0.8	1	59	0.6	1		0.1	
1933	59	1.9	3	56	0.5	1	3.7	0.1	3
1934	67	4.1	6	65	0.7	1	3.9	0.1	3
1935	74	6.0	8	73	0.9	1	4.1	0.1	2
1936	83	10.9	13	83	0.9	1	4.4	0.2	5
1937	93	11.7	13	91	1.0	1	4.6	0.3	7
1938	105	17.2	17	85	1.0	1	4.8	0.4	8
1939	130	30.0	23	91	1.3	1	5.0	1.1	22
1940	141	53.0	38	101	2.2	2	6.0	3.2	53
1941	152	71.0	47	126	13.8	11	6.8	4.1	60
1942	165	91.0	55	159	49.6	31	7.5	4.8	64
1943	184	112.0	61	193	80.4	42	8.0	5.0	63
1944				211	88.6	42	8.2	5.1	62
1945				214	75.9	36	8.3	4.4	53

From Berenice A. Carroll, *Design for Total War. Arms and Economics in the Third Reich* (The Hague/Paris, 1968), p. 184. (Carroll discusses the statistics fully in a statistical appendix.)

Table 2 The balance of power in Europe, 1939

	*Population (thousands)**	*National income ($m)**	*Reserves (million)*	*Peacetime armies (million)*	*Aircraft (first line)*	*Destroyers*	*Sub-marines*
Great Britain	47,692	23,550	0.4	0.22	2,075	184	58
France	41,600	10,296	4.6	0.8	600	28	70
USSR	167,300	31,410	12.0†	1.7†	5,000†	28	150
USA	129,825	67,600	**	0.19	800	181	99
Poland	34,662	3,189	1.5	0.29	390	4	5
Germany	68,424	33,347	2.2	0.8	4,500†	17	56
Italy	43,779	6,895	4.8	0.8	1,500††	60	100
Japan	70,590	5,700	2.4†	0.32†	1,980	113	53

* 1938 † approximate
** not available †† 1940

For comparisons

Table 3 The decline of Germany's foreign trade with its future opponents

	Percentage of total German imports				*Percentage of total German exports*			
	1929	*1932*	*1935*	*1938*	1929	1932	1935	1938
West Europe	26.2	31.9	26.1	20.8	15.7	15.1	14.1	11.9
Great Britain	9.7	7.8	8.8	6.7	6.4	5.5	6.2	5.2
USA	7.4	4.9	4.0	2.8	13.3	12.7	5.8	7.4

Based on Wolfram Fischer, *Deutsche Wirtschaftspolitik 1918–1945* (3rd edn, Opladen, 1968), p. 110.

Compare, too, these figures for German–Russian trade:

German imports (millions RM)					*German exports (millions RM)*				
1932	1935	1936	1937	1938	1932	1935	1936	1937	1938
271	215	93	65	47	626	39	126	117	32

Based on Hans-Erich Volkmann, 'Aussenhandel und Aufrüstung in Deutschland 1933 bis 1939', in Friedrich Forstmeir and Hans-Erich Volkmann (eds), *Wirtschaft und Rüstung am Vorabend des Zweiten Weltkrieges* (Düsseldorf, 1975), p. 102.

Compare these figures with those in Table 6.

Table 4 Percentage of Czechoslovak foreign trade with Germany

Year	*Exports*	*Imports*
1931	18.1	26.9
1932	19.6	22.9
1933	19.1	19.5
1934	25.3	16.4
1935	15.4	17.0
1936	15.3	17.3

From A. Polonsky, *The Little Dictators. The History of East Europe since 1918* (London, 1975), p. 181.

Table 5 Percentage of Poland's trade with Germany

Year	*Exports*	*Imports*
1928	34.2	26.8
1932	16.2	20.1
1934	16.6	13.6
1938	24.1	23.0

(Figures for 1938 include Austria.) From Polonsky, op. cit., p. 181.

Table 6 Germany's percentual share in the trade of the states of South-East Europe

	1929	*1930*	*1931*	*1932*	*1933*	*1934*	*1935*	*1936*	*1937*	*1938*
Hungary										
Imports	20.0	21.0	24.4	22.5	19.7	18.3	22.7	26.0	25.9	40.9
Exports	11.7	10.2	12.7	15.2	11.2	22.2	23.9	22.8	24.0	40.0
Romania										
Imports	24.1	25.1	29.1	23.6	18.6	15.5	23.8	36.1	28.9	40.0
Exports	27.6	18.8	11.4	12.5	10.6	16.6	16.7	17.8	22.3	26.5
Yugoslavia										
Imports	15.6	17.6	19.3	17.7	13.2	13.9	16.2	26.7	32.4	39.4
Exports	8.5	11.7	11.3	11.3	13.9	15.4	18.6	23.7	21.7	42.0
Bulgaria										
Imports	22.2	23.2	23.3	25.9	38.2	40.2	53.5	61.0	54.8	52.0
Exports	29.9	26.2	29.5	26.0	36.0	42.8	38.0	47.6	43.1	59.0

(The figures for 1938 include Austria.)
Based on C.A. Macartney and A.W. Palmer, *Independent Eastern Europe* (London, 1962), p. 315.

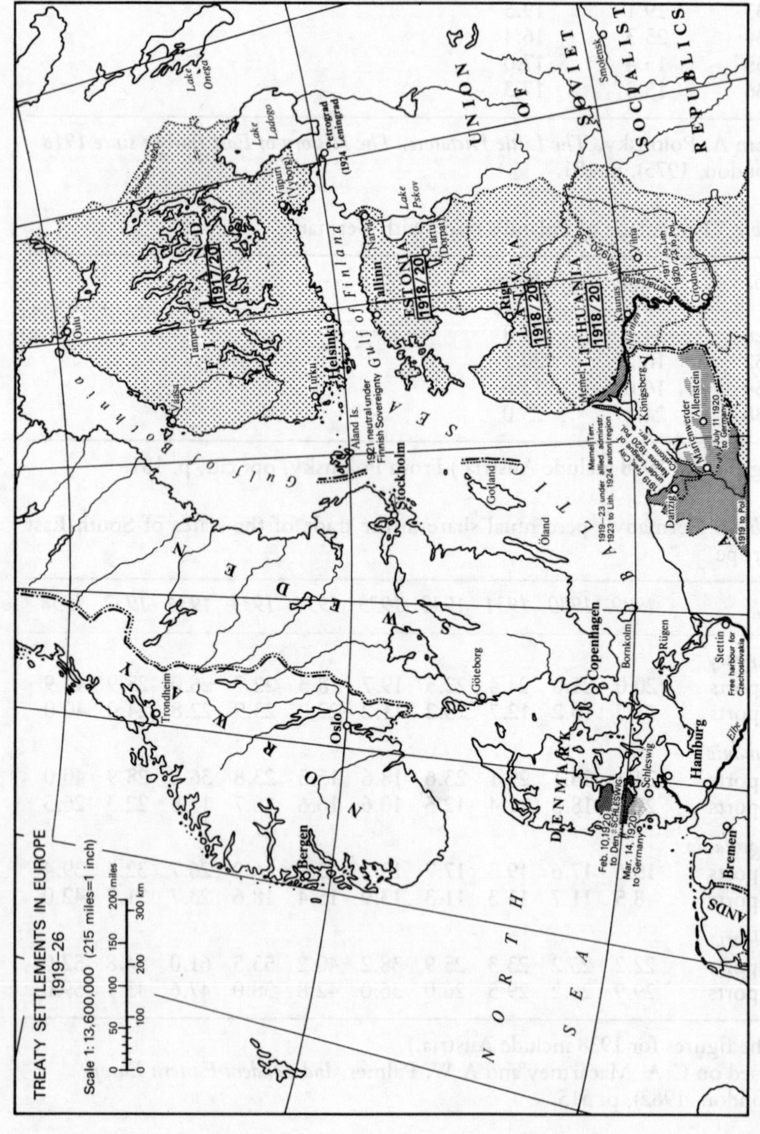
TREATY SETTLEMENTS IN EUROPE
1919–26
Scale 1: 13,600,000 (215 miles=1 inch)
0 50 100 150 200 miles
0 100 200 300 km
NORTH SEA
NORWAY
SWEDEN
FINLAND
1917/20
ESTONIA
1918/20
LATVIA
1918/20
LITHUANIA
1918/20
DENMARK
BALTIC SEA
UNION OF SOVIET SOCIALIST REPUBLICS
Gulf of Bothnia
Gulf of Finland
Lake Onega
Lake Ladogo
Lake Pskov
Boundary 1920
Oulu
Vaasa
Tampere
Turku
Helsinki
Viipuri (Vyborg)
Petrograd
(1924 Leningrad)
Narva
Tallinn
Tartu
(Dorpat)
Riga
Memel
Memel Terr.
1919–23 under allied adminstr.
1923 to Lith. 1924 auton. region
Kaunas
Vilna
Grodno
Demarcation Line 1920
1917 to Lith.
1920/23 to Pol.
Smolensk
Niemen
Aland Is.
1921 neutral under
Finnish Sovereignty
Stockholm
Gotland
Öland
Trondheim
Bergen
Oslo
Göteborg
Copenhagen
Bornkolm
Feb. 10,1920
to Den.
SCHLESWIG
Mar. 14, 1920
to Germany
Schleswig
Rügen
Hamburg
Bremen
Elbe
Stettin
Free harbour for
Czechoslovakia
Danzig
1919 Free City
under League of
Nations 1920 Pol.
Customs Terr.
Königsberg
Marienwerder
Allenstein
July 11 1920
to Germany
1919 to Pol.

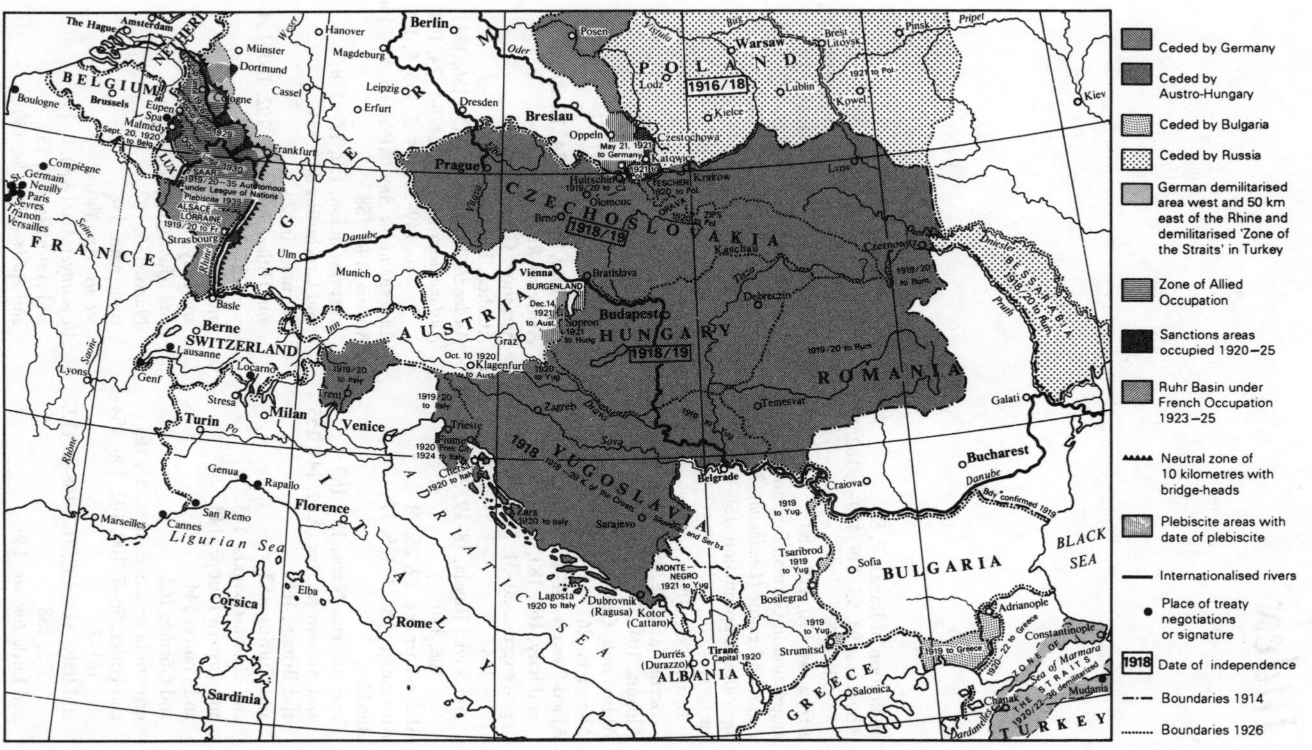
Ceded by Germany
Ceded by Austro-Hungary
Ceded by Bulgaria
Ceded by Russia
German demilitarised area west and 50 km east of the Rhine and demilitarised 'Zone of the Straits' in Turkey
Zone of Allied Occupation
Sanctions areas occupied 1920–25
Ruhr Basin under French Occupation 1923–25
Neutral zone of 10 kilometres with bridge-heads
Plebiscite areas with date of plebiscite
Internationalised rivers
Place of treaty negotiations or signature
1918 Date of independence
Boundaries 1914
Boundaries 1926
POLAND
1916/18
CZECHOSLOVAKIA
1918/19
HUNGARY
1918/19
ROMANIA
YUGOSLAVIA
1918
AUSTRIA
BULGARIA
ALBANIA
GREECE
TURKEY
ITALY
FRANCE
SWITZERLAND
BELGIUM
LUX
BESSARABIA
1918/20 to Rum.
BURGENLAND
SAAR
ALSACE LORRAINE
1919/20 to Fr.
MONTE-NEGRO
1921 to Yug
BLACK SEA
ADRIATIC SEA
Ligurian Sea
Sea of Marmara
ZONE OF THE STRAITS
Berlin
Vienna
Budapest
Prague
Warsaw
Bucharest
Belgrade
Sofia
Rome
Berne
Brussels
Paris
Versailles
Trianon
Neuilly
Sèvres
St. Germain
Compiègne
Rapallo
Locarno
Lausanne
Genua
Spa
Stresa
San Remo
Cannes
Constantinople
Salonica
Adrianople
Chanak
Mudania
Danube
Rhine
Oder
Vistula

Index